Recognition, Equality and Democracy

This volume brings together a range of theoretical responses to issues in Irish politics. Its organising ideas: recognition, equality, and democracy set the terms of political debate within both jurisdictions. For some, there are significant tensions between the grammar of recognition, concerned with esteem, respect and the symbolic aspects of social life, and the logic of equality, which is primarily concerned with the distribution of material resources and formal opportunities, while for others, tensions are produced rather by certain interpretations of these ideas while alternative readings may, by contrast, serve as the basis for a systematic account of social and political inequality. The essays in this collection will explore these interconnections with reference to the politics of Northern Ireland and the Republic. The Republic has gone through a period in which its constitution was the focus for a liberal politics aimed at securing personal autonomy, while Northern Ireland's political landscape has been shaped by the problem of securing political autonomy and democratic legitimacy. While the papers address key questions facing each particular polity, the issues themselves have resonances for politics on each side of the border.

This book was previously published as a special issue of *Irish Political Studies*.

Jurgen De Wispelaere lectures in moral and political philosophy at the Department of Philosophy, Trinity College Dublin.

Cillian McBride is a lecturer in political theory, at the School of Politics, International Studies, & Philosophy, Queen's University Belfast.

Shane O'Neill is Professor of Political Theory, at the School of Politics, International Studies, & Philosophy, Queen's University Belfast.

Recognition, Equality and Democracy

Theoretical Perspectives on Irish Politics

Edited by
Jurgen De Wispelaere, Cillian McBride and
Shane O'Neill

Routledge
Taylor & Francis Group
LONDON AND NEW YORK

First published 2008 by Routledge

2 Park Square, Milton Park, Abingdon, Oxon OX14 4RN
711 Third Avenue, New York, NY 10017, USA

Routledge is an imprint of the Taylor & Francis Group, an informa business

First issued in paperback 2016

Typeset in Times by Genesis Typesetting, Rochester, Kent, UK.

British Library Cataloguing in Publication Data
A catalogue record for this book is available from the British Library

ISBN13 978-0-415-46440-6 (hbk)
ISBN13 978-1-138-99709-7 (pbk)

Contents

1 Introduction: Theorising Politics
Cillian McBride, Jurgen De Wispelaere and Shane O'Neill 1

2 Critical Theory and Ethno-National Conflict: Assessing Northern Ireland's Peace Process as a Model of Conflict Resolution
Shane O'Neill 17

3 Illegal in Ireland, Irish Illegals: Diaspora Nation as Racial State
Ronit Lentin 39

4 Democratic Autonomy, Women's Interests, and Institutional Context
Ian O'Flynn 61

5 Comprehensive Liberalism and Civic Education in the Republic of Ireland
Graham Finlay 79

6 The Battle(s) Over Children's Rights in the Irish Constitution
Aoife Nolan 101

7 Disability Rights in Ireland: Chronicle of a Missed Opportunity
Jurgen De Wispelaere and Judy Walsh 123

8 How to Think About Marriage: Autonomy, Equality, Recognition
Peter Morriss 151

9 The Regulation of Public Space in Northern Ireland
Ciarán O'Kelly and Dominic Bryan 171

10 Identity, Unity, and the Limits of Democracy
Cillian McBride 191

Index 215

Introduction: Theorising Politics

CILLIAN MCBRIDE, JURGEN DE WISPELAERE & SHANE O'NEILL

The aim of this collection is to bring theoretical perspectives to bear upon a range of issues within the politics of Northern Ireland and the Republic. This may seem to some to be a distinctly quixotic enterprise to the extent that theory is supposed to aspire to a high level of abstraction in order to discern universal truths and avoid becoming too entangled in particular political contexts and local political disputes. The tendency to see the work of theory and the work of empirical social science as polar opposites is perhaps stronger still in Ireland where the prevailing intellectual culture has a distinctively literary-historical flavour (Kearney, 1997) rendering it somewhat inhospitable to philosophical concerns. This view of political theory as a utopian, platonic, enterprise floating above the world of real politics may still have some currency, albeit less amongst contemporary political theorists themselves than amongst non-theorists, but it is one which is firmly rejected by the contributors to this collection, who have sought to illuminate practical issues in Irish politics with a variety of theoretical tools, drawn from a range of theoretical traditions.

Of course, within political theory itself, there has been considerable disagreement over the years as to the precise nature of the relationship between theory and context, and it is possible to discern at least three main accounts of this relationship – there may, of course, be more; there are certainly nuances in each of those we have identified that we cannot do justice to here. First, there is the view that political theory is *necessarily* impractical. One popular source of this view has been the idea that the basic currency of political theory, ideas, are little more than reflections of an underlying political reality (Macpherson, 1962; Larrain, 1979). This view is recognisable as the main plank in the now largely defunct enterprise of historical materialism, and it places theory firmly on the sidelines to the extent that the most we could hope for from the study of ideas is to see them debunked as mystifications of underlying social and political realities (Skinner, 1988). Marxism always struggled with the issue of whether or not to include itself within this analysis (Lukács, 1971), an analysis which may perhaps draw some empirical support from the speed with which revolutions in the political landscape ultimately rendered Marxism itself redundant.

Naturally, there have also been versions of this view to be found on the right of the political spectrum, notably in the work of Oakeshott, for example, who argued that the work of political philosophy was fundamentally impractical, being essentially concerned with the analysis of the fundamental presuppositions underlying our practices (Oakeshott, 1990). Having identified these presuppositions, the work of the philosopher was done, and to suppose otherwise was to fall prey to the insidious disease of rationalism, of which no good could come (Oakeshott, 1991). The 'impotence' view political theory was also exemplified in the mercifully short-lived project of conceptual analysis which was briefly in vogue in Oxford 1950s and 1960s. This notoriously saw the business of mapping our use of political concepts as an end in itself, a study held to be philosophically interesting but not in any way relevant to politics. From this apparently barren soil, however, was eventually born a much more engaged, political philosophy of which more in a moment (Weldon, 1953).

The second version of the theory-context relationship is represented by a range of thinkers who came to prominence in the 1980s under the banner of 'communitarianism' (MacIntyre, 1981; Sandel, 1982; Taylor, 1985; Walzer, 1985). Communitarians reject the impotence view in favour of an altogether more *engaged* view of political theory as absolutely central to the cultural self-understanding of political communities. Michael Walzer famously set out this view of political theory as social criticism in his re-reading of Plato's cave analogy(Walzer, 1987). For Plato the business of the philosopher is to ascend out of the gloomy cave of common opinion into the light of the eternal verities, but for Walzer, the key move in this story is the philosopher's return to the cave in order to offer his fellow cave-dwellers the fruits of his reflections. Walzer points out the persistence of metaphors such as the ascent from the cave, or of prophets ascending mountains, all of which link philosophy to separation from everyday life, and he rejects them as representing an incoherent desire to occupy a disengaged 'view from nowhere' (Walzer, 1987). Instead we must embrace the fact that we are all situated in particular communities whose traditions of interpretation and particular values are what makes philosophy possible in the first place and gives it a purpose. Rather than aspire to universal truth, the role of the political philosopher is that of social critic, moving in the medium of a particular community's ethical and political tradition and offering to his fellow citizens not truths from on high, but better, richer, interpretations of that community's own practices so that the community might better live up to its own best view of itself. To do otherwise is not only mistaken, but also does violence to the ethical life of communities through the imposition of alien values and principles (Walzer, 1994).

Clearly, this communitarian view of the political philosopher as situated social critic is attractive in that it weaves the work of the philosopher into the public affairs of particular political communities, but it is also clear that it is not just a view about the relationship between philosophy and its context, but also, primarily indeed, a *normative* view about the value of community and tradition, a view at odds with liberal, impartialist, cosmopolitan outlooks (Taylor, 1995). While communitarian-inclined philosophers have reflected more thoroughly than most on issues of context and situation then, their reflections are not ultimately innocent, but are rather premised on particular, controversial, views about politics and morality.

Is there a way to think about the relationship between political philosophy and its social and political contexts, that does not rob of it practical application or commit us to a communitarian politics, a view that might be both engaged, but also more hospitable to universalist moral and political argument? There are two main sources of this sort of view in contemporary political theory, one taking its lead from the Critical Theory formulated by the unorthodox Marxists of the Frankfurt School (Adorno & Horkheimer, 1979; Marcuse, 1987), but which now embraces a range of approaches from the work of Habermas to that of Iris Young and Nancy Fraser (Young, 1990; Fraser, 1996; Habermas, 1996), and the other a more narrowly focused analytical political philosophy of a broadly liberal egalitarian character (Barry, 1995; Rawls, 1999b; Dworkin, 2000). Both share a broadly universalist, egalitarian, cosmopolitan outlook and view political theory as essentially engaged with the business of politics. For those working in the Critical Theory tradition, the goal of the critical theory of society is to identify structural obstacles to human emancipation as an essential pre-requisite of the project of social transformation, a project which has a distinctively interdisciplinary character and which may arguably also embrace elements of post-structuralist social criticism, such as that of Foucault (Foucault, 1995; Butler, 1997, 2006). The 'Rawlsian' current in contemporary political theory seems, by contrast, aridly abstract to many, but, while it is true that it eschews the sort of sociological analysis on which Critical Theory is founded, this unpromising appearance is misleading for philosophers working in this stream have, more than any other, sought to bring philosophical analysis to bear upon issue of public policy, with a particular focus on the question of distributive justice.

For this group of theorists, which is engaged with its social and political context but also is moral universalist, the business of philosophical argument is inextricably tied to political dispute, for normative issues are seen not as eternal truths to be pursued at the expense of political engagement, but as arising directly from the day-to-day business of politics. To see politics as nothing more than a sphere in which self-interest is ruthlessly pursued without reference to ideas about justice and fairness is, for these theorists, wholly misconceived, for while we may all be tempted from time to time to pursue our own self-interest at the expense of others, it is also the case that we have an interest in others abiding by the same normative principles we may occasionally wish to bend (Hume, 1960). Anyone who has ever felt resentment at what they view as unfair treatment at the hands of another has manifested this implicit commitment to some notion, however vague and ill-defined, of justice (Strawson, 1974; Habermas, 1990). While rule bending and rule breaking are all too common, the central stuff of political life is constituted by the clash between differing conceptions of justice, whether between neo-liberals, egalitarians, and communitarians, between nationalists and cosmopolitans, or between secularists and religious adherents. The task of political theory then is to make sense of these clashes and to offer some guidance as to how to resolve the underlying normative conflicts which drive them.

This view of political theory as engaged with issues at the heart of political struggles may seem to be at odds with the sort of abstract, seemingly apolitical view of theory exemplified in John Rawls's notorious idea that we should choose principles of social justice from behind a 'veil of ignorance' which deprives us of all knowledge of our identity, commitments, and social location; all of the things, surely, which make us who we are (Rawls, 1999b). This is taken by many as the very epitome of the unrealistic, abstract, quality of contemporary political theory, but whatever the precise merits of Rawls's metaphor (Barry, 1995; O'Neill, 1996) this view is entirely misleading, both with respect to Rawls, and to contemporary political theory more generally. Another of Rawls's ideas, reflective equilibrium, provides a more useful model of the relationship between theory and its context. Rawls suggests that the ordinary moral agent is engaged in an ongoing attempt to establish a 'reflective equilibrium' between his avowed moral principles, and his particular political judgements about the world (Rawls, 1999b). This is not a matter of simply imposing principles willy nilly on the real world, or of tailoring one's principles to fit the world as one finds it (Miller, 1992), but is rather a more delicate process of mutually adjusting principles and judgements until they cohere in such a way as to achieve equilibrium. The device of the veil of ignorance is just a thought experiment performed as part of this larger process and it is not meant as *description* of how we might actually converge on principles of social justice.

The significance of the notion of reflective equilibrium is first of all that it illuminates how even abstract, universalist, political theory is nonetheless inevitably engaged with particular social and political contexts, not as some sort of passive reflection of these contexts, but as part of an *active* process of deliberative problem-solving which we bring to bear in our efforts to cope with the world.[1] Second, it is suggestive of a division of labour between normative theory proper, which takes as its subject the analysis and justification of normative principles themselves, and a more empirically grounded social criticism, which takes as its subject the analysis of the constellation of particular values, discourses and institutions of particular societies – the sort of enterprise that Walzer takes to be the whole of political theory. The model of reflective equilibrium, however, suggests a more complex process, in which our responses to our context comprise both abstract normative argument and particular judgements about particular circumstances. The model of reflective equilibrium, understood to be a process not confined to philosophers, but rather as one necessarily engaged in to some degree by all citizens, not only sheds light on the link between theorising and political deliberation, but also suggests a way of thinking about the interconnections between different styles of social and political theorising. Rather than seeing Critical Theory, analytical political theory, and post-structuralist social criticism simply as three rival approaches, it may also be possible to detect possible lines of communication between them. Where the analytical political theorist one maintains a relatively narrow focus on normative argument, others working within the traditions of Critical Theory and post-structuralist social criticism can supply the sorts of rich sociological reflection which the former lacks. Both of these enterprises seem to be necessary, however, to enrich the reflective, deliberative, engagements of the democratic citizen.[2]

What, then, has political theory to offer the analysis of Irish politics at this particular historical juncture? It is clear from the contributions to this volume that two broad themes can be discerned, reflecting particular political developments within Irish politics and the wider world of contemporary political theory, namely the issues of recognition and respect, and of democratisation. Where some might like to think of these as simply superceding an older politics of left and right, centred on the issue of the distribution of economic resources, we take the view that these are rather *diversifications* of that politics, which continue to connect in a variety of ways with questions of equality as conceived through the lens of distributive justice and that these connections will become clearer still as debates on the politics of recognition and democratic legitimacy develop in the years to come(Baker *et al.*, 2004).

The politics of recognition, as it has come to be known in political theory circles, was first formulated by Charles Taylor in the early 90s, at a time when the political scene was still reverberating with the collapse of the Berlin Wall and, with it, of Marxism as a significant intellectual and political force (Taylor, 1994). This was simply the culmination of a process already at work for a number of years: the eclipse of traditional class politics by a more diffuse politics of identity, and of national and cultural identities in particular. Of course, this is a highly stylised account of events: the politics of identity, conceived as a politics centring on the complexities of gender, race and sexuality had been underway in various forms for a couple of decades by then (Benhabib, 1995). However, by the early 90s, it was clear that, both theoretically and in terms of practical politics, questions of identity were now occupying centre-stage. In some ways, this may not have been so immediately apparent in Ireland, neither jurisdiction having developed a particularly robust class politics, and the politics of each having been dominated, to different degrees, by questions of national identity and their intersection with religious traditions since their foundation.

The politics of recognition and its near cousin, the politics of difference, both react against the perceived inadequacies of the egalitarian 'distributive' paradigm (Young, 1990). For Taylor this is a matter of the insensitivity of traditional enlightenment notions of equality and of universal respect to people's attachment to their particular social identities, and the rich tapestry of cultural diversity within which these are located. Taylor contrasts the notion of universal respect with that of particular recognition, arguing that the latter enjoins a positive valuation of difference, while the former fosters an attitude of indifference to particular identities at best, and outright hostility, at worst (Taylor, 1994). The enlightenment notion of equality, is complicit in an insidious sort of fundamentalism insofar as it wrongly privileges what we have in common, even if these commonalities are little more than universalist abstractions, and it treats the rich variety of our differences as merely *accidental* to our humanity.

This has significant implications for political life. Multiculturalists have argued that liberal 'neutrality' is both unattainable and undesirable: opposing the establishment of a particular religion is all very well, but the liberal state can scarcely claim to be culturally neutral itself. Insofar as it is embedded in a particular social context, it will be biased in favour of the majority culture. On this view liberal 'pluralism', turns out, on closer inspection, to be culturally assimilationist, as the price of admission to citizenship for members of minority cultures is the surrender of their cultural distinctiveness (Kymlicka, 1995). The traditional liberal strategy for coping with difference, it has been suggested, is to treat it as essentially a private matter, rather than a public concern (Parekh, 2000; Modood, 2005). The politics of recognition adopts the opposite strategy: cultural differences must be publicly recognised. What this means in practice is that certain group rights, designed to permit groups to preserve their cultural distinctiveness ought to be recognised by the state, not only in symbolic terms but also in legal and political institutions that go beyond earlier notions of non-discrimination and of toleration in seeking to accommodate, and even celebrate, cultural diversity (Modood, 2005). These rights typically include language rights but also limited rights to political autonomy and/or special group representation in representative bodies (Kymlicka, 1995).

While it may be tempting to give in to a quasi-historicist view of the supercession of equality by difference, or of the emergence of group-inflected rights out of an individualist prehistory, this would be too simple (Kymlicka & Norman, 1994). On the normative front, despite the efforts of Will Kymlicka in particular to articulate a version of multiculturalism which presents it as a logical development of liberal principles (Kymlicka, 1989), others worry that the recognition paradigm requires undue deference to the claims of cultural conservatives and is insensitive to the problem of 'internal' hierarchies (Okin, 1999; Barry, 2001). While the politics of recognition has, in its multicultural variant, posed a significant challenge to egalitarian thought, it might be argued that in identifying the issue of recognition so closely with that of cultural and religious identities in particular, this model has taken too narrow a view of the scope of the politics of recognition. Certainly, contributions to this collection not only identify the emergence of a multicultural politics of recognition in Ireland, primarily in the Republic, but also touch on the extension of this paradigm to an even wider range of issues, notably those of children's rights and disability rights.

An alternative, more systematic, account of recognition is offered by Axel Honneth, who resists tying it so directly to cultural identity and varieties of symbolic affirmation (Honneth, 2003). Instead, he offers a tripartite analysis of recognition, with developmental aspects, which distinguishes different modes and potential sites in which struggles for recognition may take place (Honneth, 1992, 1995, 2007; Fraser & Honneth, 2003). While most theorists in the analytical tradition are content to accept the claim that there *is* a straightforward contrast between an egalitarian politics of respect and the group identity-centred politics of recognition, Honneth's model challenges this dualism, by distinguishing between recognition as love, respect and esteem (Honneth, 1992). While talk of celebrating cultural difference and moving beyond the traditional notion of toleration seems to correspond to the notion of recognition as the pursuit of esteem, or endorsement of particularity, Honneth argues that much of what appears to be a 'politics of identity' turns out, on closer inspection, to be a version of the struggle for universalist respect recognition, even when carried out in the name of particular social groups (Honneth, 2003). What matters for many marginalised groups, including but not restricted to cultural minorities, is that they count as equal members of the community, i.e. that they are respected as equals. Honneth's model arguably extends the scope of the concept of recognition, and reveals its dynamics at work in political struggles which seem far removed from traditional multicultural contexts. Even disputes that seem to be purely concerned with the distribution of resources, e.g. strikes for better pay, may turn out to have an important recognition dimension, to the extent that income can be read as a symbolic form of social esteem – even a small wage increase may signal to workers, particularly in the public sector, that their activities are deemed socially valuable (Honneth, 2003).

The second major development, that of a resurgence of democratic theory, in the form of theories of deliberation, has clear affinities with the first, insofar as multi-cultural political theory has devoted considerable attention to the issue of constitutional innovation as a pre-requisite of extending genuine political autonomy to culturally marginalised groups (Kymlicka, 1995; Tully, 1995; McBride, 2005).[3] The primary concern of deliberative democratic theorists, however, has been with the special character of public reasoning (Rawls, 1993, 1999a; Cohen, 1997), rather than with the pre-requisites of cultural survival. In contrast with thin, aggregative models of collective decision-making and democratic legitimacy (Schumpeter, 1965), deliberative theories impose a requirement of public reasoning on collective decision-making. While the traditional model follows the logic of the market in treating voters as consumers and voting as a matter, therefore, of the rational pursuit of self-interest, deliberative models regard political choices as fundamentally different to consumer choices insofar as the outcome of these collective choices will be binding on others (Elster, 1997).

This has two implications, one normative and the other institutional. First, it is argued that in virtue of the binding character of collective decision-making, voters acquire a duty to justify their political preferences to their fellow citizens, i.e. they must engage in a process of public reasoning as a central part of democratic politics. Rawls terms this the 'duty of civility', and it requires citizens to refrain from seeking to use what is in effect, their 'common coercive power' for private ends (Rawls, 1993: 217). This reading of political citizenship has distinctly counter-majoritarian implications, for to seek to mobilise a majority in support of a public policy that lacks the appropriate public justification would be a violation of the duty of civility. Second, it suggests that, in contrast to elitist models of democracy, democratic institutions should aim for greater transparency insofar as this provides incentives for political actors to engage in the business of exchanging appropriately public reasons (Elster, 1989, 1997).

The development of these public reason-centred models of democracy has been in large part a response to a growing awareness of the issue of value pluralism within the literature on distributive justice. Where societies display a deep ethical pluralism, and not merely a pluralism of opinion or interest, then this will pose a significant challenge to the project of outlining a vision of social justice on which the citizens of a diverse society might converge. For this reason, philosophers such as Rawls have been led from the problem of determining principles of justice, to the problem of democratic legitimacy: if the pursuit of social justice will inevitably be complicated by the fact of 'reasonable pluralism', i.e. a pluralism in ethical and political outlooks that cannot be explained away as the product of self-interest of poor reasoning, then we must look to democratic procedures for a way of *handling* the disputes that must arise in a manner which all can regard as fair (Rawls, 1993). For Rawls, then, this means that a genuinely public reason is one that must avoid appealing to controversial moral views that one cannot reasonably expect one's fellow citizens to endorse (Rawls, 1993: 151). As Gutmann and Thompson indicate, deliberative procedures cannot hope to resolve the deep ethical disputes that arise from the fact of value pluralism, e.g. disputes over the morality of abortion, but they can hope to manage these disagreements in such a way as to ensure that all parties can receive a fair hearing and regard democratic decisions as legitimate (Gutmann & Thompson, 1990, 1996).

Perhaps the most striking aspect of the normative conception of deliberative democracy is the way in which it sets out a radical reworking of the traditional conception of the relationship between liberty and democracy, the view set out by Mill on which democracy must always be constrained from without in order that individual liberty be protected from the tyranny of the majority. While deliberative theories are similarly counter-majoritarian, they now present individual rights and democratic politics as 'co-original' such that one presupposes the other (Habermas, 1996, 1998: 259; Cohen, 1989; Rawls, 1993: 412; Nino, 1996). On this view, restraints upon majoritarianism are justified from *within* a theory of democracy itself, and ought not to be regarded as external restraints imposed upon popular sovereignty by grudging liberals.

This, then, is the first major contribution of deliberative theories: a conception of democratic autonomy on which restraints on the majority can be seen as required by democracy, and not as deviations from it. As such it paves the way for a more nuanced understanding of the interrelations between individual rights and political autonomy than that offered by earlier theories.

The second major contribution follows from the first: this public reason-centred account moves decisively beyond the opposition of 'authentic' direct democracy on the Athenian model, to modern, representative democracy, insofar as the normative conception set out here does not simply equate political autonomy with direct involvement in decision-making (Cohen, 1997: 85). As Fishkin notes, there is no guarantee that a direct democracy will be more likely to abide by the requirements of public reasoning than a representative assembly (Fishkin, 1991: 50). The criterion for institutional design is given by the ideal of public reason, i.e. institutions should be designed with the aim of enhancing the practice of public reasoning, and while this may mandate greater direct involvement in decision-making it is also sensitive to situations in which this may in fact undermine public reasoning (Sunstein, 2002). While some have argued that there is an overly abstract quality to the deliberative literature (Phillips, 1999: 119), often this seems to mistake the role of a normative conception in our thought: it is not itself a blueprint for democratic institutions, but rather sets out an account of the criteria which should be followed when institutions are designed for particular polities. Seen in this light, deliberative conceptions of democracy can be seen to provide a coherent rationale for a tremendous range of institutional innovations, from participatory devices such as Ackerman and Fishkin's 'Deliberation Day' (Ackerman & Fishkin, 2004), through deliberative polling exercises (Fishkin, 1991), to at least some versions of special representation for marginalised groups (Phillips, 1995; Williams, 1998; Young, 2000) and, as several contributors here suggest, for the sort of consociational devices adopted in Northern Ireland under the terms of the Belfast Agreement.

Of course, deliberative theories of democracy, like any other, stand in a complicated relationship to the issue of substantive social equality. On the one hand, democratic institutions continue to be undermined by the way that social inequalities translate so reliably into political inequalities (Phillips, 1999). If the idea of genuinely equal influence on the conduct of our collective affairs is to be taken seriously, then these inequalities must be addressed. Of course, as our brief reflection on difference and equality above underlines, the very complexity of our ideas about social justice in general and about what constitutes equality (Rae, 1981; Temkin, 1993), in particular, means that there will be no legitimate way of realising any vision of social justice, outside of democratic politics. Given their contested nature, these ideas can only be thrashed out in the context of an inclusive, deliberative, set of institutions.

How, then, might we think about the relations between recognition, equality, and democracy? One tempting line to take would be to read them as part of some linear grand narrative, in the manner of Marshall's account of the development of the modern concept of citizenship: equal civil rights coming first, followed by political rights and then social, i.e. welfare, rights and now, perhaps, a new generation of identity-centred cultural or recognition based rights of some sort (Marshall, 1992). We might wonder, however, whether a linear account of any sort really does justice to the complexities of the situation? Rather then see one set of concerns giving way to another in an orderly progression as each issue is settled in some way, it might be more accurate to view this process as something more like a circle in which advances in one area have ramifications for others, which in turn may prompt a reassessment of other problems previously thought to have been settled, and so on. The pursuit of social equality, then, has not been superceded by newer concerns with identity and political inclusion, but has diversified into these areas, and has been enriched by this process. Recognition, may in some contexts be 'merely' symbolic, but in many more contexts, will involve the securing of substantial legal rights to autonomy across a range of contexts. Equally, welfare policy can no longer be regarded as confined to the allocation of resources, but rather embraces the recognition of a range of rights, not least the rights to equal participation in the formulation of those policies, and rights to challenge aspects of its administration, not merely as private individuals, but as citizens taking ownership of the institutions which shape their lives (Habermas, 1996; Olson, 2006).

The contributions to this collection amply reflect the complexity of the relations between these concepts, from the centrality of issues of national recognition to Northern Ireland's political institutions, to questions of cultural equality the Republic's school curriculum, and the complexity of discourses of inclusion and citizenship in the politics of immigration.

Shane O'Neill sets out to place the analysis of the Belfast Agreement in a larger theoretical context, arguing, in the first instance for an engaged theoretical perspective on issues of ethno-national conflict resolution that is both empirically rich but also directed to the transformation of social relations. O'Neill then argues that critics of alleged 'sectarian' nature of the consociational arrangements established under the terms of the Belfast Agreement have failed to give adequate weight to the dynamics of ethno-national identity formation. While the critical theoretical approach may, in line with its egalitarian tenor, favour some measure of transformation in the group identities involved, a theoretical approach to conflict resolution that fails to come to terms with the importance which actors place upon these aspects of their self-understanding must necessarily fail. Viewed in this light, O'Neill concludes that the Agreement should be viewed as offering a successful model of conflict resolution.

Ronit Lentin, writing about the politics of immigration in the Republic, draws on a very different set of theoretical tools, derived from the work of Foucault and Agamben, but, in common with O'Neill, sees the work of theory as inseparable from wider public debates. In this case, she details the unexpected consequences of attempts to redefine Ireland as a 'diaspora' nation in the 90s. While intended as a move towards a more inclusive understanding of Irishness, with rising levels of immigration it has come to underwrite a racially exclusive model of Irishness, which the 2004 Citizenship Referendum has stitched into the Republic's institutions in such a way that it is fair to regard it now as a 'racial state'. In particular, she argues, the effect of these changes has been to create a new category of Irish 'citizen': one that is deprived of the same constitutional protections enjoyed by other citizens. Underlining the often contradictory character of political discourses, she contrasts this willingness to expose child-citizens to arbitrary treatment, with the Irish state's eagerness to defend the rights of Irish illegals in the US.

Ian O'Flynn, like O'Neill, seeks to address criticisms of the Belfast Agreement's consociationalism, and in particular the charge that these arrangements effectively stifle the emergence of any politics other than that of Green and Orange. The early successes but subsequent failure of the Women's Coalition seems to suggest that gender-based politics may be a particularly significant casualty of these arrangements. O'Flynn cautions against uncritical acceptance of this conclusion, however, and argues that any assessment of the institutions must begin with a clear account of the concept of political autonomy. O'Flynn's analysis suggests that there may be several different modes in which women may realise their political autonomy, and that while voting for a women's party, such as the Women's coalition, is one of these it does not exhaust the range of options open to women. In view of this, and of empirical evidence about women's representation across the political spectrum in Northern Ireland, he concludes that a balanced assessment of the Belfast Agreement suggests that these institutions are not ultimately inimical to women's equal political representation.

Graham Finlay's contribution addresses a key problem in liberal political theory: how best to foster a sense of common citizenship while respecting cultural and ethical pluralism in the wider society. Where Lentin focused on the intersection of immigration with discourses of nationality and citizenship, Finlay addresses the challenges posed for civic education in an increasingly culturally diverse Ireland. Finlay argues that we should be concerned not simply with the content of education for citizenship, but also the mode of any such education. Thus, while new developments in civic education may no longer tie questions of civic responsibility as closely to religious values as in the past, there is still a risk that the new curriculum might seek to *directly* inculcate civic values, rather than foster the appropriate critical faculties in the students concerned. Rawls's apparently more 'pluralist' political liberalism, Finlay argues, turns out on closer inspection to favour an altogether too direct form of civic instruction, so he turns instead to Mill's 'comprehensive' liberalism, which, he concludes, offers a promising model for a programme of civic education that balances the liberal commitment to fostering a capacity for critical judgement with a sensitivity to cultural pluralism and diversity.

Aoife Nolan maps the legal and political debates about the place of children's rights within the Irish constitution, viewing them through an analytical framework which distinguishes primarily between rights-based constitutions and basically paternalist 'child protection' constitutions. She addresses the practical and theoretical challenges faced by attempts to treat children as right-holders, and assesses the likelihood that a rights-centred framework will be adopted in the forthcoming constitutional referendum. Nolan suggests that the prospects of the rights-based model being adopted are not particularly good – her contribution, like that of Walsh and De Wispelaere in particular, charts the resistance of the state to moves in the direction of a rights-based culture more generally, and the persistence of a traditional paternalism in matters of social policy which is resistant to rights per se, and not merely to the idea of socio-economic rights in particular.

Jurgen De Wispelaere and Judy Walsh's contribution illustrates the density of connections between rights, recognition and democracy through an examination of the 2005 Disability Rights Act in the Republic, which they argue constitutes a missed opportunity to institutionalise a sufficiently robust set of disability rights. Ideally, such rights would strengthen access to public services sufficient to meet the needs of disabled people, going beyond current legislation which restricts moves in this direction to the bare right to have one's needs assessed. While acknowledging difficulties with attempts to guarantee access to specified levels of public services, De Wispelaere and Walsh argue that the current arrangements not only fail to secure robust socio-economic rights for disabled citizens, but, in line with the deeply embedded paternalism in the welfare model of disability policy, is insensitive to issues of dignity and recognition, and to the possibility that disabled citizens are vulnerable to arbitrary treatment at the hands of state bureaucracies. Linking socio-economic rights with the more political dimensions of citizenship, they argue that a rights-based approach to public services entails that disabled citizens are guaranteed a robust legal right to hold the state to account over its disability provisions. A justiciable right to challenge administrative decisions in relation to public services, it is argued, would promote the dignity of disabled citizens while at the same time strengthening democratic control over disability policy.

The Republic has, since the early 80s, experienced a series of constitutional upheavals over issues relating to sexuality. While the moral climate of politics in the Republic is now very different to what it was then, the issue of the relations between marriage and civil partnership is likely to prove a source of significant political controversy. Pete Morriss' contribution also deals with issues of rights and of recognition, in this case, as they play out in relation to the legal status of marriage. There are significant legal and economic implications attached to the way that states give legal recognition to personal relationships, and Morriss takes issue with recent legal judgments, which, he argues, focus too narrowly on the significance of sexual relationships to the question of legal recognition. This clearly disadvantages individuals, e.g. siblings and companions, involved in domestic relationships other than traditional marriages, and Morriss argues that a fairer, more inclusive, approach would be to focus rather on the issue of interdependence between those involved in a household, even where no sexual relationship is involved. In this way, Morriss would extend the debate on the legal status of marriage beyond that surrounding the recognition of civil partnerships involving same-sex couples. He suggests that the way forward for public policy in this area would be to avoid state-endorsement of any particular understanding of the institution of marriage, while honouring any domestic arrangements voluntarily entered into by their participants, irrespective of the presence or absence of sexual relationships between those concerned.

Ciarán O'Kelly and Dominic Bryan seek to analyse the performance of the Parades Commission in regulating the use of public space in Northern Ireland. They approach this task armed with the model of the 'enforcement pyramid' drawn from regulation theory, and use this to identify the various factors that have frustrated the efforts of the Commission to effectively regulate parades in Northern Ireland. They argue that, while it is true that viewed through this lens the Commission has not been as efficient at regulating parades as one would like, we should not underestimate the significant successes it has ensured in terms of reducing the violence associated with parades. Its status as an independent agency has helped to drastically reduce the incentives for opposing sides of the parades issue to escalate the use of violence and, while it has not resolved the parading issue per se, this is more a result of the larger political landscape in which the Commission exists, rather than of any particular flaws in its design. Successful governance, in Northern Ireland, as elsewhere, must rely ultimately on the degree to which the wider body of citizens regard the operations of the state as legitimate and not merely as arbitrary interferences in their lives.

Finally, Cillian McBride's contribution addresses the boundary problem in democratic theory in relation to the politics of Northern Ireland. This, he suggests, has two dimensions: one pertaining to the issue of the preconditions of creating common citizenship within Northern Ireland, and the second to do with the question as to whether it is possible to conceive of a democratic politics developing around the issue of state boundaries, or whether, as a matter of logic, this must remain outside the purview of purely democratic politics, as opposed to one which rests on ideas of pre-political cultural membership, whether nationalist or multiculturalist. McBride offers a conception of public-reason centred politics which indicates, first, how a common citizenship may be forged through the practice of public reasoning itself, and, second, how we might conceive of a democratic politics of borders that does not lapse into a version of nationalism. This serves not to resolve Northern Ireland's constitutional question in favour of one side or the other, but to indicate the rational legitimate form which a civic Unionism or a civic Nationalism should adopt.

It is evident that there is a clear division here between those contributions dealing with Northern Ireland, and those dealing with the Republic: while the latter are focused on issues arising over struggles for civil and social rights, contributions dealing with the former deal primarily, although not exclusively, with struggles over political rights. This should not, of course, be surprising: it simply reflects the fact that the politics of Northern Ireland has, since partition been unable to put the constitutional question to bed, and it is too early to say yet whether the current settlement has finally succeeded if not in resolving the issue, at least in providing a framework within which it might become the subject of normal democratic politics. By contrast, the Republic's constitutional upheavals have focused primarily on issues of personal autonomy: abortion, divorce, etc. We conclude by suggesting that it would be a mistake to suppose that it will be ever thus. Clearly, ethno-national conflict in Northern Ireland, together with the machinery of direct rule, has displaced a whole range of social problems from the political agenda, but it seems likely that we will gradually see greater mobilisation around these issues (no doubt still inflected by the traditional divisions for the foreseeable future) now that there is a devolved administration to serve as the focus for such mobilisation. Equally, as the politics of rights continues to develop and diversify in the Republic, this must inevitably raise more fundamental questions about the appropriateness of existing political institutions for dealing in a fair and accountable way with these issues. The sorts of social policy issues discussed here in relation to the Republic may in time come to resonate with the politics of Northern Ireland, just as some of the fundamental questions about democratic legitimacy raised in relation to that jurisdiction may equally come to resonate in the Republic. To predict how the complex relations of recognition, equality and democracy will be come to be configured in each context lies beyond the reach of theory, but we would argue that, however these processes play out in practice, the work of theorising is indispensable for those caught up within them.

Notes

Shane O'Neill acknowledges support from the British Academy that allowed him to spend some months at the Solomon Asch Center for the Study of Ethnopolitical Conflict, University of Pennsylvania in 2005. The research he conducted there helped to shape his contribution to this project. The editors would like to thank the AHRC for its support of the Democracy, Division, & the Public Sphere seminar, held at Queens University, Belfast in November 2006, from which some of the contributions collected here were drawn. This seminar was part of a series of Arts and Humanities Research Council (AHRC) funded seminars on 'Toleration and the Public Sphere'. We would like to thank the participants in that seminar, and the series organisers, Gideon Calder, Jonathan Seglow and Philip Cole. We would also like to record our gratitude to all those who participated in the 'Recognition, Equality, Democracy' workshop held at the School of Politics, Queens University, Belfast, 8 June 2007, especially Keith Breen and Ian Hughes. More general debts of gratitude are owed to Jonathan Seglow, the PSAI, and, of course, John Garry for his enthusiasm and patience throughout.

1. Hume argued that justice was an 'artificial virtue' which was only needed because of the circumstances we happened to find ourselves in, those of scarcity and limited generosity. If the world were different we would have no need of any theory of justice. Normative theorising is, then, a particular way of responding to the world and not a pursuit of eternal truths for their own sake.
2. This is not to deny, of course, that there will not remain in many cases substantive normative and philosophical disagreements between adherents of these views, but only to suggest that each may have something to learn from the other, even if that 'learning' may necessitate some reinterpretation.
3. Kymlicka endorses a deliberative conception of democracy in (Kymlicka, 1995). Miller, however, argues that deliberation requires a more unified public culture, i.e. that provided by a civic nationalism. See also McBride (2005) for consideration of the tensions between the dominant version of the politics of recognition and deliberative democracy.

References

Ackerman, B. & Fishkin, J. (2004) *Deliberation Day* (New Haven, CT: Yale University Press).
Adorno, T. W. & Horkheimer. M. (1979) *Dialectic of Enlightenment* (London: Verso).
Baker, J., Lynch, K., Cantillon, S. & Walsh, J. (2004) *Equality* (Basingstoke: Palgrave).
Barry, B. (1995) *Justice as Impartiality* (Oxford: Oxford University Press).
Barry, B. M. (2001) *Culture and Equality: An Egalitarian Critique of Multiculturalism* (Cambridge, MA: Harvard University Press).
Benhabib, S. (1995) *Feminist Contentions: A Philosophical Exchange* (London: Routledge).
Butler, J. (1997) *Excitable Speech* (London: Routledge).
Butler, J. (2006) *Gender Trouble* (London: Routledge).
Cohen, J. (1989) Democracy and Liberty, in: J. Elster (Ed.) *Deliberative Democracy*, pp. 185–231 (Cambridge: Cambridge University Press).
Cohen, J. (1997) Deliberation and Democratic Legitimacy, in: J. Bohman & W. Regh (Eds) *Deliberative Democracy*, pp. 67–92 (Cambridge, MA: MIT Press).
Dworkin, R. (2000) *Sovereign Virtue* (Cambridge, MA: Harvard University Press).
Elster, J. (1989) Deliberation and Constitution Making, in: J. Elster (Ed.) *Deliberative Democracy*, pp. 97–122 (Cambridge: Cambridge University Press).
Elster, J. (1997) The Market and the Forum: Three Varieties of Political Theory, in: J. Bohman & W. Regh (Eds) *Deliberative Democracy*, pp. 3–34 (Cambridge MA: MIT Press).
Fishkin, J. S. (1991) *Democracy and Deliberation* (New Haven, CT: Yale University Press).
Foucault, M. (1995) *Discipline and Punish: The Birth of the Prison* (New York: Vintage).
Fraser, N. (1996) *Justice Interruptus: Critical Reflections on the 'Postsocialist' Condition* (New York: Routledge).
Fraser, N. & Honneth, A. (2003) *Redistribution or Recognition?* (London: Verso).
Gutmann, A. & Thompson, D. (1990) Moral Conflict and Political Consensus, *Ethics*, 101(1), pp. 64–86.

Gutmann, A. & Thompson, D. F. (1996) *Democracy and Disagreement* (Cambridge, MA: Belknap Press).
Habermas, J. (1990) Discourse Ethics: Notes on a Program of Philosophical Justification, in: J. Habermas (Ed) *Moral Consciousness and Communicative Action*, pp. 41 115 (Cambridge MA: MIT Press).
Habermas, J. (1996) *Between Facts and Norms* (Cambridge: Polity).
Habermas, J. (1998) On the Internal Relation Between Law and Democracy, in: C. Cronin & P. DeGrieff (Eds) *Inclusion of the Other*, pp. 253–264 (Cambridge MA: MIT Press).
Honneth, A. (1992) Integrity and Disrespect: Principles of a Conception of Morality Based on the Theory of Recognition, *Political Theory*, 20, pp. 187–201.
Honneth, A. (1995) *The Struggle for Recognition* (Cambridge: Polity).
Honneth, A. (2003) Redistribution as Recognition: A Response to Nancy Fraser, in: N. Fraser & A. Honneth (Eds) *Redistribution or Recognition?*, pp. 110–197 (London: Verso).
Honneth, A. (2007) *Disrespect* (Cambridge: Polity).
Hume, D. (1960) *A Treatise of Human Nature* (Oxford: Clarendon Press).
Kearney, R. (1997) *Postnationalist Ireland* (London: Routledge).
Kymlicka, W. (1989) *Liberalism, Community and Culture* (Oxford: Oxford University Press).
Kymlicka, W. (1995) *Multicultural Citizenship* (Oxford: Oxford University Press).
Kymlicka, W. & Norman, W. (1994)Return of the Citizen: A Survey of Recent Work on Citizenship Theory, *Ethics*, 104, pp. 352–381.
Larrain, J. (1979) *The Concept of Ideology* (London: Hutchinson).
Lukács, G. (1971) *History and Class Consciousness* (London: Merlin Press).
MacIntyre, A. (1981) *After Virtue* (London: Duckworth).
Macpherson, C. B. (1962) *The Political Theory of Posessive Individualism* (Oxford: Oxford University Press).
Marcuse, H. (1987) *Eros and Civilisation* (London: Ark).
Marshall, T. H. (1992) *Citizenship and Social Class* (London: Pluto Press).
McBride, C. (2005). Deliberative Democracy and the Politics of Recognition, *Political Studies*, 53, pp. 497–515.
Miller, D. (1992) Distributive Justice – What the People Think, *Ethics*, 102(3), pp. 555–593.
Modood, T. (2005) *Multicultural Politics* (Minneapolis, MN: University of Minnesota Press).
Nino, C. S. (1996) *The Constitution of Deliberative Democracy* (New Haven, CT: Yale University Press).
O'Neill, O. (1996) *Towards Justice and Virtue* (Cambridge: Cambridge University Press).
Oakeshott, M. (1990) *On Human Conduct* (Oxford: Oxford University Press).
Oakeshott, M. (1991) *Rationalism in Politics* (Indianapolis, IN: Liberty Press).
Okin, S. M. (1999) *Is Multiculturalism Bad for Women?* (Princeton, NJ: Princeton University Press).
Olson, K. (2006) *Reflexive Democracy: Political Equality and the Welfare State* (Cambridge, MA: MIT Press).
Parekh, B. (2000) *Rethinking Multiculturalism: Cultural Diversity and Political Theory* (Basingstoke: Macmillan).
Phillips, A. (1995) *The Politics of Presence* (Oxford: Oxford University Press).
Phillips, A. (1999) *Which Equalities Matter?* (Cambridge: Polity Press).
Rae, D. W. (1981) *Equalities* (Cambridge, MA, London: Harvard University Press).
Rawls, J. (1993) *Political Liberalism* (New York: Columbia University Press).
Rawls, J. (1999a) The Idea of Public Reason Revisited, in: S. Freeman (Ed.) *Collected Papers*, pp. 573–615 (Cambridge, MA: Harvard University Press).
Rawls, J. (1999b) *A Theory of Justice* (Oxford: Oxford University Press).
Sandel, M. J. (1982) *Liberalism and the Limits of Justice* (Cambridge: Cambridge University Press).
Schumpeter, J. A. (1965) *Capitalism, Socialism and Democracy* (London: Allen & Unwin).
Skinner, Q. (1988) Meaning and Context in the History of Ideas, in: J. Tully (Ed.) *Meaning and Context*, pp. 29–67 (Cambridge: Polity), pp. 29–67.
Strawson, P. F. (1974) *Freedom and Resentment, and Other Essays* (London: Methuen).

Sunstein, C. R. (2002) The Law of Group Polarization, *Journal of Political Philosophy*, 10(2), pp. 175–195.
Taylor, C. (1985) *Philosophy and the Human Sciences* (Cambridge: Cambridge University Press).
Taylor, C. (1994) The Politics of Recognition, in: A. Gutmann (Ed.) *Multiculturalism*, pp. 25–74. (Princeton, NJ: Princeton University Press).
Taylor, C. (1995) Cross-Purposes: the Liberal-Communitarian Debate, in: C. Taylor (Ed) *Philosophical Arguments*, pp. 181–203 (Cambridge, MA: Harvard University Press).
Temkin, L. S. (1993) *Inequality* (New York: Oxford University Press).
Tully, J. (1995) *Strange Multiplicity* (Cambridge: Cambridge University Press).
Walzer, M. (1985) *Spheres of Justice: A Defence of Pluralism and Equality* (Oxford: Blackwell).
Walzer, M. (1987) *Interpretation and Social Criticism* (Cambridge, MA: Harvard University Press).
Walzer, M. (1994) *Thick and Thin: Moral Argument at Hhome and Abroad* (Notre Dame: University of Notre Dame Press).
Weldon, T. D. (1953) *The Vocabulary of Politics* (Harmondsworth: Penguin).
Williams, M. (1998) *Voice, Trust, and Memory* (Princeton, NJ: Princeton University Press).
Young, I. M. (1990) *Justice and the Politics of Difference* (Princeton, NJ: Princeton University Press).
Young, I. M. (2000) *Inclusion and Democracy* (New York: Oxford University Press).

Critical Theory and Ethno-National Conflict: Assessing Northern Ireland's Peace Process as a Model of Conflict Resolution

SHANE O'NEILL

Introduction

Many of the most intractable political conflicts of the late modern era have been those in which the sovereignty of a particular piece of territory has been contested by antagonistic ethno-national communities. Such disputes have often led to widespread public disorder and to violent inter-communal conflict as has been the case in Palestine/Israel, successor states of the former Yugoslavia, Sri Lanka, the Basque Country, Cyprus and elsewhere. Many other social and economic disorders have typically followed as consequences of state-building failures to establish political institutions that are acknowledged across an ethno-national divide to be sufficiently legitimate, fair and just. This has made the task of securing effective grounds for peace and long-term stability extremely difficult in such divided regions or states.

Northern Ireland was considered for many years to be one of the most intractable of such conflicts (Giliomee & Gagiano, 1990), and some even viewed the quest for a solution as hopeless (Whyte, 1991: 234–235). For more than a decade now, however, it has been looked to, by all but the most disconsolate of commentators (more on some of them later), as a relative success story, as one of the few positive examples where the parties to conflict have been engaged effectively in a process of conflict resolution. This view has been reinforced strongly by the establishment of an executive at Stormont on 8 May 2007 led by Ian Paisley of the DUP and Martin McGuiness of Sinn Féin, particularly when we consider that the antagonistic relationship between these parties has been a key dimension of a political context that was marked by a quarter of a century of political violence. My aim here is to provide a brief critical assessment of the peace process in Northern Ireland with a view to evaluating its merits as a potential model for conflict resolution elsewhere, particularly in comparable cases involving two historically antagonistic national communities. I will be doing so from the perspective of a critical theory, the main contours of which I will outline in the course of the argument.

Northern Ireland's Peace Process in Context

For the sake of providing some clarification regarding empirical categories, before focusing on the case of Northern Ireland, I will briefly define in the second section what I mean by ethno-national conflict. I will do so by considering it in the broader context of ethnic politics. There are various types and varieties of ethnic politics, situations where ethnic diversity interwoven in multiple, complex, and varied ways with racial, cultural, religious, linguistic or national differences, can potentially lead to political strife and conflict. It will be useful to make some analytical distinctions in that section, so as to avoid confusion, to minimise the danger of false analogy, and to give a clear focus to the argument that follows.

In the subsequent methodological section (III), I set out some of the key features of a critical-theoretical approach to ethno-national conflict. One of the distinctive characteristics of this approach is that it seeks to *engage with* rather than *abstract from* the deeply divergent interpretations of historical events that fuel such conflicts as well as the values and identities that shape these interpretations. Deep interpretive divergence of this kind is a highly significant factor in the relative intractability of ethno-national conflicts. The depth of divergence reflects the significance of what is at stake since typically these conflicts involve struggles between national communities regarding the 'fit' between citizenship status in the constitutional order and their differing national identities. Getting that 'fit' right for all major citizen groups usually brings basic constitutional arrangements or state boundaries into question, with implications for the political identities of all concerned (O'Neill, 2003a).

A distinctive feature of critical theory as an approach to social-scientific research is that it claims to be at once explanatory, normative and practical (Hoy & McCarthy, 1994; Rush, 2004; Bohman, 2005). Turning to an analysis of ethno-national conflict, I begin to draw out the connections between these dimensions (section IV), with particular reference to Northern Ireland. The critical approach I adopt is not only concerned to work out how best to bring an end to violence but it also seeks to identify and eliminate the roots of conflict so as to ensure that peace is grounded in a just resolution that offers long-term stability on a basis that is fair to all and in accord with a the demands of equal citizenship. This requires a process of social transformation that involves the dismantling of the structures of domination that generated the conflict, and the achievement of a robustly egalitarian constitutional order.

Other scholars have sought to intervene in the recent history of Northern Ireland from a critical perspective that has some similarity to the approach I advocate (Ruane & Todd, 1996). They seek to emphasise the need for critical reflection and a process of social transformation that will lead to a dismantling of the causes of conflict. Others give the critical approach a more deconstructive emphasis, inspired by post-structuralist accounts of ethnic conflict elsewhere (Campbell, 1998) or by agonistic theories of democracy (Mouffe, 2000). The impulse in the latter strand of inquiry has been to transform the conflict in Northern Ireland by deconstructing the oppositions on which it is based, and by problematising standard assumptions that are made in representing the nature of the antagonism (Little, 2004; Finlayson, 2006; Vaughan-Williams, 2006). Although it is often less explicit in the latter cases, all of these critical approaches can be thought of as transformative interventions that are driven by conceptions of freedom, equality and democracy, or some combination of these values. Conceptions of the same democratic values also feed into the analyses of a number of commentators who, while not explicitly committed to a critical-theoretical research agenda, argue from the perspective of cosmopolitan liberalism (Taylor, 2001, 2006; Wilford & Wilson, 2003, 2006 ; O'Flynn, 2003; Oberschall & Palmer, 2005). All of these writers, critical theorists, post-structuralists and cosmopolitan liberals alike, advocate some conception of egalitarian democracy and many of them have delivered negative assessments of the most significant political developments that have taken place in Northern Ireland since the mid-1990s. I will focus here on the criticisms made from the egalitarian democratic perspective of cosmopolitan liberalism, although some of the anxieties they express about recent developments in Northern Ireland are shared by those commentators who identify themselves explicitly with critical or post-structuralist traditions of social scientific research inquiry.

The cosmopolitan critics of the peace process have found key aspects of the 1998 Agreement, and the political institutions and constitutional arrangements it has established, to be deeply troubling. They are troubled not because they are committed, explicitly at least, to either Irish nationalism or to unionism. They don't believe that the process has been unfair in the sense that they their favoured 'side' has been losing out or has been forced to concede too much with respect to the 'other'. It is rather for broadly *egalitarian liberal*, and intentionally non-partisan reasons, that they reject those features of the new Northern Ireland that appear to have carved into the political landscape a form of national group recognition. They have in mind the bi-national, consociational features of post-Agreement politics (Lijphart, 1978;

McGarry & O'Leary, 2004). For reasons to be explored in later sections, many of these cosmopolitan critics consider these features of the settlement to prevent satisfaction of the demands for transformation they presume to follow from the progressive values they espouse. Some even consider the arrangements that are now in place to take us in the wrong direction altogether (Taylor, 2006), as they are said to 'entrench' (Wilford & Wilson, 2003: 11–12; Oberschall & Palmer, 2005: 77) or 'exacerbate' (O'Flynn, 2003: 141) the very structures of group difference that have generated the conflict in the first place, thus making those structures harder than ever to dismantle.

I do not share the views of these particular egalitarian democrats. From the perspective I develop here, it seems clear that if we have an interest in establishing an egalitarian political order in Northern Ireland, one that will allow people to find a way beyond the destructive conflict they have endured, then we should acknowledge the hugely positive advances that have been made possible by the process of mutual national recognition that is at the heart of the Agreement and its political outcomes. The arguments made by the Agreement's egalitarian critics have therefore, to my mind, been largely counterproductive. Some of the critics might also be accused of being politically irresponsible, since attacking the Agreement has thrown them together with some strange bedfellows, notably those less progressive opponents of the Agreement, who would rather squander this historic opportunity to move beyond conflict and violence than compromise on their exclusive Irish republican or unionist agendas that involved the assimilation of the other within their preferred nation-state. By playing down the significant gains of peace in the years after the 1994 ceasefires some cosmopolitan critics (Wilford & Wilson, 2003: 8–10) may have lost sight of the numerous lives that have in all probability been saved, and the unnecessary suffering that has thereby been averted in recent years. My assumptions regarding such a peace dividend seem to be borne out by any plausible reading of police statistics on security related incidents, and deaths caused by them, from 1969 to the present (PSNI, 2007).

In the final section, I focus on the question as to how ethno-national conflicts might best be transformed, and I assess current arrangements in Northern Ireland in this light. There will be no detailed recommendations there for specific comparable cases of ethno-national conflict, as my main purpose is to investigate the extent to which Northern Ireland's peace process can be said to have succeeded as a normatively sound process of conflict resolution. This will give me an opportunity to make it clear why I disagree with many of my fellow egalitarian commentators on the key bi-national, consociational aspects of Northern Ireland's new, agreed constitutional order. While the critics consider those features of national group recognition that have been central to the peace process as obstacles to the social transformation that is required to end the conflict, it is from my perspective only through a process of constitutional change that embodies the mutual recognition of rival national groups that this transformative process can get underway.

When considering what is required in order to transform such cases of national conflict, those cosmopolitan critics of post-Agreement Northern Ireland tend to opt for: (i) a democratic regime with no need for formal group affiliation or recognition, where individuals are free to act, vote and represent without any such group-based restrictions; (ii) political and social integration rather than consociation and national group autonomy; (iii) a post-national constitutional order rather than one that is constantly vulnerable to the destabilising effects of a zero-sum conflict over sovereignty; and finally (iv) a political process focused on tackling injustices of class and gender rather than one that feeds the aspirations of alleged ethnic entrepreneurs. I will take up each of these four issues in turn and will argue that advocates of a strongly individualistic, integrated, post-national, liberal order in Northern Ireland have typically failed to grasp the group-differentiated realities of structural injustice that must be addressed if the transformation of such a conflict is to be effective and durable. The cosmopolitan conception of egalitarian democracy that these critics rely on fails to deliver an adequate normative framework for dealing with the challenges that have been faced by those engaged in this peace process.

Ethno-National Conflict and Other Forms of Ethnic Politics

I take the conflict in Northern Ireland to be representative of one variety of ethnic politics, a clash between antagonistic modern, ethno-national communities involving disputed claims to sovereignty made by at least one state. In order to respect fully the important differences between the range of types and varieties of ethnic politics (Kymlicka, 1995, 2001; Guibernau & Rex, 1997; May *et al.*, 2004), and the conflicts they can potentially generate, I will outline here a set of categories to facilitate a differentiated analysis of ethno-political conflict and to highlight some important distinctions between types. Without such an analysis there a danger of treating all forms of ethnic politics in the same way, a danger associated with those elements of cosmopolitan thought that are hostile to group recognition in all it guises (Barry, 2001). Ethnic politics presents a very wide range of varied challenges depending on the political and historical context, and these challenges will not be met in an appropriate manner if policy makers fail to spot the differences. I suggest that we consider three main types of ethnic politics, with some further subdivisions of varieties within some types. First, there is potential for internal conflict between ethnic groups *within* established states where sovereignty is not itself in dispute, and there are at least three varieties of such internal strife. Second, there are conflicts *about* the fundamental structure of at least one state, of which there are also three varieties, one of these being my immediate concern. There are also, third, conflicts *beyond* the order of states, between ethno-political groups that transcend state boundaries.

Ethno-political conflicts *within* a state (A) can arise amongst ethnic groups who are integrated differently, or who are at different stages of integration, as groups of citizens within a particular state. The circumstances of such conflicts are almost always dependent on differing historical patterns of migration and there are at least three varieties of such conflicts. We can, first, have ethno-political conflict *within* a state when groups of relatively recent immigrants struggle to achieve equal citizen status in a political context marked by a strong national tradition (A1), take France, Britain and, increasingly, both parts of Ireland as examples. But we can also, second, have such conflict in societies where most citizens have an immigrant heritage but where the patterns of political integration amongst immigrant groups have had very different historical trajectories (A2). Typically these conflicts occur amongst ethnic groups in immigrant societies such as the United States, Canada, Australia and New Zealand. In the case of the first of these examples, in particular, these conflicts are driven by antagonistic race relations shaped by the legacy of slavery, but there are also ethno-political conflicts in such societies between more recent immigrant communities and these can be driven by competition for scarce material resources as well as by matters of cultural and linguistic, as well as racial difference.

Given the post-colonial features of many immigrant societies, a third variety of conflict *within* a state can arise. This type of conflict is caused by political tensions between indigenous peoples and the 'new political order' that was constructed on historical foundations established by colonial settlers and developed further by subsequent generations of immigrants (A3). This third variety, post-colonial conflict, can in some instances lead to a more fundamental questioning of the constitutional order itself, in which case it may be transformed from an internal conflict into one variety of ethno-national conflict, a form of ethno-political conflict in which national claims to sovereignty are in dispute (B). In many cases of post-colonial conflict, the antagonism between indigenous peoples and dominant settled populations does not lead to questions about sovereignty or national self-determination but rather to internal matters concerning material distribution or policies related to cultural, religious and linguistic differences. Depending on the nature of the disputes in particular contexts, post-colonial conflicts can, therefore, either be contained within a state (A3) or become disputes about the basic constitutional order itself (B1).

The distinctive characteristic of all conflicts of the first form, those I've discussed as being contained *within* a state (A1-3), is that while the terms of political integration are at stake, the constitutional order in which these terms are disputed is itself accepted at least in its most fundamental features. When those constitutional fundamentals are themselves up for grabs, then we are dealing with an ethno-political conflict about at least one state. In these cases the citizen-ethos and political identity of a nation-state, or the state's external territorial boundaries, or the fundamental structure of the constitutional order are in dispute. We have already seen how post-colonial conflicts involving claims to sovereignty made by indigenous peoples (B1) take this form. But there are numerous other examples of ethno-national conflict about at least one state that involve disputes between two or more (modern) national communities. Some of these conflicts are bi-polar in that the key dispute about sovereignty is between two national communities (B2), including the cases of Israel/ Palestine, Sri Lanka, Cyprus and Northern Ireland. The dynamics of conflict differ when more than two communities have had key stakes in the conflict (B3), as in the cases of Bosnia, Iraq or Lebanon. My focus in the article is with bi-polar ethno-national conflict about disputed state sovereignty claims (B2) and I take the political struggle about the constitutional status of Northern Ireland to fit squarely into that sub-category.

One might also distinguish a third form of ethno-political conflict that transcends the state altogether by going beyond, in some important respects at least, all questions as to how particular constitutional states are ordered. Such global ethno-political conflict may occur between competing world-views informed by religious and geo-political considerations (C). There is little doubt that this last form of ethno-political conflict presents us with one of the greatest challenges we face today both in terms of global security and of global justice. While I will have little to say about it here, it is worth noting that such global conflicts do continue to be played out in various conflicts both within particular states and about states. It might even be suggested that one key variable in ethno-national conflict is the extent to which a global ethno-political conflict is being played out in that context, as is the case in Iraq and also Israel/Palestine. It appears to be the case that the absence of any such global conflict in the case of Northern Ireland was favourable to the prospects for resolution. This meant that it was possible in the Northern Irish case for third parties, particularly the United States (McGinty, 1997), to engage in acts of benign intervention, whereas in the other cases mentioned above it is difficult for any international actors, particularly the United States in the post-2001 global order, to intervene without their acts being perceived for various reasons as malign, by at least one of the relevant parties.

One of the most significant features of the variety of ethno-national conflicts with which we will be concerned, those involving disputes about sovereignty between two antagonistic modern national communities (B2), is the propensity in such cases for significant levels of political violence (Gurr & Harff, 2002). Certainly the contrast in this regard is stark between such conflicts (also B3) and the varieties of ethno-political conflict that are contained within a state (A1-3 above). Much of the social scientific debate on ethno-national conflict has therefore, understandably, focused on the most effective means of bringing about an end to violence in such contexts. Ending the violence, be that paramilitary or state violence, has certainly been a priority for many of the people involved in such conflicts. The experience of violence or its threat leads many participants to recognise (some more quickly than others) that the cost of violent conflict may be too high, regardless of the importance they attach to the disputed political goals. The concern to end violence, while it often competes with other goals, is typically shared in such contexts by many ordinary citizens across the ethno-national divide as well as their political representatives, and those with governmental responsibility for the states in dispute. It is also a concern shared by those external observers who view the conflict with some dismay, including those from neighbouring states or beyond in the wider international community who may, in some cases, feel a sense of responsibility to intervene, or at least to do something practical that will help minimise unnecessary suffering. We will bear these concerns in mind when we assess the merits of Northern Ireland's peace process as a model of conflict resolution in later sections, but before that an outline of the key features of a critical-theoretical approach to social scientific research is in order.

Explanation, Interpretation and Critique

Naturalistic social scientists, those who model their methods on the natural sciences, seek to present addressees with a rationally disengaged, external, scientific perspective on the object of inquiry. With respect to ethno-national disputes, it might be thought that such a disengaged approach provides the only way to ground an objective, neutral basis for resolving conflict, a position that will not be tainted by the multiplicity of biased and conflicting points of view that participants will have on the situation. In contrast, critical theorists seek to *engage with* rather than *abstract from* the conflicting interpretations that are operative in the minds of participants. This allows the critical theorist to take seriously, in ways that disengaged naturalists may find more difficult, the complex and potentially problematic relationship between their analysis of the conflict and participants' perspectives. A critical-theoretical analysis is itself a self-conscious intervention in the world, not just an appeal that addressees might consider some advice, given from an apparently rational and neutral point of view, to act in this way or that so as to tackle a particular problem. The critical theorist engages in a form of transformative action since the purpose of analysis is to explore *with* participants new and better ways of thinking about and acting in the world. In particular critical theory seeks to articulate the aspirations of those who endure forms of unnecessary suffering, including the consequences of political violence, by casting a critical gaze on the causes of such suffering. Critical theory is of necessity inter-disciplinary since it always has normative-philosophical, interpretive-historical and explanatory-social scientific dimensions to it.

The emphasis on engagement with rather than abstraction from participants' perspectives gives a central place in the analysis to the social meaning that historical events have for participants. In particular it allows for an engagement with the conflicting historical interpretations that are so central to ethno-national disputes. Once questions of meaning are placed at the heart of the practice of social science, it becomes a fundamentally different enterprise from natural science (Taylor, 1985; Flyvbjerg, 2001). This is one of the reasons why critical theorists consider it impossible to conduct social research entirely from the perspective of a neutral, rationally disengaged, external observer. They recognise their own role as participants in the object of inquiry since they think that all social scientists are always already participating in the phenomena they investigate. As a participant, the critical theorist does not merely observe but rather interprets data, a distinction that can be drawn out with reference to the famously ambiguous duck-rabbit drawing as discussed by Ludwig Wittgenstein (1978: 193–230).

Observers of the drawing in Figure 1 will first, instinctively, see either a duck looking to the observer's left, or else a rabbit looking to the observer's right. We can take a second look and switch from one to the other but we cannot see both at the same time. It's not a duck or a rabbit but a duck-rabbit. What we observe in the world depends very much on what we think we are observing. There is no raw historical data just waiting to be picked up by social scientific researchers but there are all sorts of meanings in the social world and researchers have to try to make

Figure 1. Duck-rabbit drawing.

sense of them. We are actively interpreting this data as we observe it and this means that we always already have a theory as to what we think we are reading in our observations of the world. Some people are likely to read certain things that are happening in the world with one interpretive frame (a 'duck' frame) while others will read it through another interpretive frame (a 'rabbit' frame) and there may be many other frames through which we could view the same events. Clearly it makes a difference to our observation which interpretive frame we use, instinctively or by design. If this is true of a simple duck-rabbit drawing, then surely its truth will hold and will carry significantly greater weight when we are investigating ethno-national conflicts, such as that in Northern Ireland. One of the key aspects to the most entrenched of these conflicts is that it is not near so easy for those involved to exchange one frame for another as it is for us to switch from duck to rabbit theory when looking at this simple drawing.

Two additional considerations add further weight to the view that a theory of ethno-national conflict cannot but be critically engaged rather than abstractly neutral. First, terms like violence, security and peace, and many others related to ethno-national conflict, have meanings that are highly contested, and some might say essentially so (Connolly, 1993). Any such contest of meaning will typically reflect some deeper differences of perspective on such conflicts shaped by participants' values and by considerations of individual and group identity. So it is difficult to argue that we can approach this research topic in a neutral way, even when it comes to the language we use in our analysis. Second, we can never be sure that the theory that guides our observations and interpretations are not shot through with assumptions that privilege without justification one perspective over others. No matter how hard we try to divest ourselves of any source of bias, it is impossible to do so since we will not even be conscious of many of the interests and identity-related considerations that may be shaping our perspective on things. It is the matters that have the most profound impact on our thinking that we may be least willing to acknowledge or to examine.

For all these reasons, critical theorists see a need to be up front about the fact that they bring a particular, engaged perspective to their research. In addition, critical theorists are sceptical of the view that the object of inquiry should itself be thought of as a neutral domain, since they consider virtually all of the most interesting aspects of social reality to be typically structured in ways that operate in the interests of some people and at the expense of others. If we try to investigate the world from a neutral perspective, therefore, our research is very likely to reflect the current constellation of power relations, while missing (or worse masking) relations of domination and subjugation under a cloak of apparent neutrality. At best, this alleged neutrality represents a failure to expose to scrutiny the values that are actually seeping into the research, but at worst it might well bolster the power of the privileged while denying voice to those who are marginalised in the current order. Since the world is assumed by the critical theorist to be structured at a deep level by relations of privilege and domination, this underscores the need for a stance of practical engagement rather than one that claims neutrality. The point is to pursue what Paul Ricoeur (1981: 34) referred to as a 'hermeneutics of suspicion', with the intention of exposing the ways in which certain social meanings underpin unwarranted and unearned privileges in the world. In the final section I will argue that cosmopolitan analysts of the conflict in Northern Ireland have tended to abstract from rather than engage with participants' perspectives. Their abstractions have involved the same problematic assumption regarding the neutrality of their own perspective as that which besets naturalistic social scientists.

The broad purpose of critical theory, therefore, is not to facilitate social control through the application of scientific reasoning but rather to generate insights that will facilitate a transformation of society that will lead to greater human freedom. It is not value-free but it remains committed to objectivity in research since it is driven by those human values of freedom, equality, and democracy that many can share even as we contest their meaning. There are, it seems, three key dimensions to any theory of ethno-national conflict that will be critical in an appropriate sense. It should (I) be capable of offering some explanation of the obstacles to human freedom that cause the conflict; (II) articulate and justify normatively a substantive criticism of the way in which such obstacles have been maintained; and (III) present some practical guidance as to what needs to be done and by whom so that the social conditions that limit this freedom are best to be transformed.

Dismantling the Causes of Ethno-National Conflict in Northern Ireland

In this section I will explore the connections between the explanatory, normative and practical dimensions of this critical-theoretical approach to ethno-national conflict by providing a very brief account of the kind of transformation that appears to be required if the conflict in Northern Ireland, as one particular case of bi-polar, ethno-national conflict, is to be resolved. The focus on this one case allows the more practical considerations as to what should be done, and by whom, to come more readily into focus, and these questions of application will be taken up in more detail in the following section. The intention here is to sketch a critical-interpretive, explanatory analysis driven by the widely shared (if interpretively contested) values of freedom, equality and democracy. The analysis seeks to be responsive to, and to engage with, the broad historical aspirations, political demands and rival perspectives of the key participants in this conflict. What have the key obstacles been to human freedom in this context, and how are they to be dismantled?

Let us begin with some basic ontological considerations. In other words, what is going on in the world when an ethno-national conflict breaks out? These conflicts occur between national communities rather than individuals as such. Like all social groups national communities are relationally constructed, which means that they are differentiated in any given context by the ways in which members of a group stand in relation to others, particularly with regard to structures of power and privilege (Young, 2000: 92–102; O'Neill, 2003b). Hierarchical relations that privilege one national community, typically but not always the majority, will be oppressive of other national communities. When those hierarchies impact profoundly and from the start of life on the capacities that members of different groups have to realise their full potential, then we have a deep structural inequality and a relation of domination. Whenever there are relations of domination, there is always also the potential for political antagonism, conflict and resistance. In the context of the conflict in Northern Ireland, Irish nationalists have sought to resist any constitutional arrangement that would subject them to domination as national minority within one region of the United Kingdom. Unionists have, on the other hand, resisted incorporation into a united Ireland as that would leave them vulnerable to domination as a national minority within that constitutional order.

Given the fact that national communities are the basic unit of this analysis, we need to account for the ontological status of individuals. Individual identities are inextricably connected to group identities. Each individual identity is constituted within a network of group affiliations, many of which will not have been chosen, as is often the case with class, gender, race, sexual orientation and, crucially in this context, nationality. Individual freedom is, on the account I am developing here, conditional on the freedom of those groups that are constitutive of that individual's identity. A group is free if its members can express and celebrate their distinctiveness without cost to their status as equals within relevant social and political contexts. Freedom depends, in other words, not on toleration but rather on the positive recognition of group identities by members of other groups (Honneth, 1995, 2007; Tully, 1995). The struggle for positive group recognition has provided much of the impetus behind many of the most significant social movements of the later modern era including socialism, feminism and liberation movements confronting racism, colonialism, homophobia, sectarianism and, of course, ethno-national domination. In each case the capacity of individual group members to achieve their full potential has depended on the group's capacity to attain equality without having to abandon its distinctiveness.

This retention of distinctiveness means resisting assimilation into the mainstream if that process of assimilation requires the acceptance of a set of normative standards that reflect disproportionately the interests of the dominant group. This is why Irish nationals in Northern Ireland would not consider themselves to be free from domination were they to achieve formal equality for each of them as individuals within an integrated, and exclusively British, United Kingdom. Under such an arrangement there would remain a deep inequality with respect to fit between the national communities and the constitutional ethos that provides a context for citizenship. In that unambiguously and exclusively British context the constitutional ethos would provide a neat fit for those who identity themselves as British nationals, in other words for unionists. This kind of fit is something that can easily be taken for granted by members of dominant national groups in similar contexts, but in such an arrangement there would clearly be no such fit for the Irish national minority. The opposite would be the case for unionists in a strongly integrated and similarly exclusive, united Ireland. Formal equality of citizenship status under such circumstances, within an exclusive nation-state, has clearly been seen by members of both national groups to be insufficient, as should be clear given the claims and issues that have been at stake in their historic struggle to secure within the constitutional order positive recognition of their distinctiveness as national communities.

Given these ontological considerations, the focus of a critical-theoretical explanation of ethno-national conflict will be on those structural relations between ethno-national groups that systematically privilege members of a dominant group over others. Typically in such cases dominant groups are privileged by constitutional arrangements within a political regime or claims to sovereignty that are made in the name of one faction, even if it is a large majority, rather than all of the people. In all such cases there is a political failure to provide an appropriate context for relations among equal citizens because the constitutional ethos in which the state institutions are embedded will be insufficiently inclusive of the diversity of ethno-national groups in the society. If political institutions are exclusively, or disproportionately, expressive of the dominant ethno-national group's identity, then those institutions will be sources of alienation for others. This suggests that an important cause of ethno-national conflict is the experience of political alienation of a national community that has been subjected to the systematic political institutionalisation of a hierarchical relation of group domination. Here we have grounds for a substantive normative critique of such political arrangements since the systematic privileges that one national community enjoys over another creates unnecessary obstacles to human freedom. Group hierarchies that have these effects ought to be dismantled as key elements of the process of transformation that will allow the causes of ethno-national to be overcome.

In its engagement with participants' perspectives, critical theory needs some way of assessing the validity of those claims that might be made by different groups as to why they feel alienated from political institutions or processes. The theory should direct our attention to those claims that can be justified in relation to some actual structures of domination, as opposed to claims of alienation that arise from other, subjective sources (O'Neill, 2003b: 371–372). A subjective feeling of alienation is only of interest to a critical-theoretical account of conflict if it is has a real basis in the experience of domination, not for example if it arises from the boredom that some relatively privileged people may feel with respect to political attempts to grapple constructively with the causes of conflict. The normative framework of the theory should put some critical distance between objective causes of alienation and subjective feelings that are rooted in ill-founded sources of ethnic resentment, such as sectarianism or nationalistic xenophobia. The critical theorist needs to identify, by drawing on relevant sources of social scientific research, those structures that have institutionalised social hierarchies historically, so that their explanatory role in causing conflict can be addressed.

The best way to get to grips with the objective alienation that is at the root of such conflict is to pursue political strategies and policies that facilitate and motivate inclusive compromises and just peace agreements between conflicting parties. This will require a process of dialogue between participants that will afford them opportunities to listen to others so as to understand better the sources of their alienation, fears and frustrations. A dialogue of this kind is also known as a peace process. Before we assess the key features of the peace process in Northern Ireland, let me draw out some further aspects of the normative substance of this critical perspective. Agreements that are most likely to bring long-term peace and stability are those that are most effective in dismantling ethno-national group hierarchies thereby creating an inclusive political ethos that sustains egalitarian relations between all citizen-groups. This suggests a normative imperative to direct efforts to secure fair agreements in such contexts. Peace processes should seek to be effective in:

> Dismantling all structures of inequality that allow differences in national group identity to be converted into systematic advantages by one group, thereby establishing a constitutional ethos that guarantees to members of all national groups equal dignity within their identity-forming contexts.

This imperative requires the deconstruction of all legal or social arrangements that allow a dominant ethno-national group to enjoy political, cultural, economic, linguistic or religious privileges that are denied to others. A deconstructive process of this kind will bring the dominance of that group to an end as it will establish an egalitarian political order that facilitates stability and justice. This order will need to ensure that opportunities for self-realisation of all individual citizens are placed on an equal footing, as they would almost certainly not be within a political system that facilitates group dominance in a nationally divided society by allowing, for example, a strongly majoritarian decision-making process.

If we are to eliminate the causes of national conflict, therefore, what is needed is a constitutional arrangement in which members of each national group can recognise themselves as equals without abandoning their group distinctiveness. Equal citizenship requires an integrated and shared political culture and an inclusive constitutional ethos. This inclusiveness will have to be reflected not only in the basic constitutional principles themselves but also in the symbolic order of the state. Flags, anthems and official emblems should be expressive of citizen unity not divisive symbols of group oppression. The achievement of such an inclusive ethos can only be built on new relations between identity groups, and that will typically require a change in the understanding of both self and other, on all sides. Political integration in societies that are marked by deep divisions of nationality require such a transformation of relations between historically antagonistic national communities, since only that will establish an inclusive politics of mutual recognition that grounds substantive equality without eradicating national differences.

The Northern Ireland Process as a Model?

Should the peace process in Northern Ireland be presented as a model for the resolution of comparable ethno-national conflicts elsewhere? The normative imperative that was presented in the previous section provides an appropriate critical standard according to which we can reach a considered view as to the successes and limitations of this process. The more fully it can be considered to have satisfied that imperative, the stronger the case will be for viewing it as a model from which those interested in resolving other comparable conflicts might learn. Our assessment will also allow us to ask whether or not the process has served participants well by facilitating the social and political transformations required in order to bring their historic conflict to an end. This will lead me to return to the claims made by cosmopolitan critics of the Agreement and of the main institutional features of the post-Agreement order, and to take up in turn the four main concerns they have about the prospects for egalitarian democracy in Northern Ireland.

The imperative demands the dismantling of any structure of inequality that grants systematic advantages to one national group over the other. The question we need to ask is whether or not the peace process has been effective in facilitating the establishment of egalitarian relations between the national communities in Northern Ireland. This would be the case if membership of one national community, unionist or Irish nationalist, rather than the other were to be of no advantage to individuals with respect to the effective opportunities they would have to realise their full potential. Have all economic, cultural or political opportunities been effectively equalised between members of the national groups, or does ethno-national difference bring benefits to one group at the expense of the other?

With respect to matters of material distribution such as employment, housing, welfare and income, there have been significant changes since the late 1960s, just before the start of a quarter of a century of sustained political violence. Irish Nationalists claimed at that time through their demand for civil rights that they were suffering from unjustifiable disadvantages that were supported by practices of discrimination in the distribution of these goods. The narrowing of the economic gap between the communities has been a vitally significant change in Northern Irish society in the past decades, a change made possible by the legal and political measures that were taken in that period to end all forms of discrimination (McGarry

& O'Leary, 1995: 265–310). Survey research suggests that it is now widely perceived across both communities that there is equal treatment with respect to employment, housing, welfare and other economic goods (Northern Ireland Life and Times Survey, 2007). This important change in perceptions allowed the parties to the Agreement to cover this issue under the general provisions for 'Rights, Safeguards and Equality of Opportunity' (*Agreement*, 1998: section 6), but no claim regarding perceived material inequalities between national communities has presented significant impediments to the process of negotiating a settlement. This is not to say, however, that material inequalities or the distribution of opportunities do not continue to raise significant challenges for Northern Ireland, but I will return to this matter shortly.

The issues that have been more contentious in this process are those involving claims to recognition, where constitutional politics and national-cultural concerns have intersected. The Agreement sought to resolve the dispute regarding sovereignty by enshrining a principle of consent whereby a right of self-determination would reside with the people of both parts of Ireland, with any change in status requiring concurrent consent 'North' and 'South' of the border. On the one hand, this assures unionists that a united Ireland could only come about with the consent of the majority in the North, and the Irish Constitution was subsequently changed to reflect this. On the other hand, Irish nationalists are assured by the requirement that the people of both jurisdictions can exercise a right of Irish self-determination together, leaving open the possibility that they could act jointly to end partition and to unite.

Strands 2 and 3 of the Agreement (sections 4–5) established North–South Ministerial Council, the British–Irish Council and the British–Irish Intergovernmental Conference, all designed to secure a bi-national framework to support the internal mechanisms for democratic government agreed under strand 1 (*Agreement*, section 3). The architecture of the Agreement reflects a process that embodies the mutual recognition of national difference, whereby both national communities recognise the legitimacy of the conflicting national aspiration of the other, while agreeing to a set of institutions that allows them to manage that difference fairly and effectively (O'Leary 1999). This framework establishes a bi-national constitutional arrangement that affords the two national traditions 'parity of esteem' by recognising their conflicting claims and aspirations to be equally legitimate. It is very clear that the main thrust of this settlement has been to dismantle any hierarchical relationship between the national communities so that neither can acquire systematic political or constitutional advantages at the expense of the other. The bi-national constitutional ethos that has emerged affords equal dignity to citizens of both traditions in their own identity-forming contexts.

The internal democratic institutions that were revived in May 2007 following the Agreement at St Andrews of November 2006, must be understood to operate in this bi-national context, supported by the new relationship between the United Kingdom and the Republic of Ireland that is enshrined in the 1998 Agreement. While of course the institutions revived in May 2007 are certainly not guaranteed to last, they are much less likely to be brought down as a result of any crisis concerning matters of security that was the case previously. There have been numerous important achievements in recent years on matters such as police reform, decommissioning, de-militarisation, and a massive scaling back of para-military activity as confirmed by a succession of positive reports (Independent Monitoring Commission, 2007). All of these achievements have helped to build confidence and mutual trust and they have created a new context in which these institutions have a much better opportunity to function effectively in a relatively stable political environment.

Many of the key features of these internal democratic institutions are designed to ensure that power can be shared effectively and inclusively across the national divide. These features mark this bi-national settlement out as a consociational one (O'Leary, 1999; McGarry & O'Leary, 2004) and they include: the choice of PRSTV as an electoral system; the rules for designation of MLAs and the role such designation plays in the passage of important legislation requiring cross-community support; the process for nominating the First Minister and Deputy First Minister as co-leaders of the executive; the d'Hondt formula for the allocation of ministerial portfolios; and the role of Assembly Committees in holding ministers to account. All of these measures are designed to ensure that unionists and Irish nationalists can engage in the political process an equal footing, with no systematic advantages being afforded to members of one or the other national group.

Before concluding our assessment we must now return, as promised, to the main cosmopolitan criticisms of post-Agreement politics in Northern Ireland. The critics worry (i) that the arrangements that are in place now privilege certain national group identities over others group identities, and that they also fail to give due and equal weight in the political process to individuals who have weak (if any) sense of belonging to national groups (Taylor, 2006: 218–221; O'Flynn, 2003). These critics do not fully appreciate the extent to which the institutional framework of the Agreement is, as its main advocates would have it, a liberal and not a corporate consociation (McGarry & O'Leary, 2004). Apart from the explicit provisions in the Agreement (section 6) on rights and equality, it must be noted that political parties engage under this system in an unrestricted competition for votes. In the ballot box, voters support any candidate or party they wish to in order of their own choices. Likewise, the allocation of ministerial portfolios is based not on the national identity of the parties but rather on the strength of their representation in the Assembly. The membership of the Assembly and of the Executive, therefore, reflect the free choices of individual voters under an electoral system that is far more likely to secure representation for smaller parties (without any clear affiliation to a national tradition) representing minority interests than would the alternative, majoritarian AV system that is favoured by many of the Agreement's liberal critics (Horowitz, 2001; O'Flynn, 2003: 142–143; Wilford & Wilson, 2003: 14–15).

What the critics seem not to have fully appreciated are the reasons why political participants in Northern Ireland continue to vote as they do for parties that are representative of national blocs, with much of the electoral competition occurring between rather than across those blocs (Mitchell, 2001). This reflects the political priorities of the voters and the need they have for reassurance that their national identities will be recognised and respected. That should come as no surprise to us considering the long history of antagonism between the two national communities, and the strong resistance that both national groups have engaged in with respect to the integrationist ambitions of some members of the other community. The rules of designation in the Assembly that govern the voting procedures for important legislation requiring cross-community support must be considered in this context. They are there to ensure that neither national community should be denied an effective voice on key matters that affect them but these rules could be modified by agreement at any stage should they no longer be needed.

Another worry (ii) that cosmopolitan critics have expressed is that the consociational architecture of the Agreement entrenches or exacerbates community divisions (Wilford & Wilson, 2003: 11–12; Oberschall & Palmer, 2005: 77; O'Flynn, 2003: 141), thereby reproducing and fostering sectarianism across society. Cosmopolitans stress the benefits of political and social integration over national group autonomy which they associate with consociationalism. But once again, they seem to have failed to notice what kind of society Northern Ireland actually is, and they underestimate the need that members of the main national groups have for positive recognition of their group differences. The agreed institutions are designed to defuse and to render manageable any causes of division between the national communities by facilitating a power-sharing arrangement in a bi-national context in which each tradition enjoys a 'parity of esteem'. Enforcing integration would hardly be a liberal solution to the realities of group difference and the enduring strength of the national traditions, reinforced as they are by cultural, educational and religious structures. It would not only be unproductive but also unjust to force one or the other national community to assimilate to an exclusively British or Irish ethos. Within the bi-national context that seems to be required as a matter of justice, some significant challenges remain particularly with respect to the public expression of cultural and national differences.

There is certainly the potential for flags, emblems, marches and cultural activities to be exploited for malign reasons, to foster sectarian division and to undermine the achievements of recent times. While there has been some thinking on the best way to manage these contentious issues of cultural, national and religious expression matters (OFMDFM, 2005; Bryan & Gillespie, 2005) it will take some considerable time to put measures in place that will allow these matters to be managed effectively. The key challenge is to ensure that they are handled in ways that give voice, through practices of dialogue, to all affected and that do not privilege one tradition over others (O'Neill, 2000) and this might require further legislation in the future to ensure cultural equality across Northern Ireland. The goal must be to bring these cultural practices into line with an inclusive political ethos that allows each citizen to celebrate their differences under conditions of equality.

The Agreement's cosmopolitan critics have also argued (iii) that the way in which the key constitutional question has been handled encourages an on-going conflict over sovereignty, instead of establishing a post-national form of politics in Northern

Ireland (Wilford & Wilson, 2003: 13–14; O'Flynn, 2003: 146–148; Oberschall & Palmer, 2005: 81). They fail to notice that the Agreement's North–South and East–West features go some way to defusing such a conflict over national sovereignty, and once again overlook the importance that most supporters of the main parties in Northern Ireland attach to the question of its constitutional status. The bi-national features of the Agreement and the constitutional ethos in which it is embedded represents a significant break from the politics of nationalism, if by that we understand the attempt to divide the world up according the a principle of 'one nation, one state'. The Agreement is certainly post-nationalist by those standards but it is not based on a naïve assumption that we can thereby move beyond the conflicting aspirations that are held dear within these two national traditions that have had such a long history of antagonism.

Finally, cosmopolitan critics argue (iv) that the agreed institutions, by privileging the politics of nationalism, leave us ill-equipped to tackle the more serious challenges that arise from inequalities based on class and gender. There clearly are serious economic inequalities within Northern Ireland that cut across the ethno-national divide, given the significant numbers of relatively rich and poor in both communities. In so far as these are supported by structures that provide systematic advantages for those born into relatively privileged socio-economic contexts, they should as a matter of justice be dismantled. The same might be said of gender imbalances in Northern Irish society, another inequality that obviously cuts across the national divide. There are also important egalitarian concerns regarding the status and socio-economic position of members of those cultures, races and ethnicities that identify with neither of the major ethno-national blocs, many of them representative of the growing numbers of immigrants in Northern Ireland. The question is whether or not these issues are more likely to be tackled under the bi-national, consociational arrangements that are in place than they were previously. Certainly by achieving an effective end to political violence, the peace process has already brought considerable benefits to those relatively underprivileged communities who suffered the worst consequences of the conflict and its associated communal tensions. It is clear, however, that much remains to be done and that the responsibility for tackling these challenges of justice is shared across the ethno-national divide by all parties represented in the Assembly. The hope is that these issues might provide a focus that will enable politicians and citizens to move in time beyond the constitutional issue, but that is something that will happen of its own accord if it happens at all. It is certainly not something that can be demanded by those who find the politics of nationalism somewhat distasteful.

Conclusion

Has the ethno-national conflict in Northern Ireland been resolved? It is clear that the main ethno-national traditions of unionism and Irish nationalism remain vibrant and strong both culturally and politically. National differences are recognised and accommodated by the political arrangements that have been agreed, and they continue to be reinforced by cultural, educational and religious structures and practices. Within this bi-national context, both groups continue to pursue long-term nationalist projects that set the two traditions into deeply opposed positions. From the perspective of this critical theory, none of this is a major cause for worry as long as it is all played out within a context that is governed by egalitarian relations between the communities, where neither side enjoys systematic privileges over the other and where the constitutional ethos is inclusive and representative of all. When we compare this to decades of on-going political violence, or to the unjust order suffered by Irish nationalists for half a century before that, the new Northern Ireland satisfies to a very high degree the normative imperative driving this analysis.

What Northern Ireland now enjoys is the politics of national and cultural pluralism and when this is pursued peacefully, as hopefully it will continue to be in this context, we have a model of political engagement that is likely to be of significant relevance to other nationally divided societies. While many egalitarian democrats may will Northern Ireland, and the rest of the world, into a post-national era in which we can focus our political energies on maximising conditions for individual autonomy by minimising the unjust effects of those structures of inequality based on differences of social class, gender, or identity, we can only encourage the creation of such a context and not simply will it into existence. If the vast majority of a population wishes to pursue conflicting nationalist agendas, and to maintain separate cultures and education systems, then the challenge is to create a set of just political institutions that will allow them to do this without unnecessary antagonism, thereby minimising the danger of relations descending into violence, and maximising the potential for those other serious inequalities to be tackled effectively. If people eventually change their political priorities and start voting for political parties without nationalist agendas, then this will be an important sign of the emergence of a post-national era. But this should not be viewed as a condition for the success of a peace process. In fact, by accommodating the exclusive agendas of the politics of nationalism effectively, the institutions agreed in Belfast on Good Friday of 1998, have succeed where a more ambitious programme of post-national integration would almost certainly have failed.

While it may well be argued that Northern Ireland could have arrived at this point by a shorter historical route that would be to underestimate the time that was required to grapple with the wide range of complex conditions that have impacted on the conflict. There were considerable difficulties with respect to the internal relations between the national communities and external relations between Britain and Ireland. One sign that the process in Northern Ireland can be considered as a useful model of resolution for other ethno-nationally conflicted societies is that the major challenges it now faces, the injustices of class, gender and identity differences, are shared by most other modern societies that have never experienced such strife. Northern Ireland is undergoing a process of 'normalisation', which for a society with a history of such instability, violence and mutual hostility is no mean achievement.

References

Agreement Reached in the Multiparty Negotiations (1998) available online at: http://www.nio.gov.uk/agreement.pdf

Agreement at St Andrews (2006) available online at: http://www.nio.gov.uk/st_andrews_agreement.pdf

Barry, B. (2001) *Culture and Equality: An Egalitarian Critique of Multiculturalism* (Cambridge: Polity).

Barry, J. & Zalewski, M. (Eds) (2006) *Intervening in Northern Ireland: Critically Re-thinking Representations of the Conflict*, Special Issue of *Critical Review of International Social and Political Philosophy*, 9(4).

Bohman, J. (2005) Critical Theory, in: *Stanford Encyclopaedia of Philosophy*, available online at: http://plato.stanford.edu/entries/critical-theory/

Bryan, D. & Gillespie, G. (2005) Transforming Conflict: Flags and Emblems, Belfast: Institute of Irish Studies, Queen's University, available online at: http://www.asharedfutureni.gov.uk/flags.pdf

Campbell, D. (1998) *National Deconstruction: Violence, Identity, and Justice in Bosnia* (Minneapolis, MN: University of Minnesota Press).

Connolly, W. (1993) *The Terms of Political Discourse* 3rd edn (Princeton, NJ: Princeton University Press).

Flyvbjerg, B. (2001) *Making Social Science Matter* (Cambridge: Cambridge University Press).

Finlayson, A. (2006) 'What's the Problem?': Political Theory, Rhetoric and Problem-Setting, in: J. Barry & M. Zalewski (Eds) *Intervening in Northern Ireland: Critically Re-thinking Representations of the Conflict*, Special Issue of *Critical Review of International Social and Political Philosophy*, 9(4), pp. 541–557.

Giliomee, H. & Gagiano, J. (Eds) (1990) *The Elusive Search for Peace: South Africa, Israel and Northern Ireland* (Cape Town: Oxford University Press).

Guibernau, M. & Rex, J. (Eds) (1997) *The Ethnicity Reader: Nationalism, Multiculturalism and Migration* (Cambridge: Polity).

Gurr, T. & Harff, B. (2002) *Ethnic Conflict in World Politics*, 2nd edn (Boulder, CO: Westview).

Honneth, A. (1995) *The Struggle for Recognition*, trans. J. Anderson (Cambridge: Polity Press).

Honneth, A. (2007) *Disrespect: The Normative Foundations of Critical Theory* (Cambridge: Polity).

Horowitz, D. (2001) The Northern Ireland Agreement: Clear, Consociational and Risky, in: J. McGarry (Ed.) *Northern Ireland and the Divided World: Post-Agreement Northern Ireland in Comparative Perspective*, pp. 89–108 (Oxford: Oxford University Press).

Hoy, D. C. & McCarthy, T. (1994) *Critical Theory* (Oxford: Blackwell).

Independent Monitoring Commission (2007) 'Reports' available online at: http://www.independentmonitoringcommission.org/

Kymlicka, W. (1995) *Multicultural Citizenship* (Oxford: Oxford University Press).

Kymlicka, W. (2001) *Politics in the Vernacular: Nationalism, Multiculturalism and Citizenship* (Oxford: Oxford University Press).

Lijphart, A. (1978) *Democracy in Plural Societies* (New Haven, CT: Yale University Press).

Little, A. (2004) *Democracy and Northern Ireland: Beyond the Liberal Paradigm?* (Basingstoke: Palgrave).

May, S., Modood, T. & Squires, J. (2004) *Ethnicity, Nationalism and Minority Rights* (Cambridge: Cambridge University Press).

McGarry, J. & O'Leary, B. (1995) *Explaining Northern Ireland* (Oxford: Blackwell).

McGarry, J. & O'Leary, B. (2004) *The Northern Ireland Conflict: Consociational Engagements* (Oxford: Oxford University Press).

McGinty, R. (1997) American Influence on the Northern Ireland Peace Process, *Journal of Conflict Studies*, 17(2), available online at: http://www.lib.unb.ca/Texts/JCS/FALL97/articles/MACGINTY.html

Mitchell, P. (2001) Transcending an Ethnic Party System? The Impact of Consociational Governance on Electoral Dynamics and the Party System, in: R. Wilford (Ed.) *Aspects of the Belfast Agreement*, pp. 28–48 (Oxford: Oxford University Press).

Mouffe, C. (2000) *The Democratic Paradox* (London: Verso).

Northern Ireland Life and Times Survey (2007) Module: Community Relations, Equality, available online at: http://www.ark.ac.uk/nilt/results/comrel.html=uality

Oberschall, A. & Palmer, L. K. (2005) The Failure of Moderate Politics: The Case of Northern Ireland, in: I. O'Flynn & D. Russell (Eds) *Power Sharing: New Challenges for Divided Societies*, pp. 77–91 (London: Pluto Press).

Office of the First Minister and Deputy First Minister (2005) A Shared Future: Policy and Strategic Framework for Good Relations in Northern Ireland, available online at: http://www.asharedfutureni.gov.uk/gprs.pdf

O'Flynn, I. (2003) The Problem of Recognising Individual and National Identities: A Liberal Critique of the Belfast Agreement, *Critical Review of International Social and Political Philosophy*, 6(3), pp. 129–153.

O'Leary, B. (1999) The Nature of the Agreement, *Fordham Journal of International Law*, 22(4), pp. 1628–1667.

O'Leary, B. (2005) Debating Consociational Politics: Normative and Explanatory Arguments, in: S. Noel (Ed.) *From Power-sharing to Democracy*, pp. 3–43 (Montreal: McGill-Queen's University Press).

O'Neill, S. (2000) Liberty, Equality and the Rights of Cultures: The Marching Controversy at Drumcree, *British Journal of Politics and International Relations*, 2(1), pp. 26–45.

O'Neill, S. (2003a) Are National Conflicts Reconcilable? Discourse Theory and Political Accommodation in Northern Ireland, *Constellations*, 10(1), pp. 75–94.

O'Neill, S. (2003b) Justice in Ethnically Diverse Societies: A Critique of Political Alienation, *Ethnicities*, 3(3), pp. 369–392.

PSNI [Police Service of Northern Ireland] (2007) Security Statistics, available at http://www.psni.police.uk/index/statistics_branch/pg_security_stats.htm

Ricoeur, P. (1981) *Hermeneutics and the Human Sciences*, J. Thompson (Ed.) (Cambridge: Cambridge University Press).

Ruane, J. & Todd, J. (1996) *The Dynamics of Conflict in Northern Ireland: Power, Conflict, Emancipation* (Cambridge: Cambridge University Press).

Rush, F. (Ed.) (2004) *The Cambridge Companion to Critical Theory* (Cambridge: Cambridge University Press).

Taylor, C. (1985) *Philosophical Papers II: Philosophy and the Human Sciences* (Cambridge: Cambridge University Press).

Taylor, R. (2001) Consociation or Social Transformation?, in: J. McGarry (Ed.) *Northern Ireland and the Divided World: Post-Agreement Northern Ireland in Comparative Perspective*, pp. 36–52 (Oxford: Oxford University Press).

Taylor, R. (2006) The Belfast Agreement and the Politics of Consociationalism: A Critique, *The Political Quarterly*, 77(2), pp. 217–226.

Tully, J. (1995) *Strange Multiplicity: Constitutionalism in an Age of Diversity* (Cambridge: Cambridge University Press).

Vaughan-Williams, N. (2006) Towards a Problematisation of the Problematisations that Reduce Northern Ireland to a 'Problem', in: J. Barry & M. Zalewski (Eds) *Intervening in Northern Ireland: Critically Re-thinking Representations of the Conflict*, Special Issue of *Critical Review of International Social and Political Philosophy*, 9(4), pp. 513–526.

Whyte, J. (1991) *Interpreting Northern Ireland* (Oxford: Clarendon Press).

Wilford, R. & Wilson, R. (2003) A Route to Stability: The Review of the Belfast Agreement, paper published by Democratic Dialogue, available online at: http://cain.ulst.ac.uk/dd/papers/dd03agreview.pdf

Wilford, R. & Wilson, R. (2006) *The Trouble with Northern Ireland: The Belfast Agreement and Democratic Governance* (Dublin: TASC).

Wittgenstein, L. (1978) *Philosophical Investigations*, trans. G. E. M. Anscombe (Oxford: Basil Blackwell).

Young, I. M. (2000) *Inclusion and Democracy* (Oxford: Oxford University Press).

Illegal in Ireland, Irish Illegals: Diaspora Nation as Racial State

RONIT LENTIN

Introduction

In May 2006, 41 Afghan asylums seekers held a hunger strike in St Patrick's Cathedral, Dublin. The group, aged between 16 and 45, had been living in Ireland between one and five years. All were seeking leave to remain in Ireland and claimed that their action was precipitated by several of their asylum applications being turned down by the Office of the Refugee Applications Commissioner.[1] According to media reports, most of the group had been trafficked into Ireland, travelling out of Afghanistan to Iran, Turkey, Italy, Germany and France before reaching Ireland. Osman Hotak, spokesperson for the group, said the Refugee Appeals Commissioner had not given full attention to their applications and had unlawfully refused most of them, and appealed to the 'people of Ireland to help them on the ground of compassion' (Gartland & Reid, 2006).

The strike attracted much media attention and support by anti-racism groups demonstrating outside the Cathedral. Support was also offered by the Church of Ireland Archbishop of Dublin John Neill, who visited the men. Although he deemed the action inappropriate, as the Cathedral lacked the facility to cope with the group, the Cathedral authorities made no move to remove the men (Gartland & Reid, 2006).

The Department of Justice Equality and Law Reform refused to negotiate with the strikers, claiming, in the words of the then Minister for Justice Michael McDowell, that Ireland's immigration regime 'is one of the best in Europe' and is 'good and fair and transparent' (Lally, 2006). The six-day strike, which ended peacefully and without loss of life, rekindled the debate on the transparency and fairness of the Irish asylum system. But, perhaps contradictorily, state actors also linked it with the debate on the entitlement of Irish illegals in the US which was aired around the same time.

The Minister for Justice insisted that Ireland's asylum system 'does not work on who decides to occupy a church or who decides to go on hunger strike', and that 'we don't deal with people in the lump so to speak. We deal with every individual case' (Gartland & Reid, 2006). At the same time, the Minister for Foreign Affairs Dermot Ahern, speaking in Washington in May 2006, as the US Senate was preparing to discuss the immigration reform bill, while also praising the Irish immigration regime, explicitly juxtaposed the Cathedral hunger strike with the situation of illegal Irish immigrants in the US – dealt with 'in the lump' as it were, not as individual cases. According to Ahern, since most recent Irish illegals came to the US after 11 September 2001, they were therefore entitled to stay; their 'entitlement' to be in America, he insisted, cannot be compared with that of illegal immigrants in Ireland: 'When people try to compare what happened recently in Ireland with the Afghans with what's been happening here in the US, you're not comparing like with like. Completely different. When you look at the reference the UNHCR people made to the immigration system, they more or less said it's second to none in the world, that it's a transparent, fair process' (Staunton, 2006).

On 11 June 2004, the government of the Republic of Ireland asked the electorate to vote in a referendum to amend article 9 of the Constitution to remove birth-right citizenship from children born in Ireland who do not have at least one parent who is an Irish citizen or who is entitled to Irish citizenship. Birth right (*jus soli*) citizenship was in existence since the establishment of the Free state in 1922. The proposed 2004 amendment did not include the children of the 1.8 million holders of Irish passports not born in Ireland who have one Irish grandparent and who are therefore entitled to blood-based (*jus sanguinis*) Irish citizenship without having to set foot in Ireland. 79.8 per cent of the electorate voted in favour of the government's proposal.

Alice Feldman's (2006) theorisation of Ireland as the ultimate 'diaspora nation', while providing a sophisticated analysis of the centrality of diaspora to her respondents' self-understanding, does not take on board the normative meaning of diaspora for the discursive constructions of Irishness and otherness by the state. This article aims to theorise Ireland as a 'diaspora nation' in different terms, arguing explicitly, following Elaine Moriarty (2007), that the Citizenship Referendum was facilitated, *inter alia*, by the state expanding the notion of 'the Irish nation' in bloodline terms through formally conceptualising Irishness as including the Irish diaspora, a process publicly begun by former president Mary Robinson in the early

1990s (Gray, 1999). This discursive expansion – while initially aimed at emphasising the enrichment of Irishness through the diaspora – arguably led to enabling the substitution of the historical *jus soli* principle of Irish citizenship with *jus sanguinis* as conceptualised by the Citizenship and Nationality Act, enacted following the outcome of the 2004 Citizenship Referendum. This discursive political reformulation of Ireland as 'diaspora nation', while explaining the narrowing of citizenship entitlement of non-citizen migrants resident in Ireland, paradoxically also makes sense of the juxtaposition of 'entitled' Irish illegals in the US with 'unentitled' illegals in Ireland, which my example of the political juxtaposition of the 'illegal' Cathedral hunger strikers with Irish illegals in the US serves to illustrate.

This article is underpinned by the argument that the 2004 Citizenship Referendum was a major turning point in the racialisation of Irishness, leading to the state being able to argue that neither it, nor nearly 80 per cent of the voters who supported the Referendum, can be dubbed 'racist'. Denying racism – and making a distinction between entitlements as was explicitly argued in the case of the hunger striking Afghan asylum seekers – enables the Irish State to continue to construct migrants as 'a problem' or at best as economic stopgaps, leading to what Etienne Balibar (1991) terms 'crisis racism'. It has also created a context in which, freed from accusations of racism, it becomes 'sensible' for the state to use biopolitical measures in 'managing', 'regulating' and 'mainstreaming' immigration, with the support of almost all social policy analysts, from the government-funded Equality Authority and National Consultative Committee on Racism and Interculturalism (NCCRI), to NGOs such as the Immigration Council of Ireland (ICI). At this point – and dialectically positioned against the Irish State directly campaigning for the legalisation of illegal Irish immigrants in the US – the politics of immigration control, which only a decade ago appeared to be the preserve of the 'loony right', becomes a core principle of the developing racist state (Lentin & McVeigh, 2006).

I begin by contextualising my argument by briefly presenting some facts and figures on the racialisation of immigration in contemporary Ireland. The following sections use social and political theory to further develop my argument. The third section theorises Ireland, after David Theo Goldberg (2002), as a racial state, and, after Giorgio Agamben (2005) as a 'state of exception', where Foucauldian biopolitics structures state racism. This set of arguments assumes specific gendered meanings as 'non-national'[2] women were made central to the public debates surrounding the Citizenship Referendum, and thus to new racial configurations in twenty-first-century global Ireland, as I argue in the fourth section. The fifth section explicitly theorises Ireland as 'diaspora nation' where citizenship is granted through blood rather than soil entitlements – an argument I illustrate by outlining the controversy surrounding citizen children of migrant parents, which preceded, and arguably enabled, the 2004 Citizenship Referendum. The sixth section further proposes that, in the 'Boston or Berlin' debate, Ireland is opting to resemble the US in regulating immigration in relation to the state's needs. This leads me to conclude by linking the position of Irish illegals with illegal immigrants in Ireland as the ultimate achievement of the 'diaspora nation' logic.

Before outlining my theoretical argument, I would like to briefly present some facts and figures in relation to immigration in twenty-first-century Ireland.

Immigration and Race in Twenty-first-Century Ireland

The 1990s advent of the so-called 'Celtic Tiger' economic boom (Kirby, 2002) transformed the situation where emigration outstripped in-migration into Ireland. In 1996 Ireland reached its 'immigration turning point' and has been a country of in-migration ever since (Ruhs, 2005). According to the 2006 census, the number of migrants, described as 'non-Irish nationals', living in Ireland has almost doubled in the past four years to 420,000, or 10 per cent of the population (O'Brien, 2007). However, claims based on 2006 census figures of a '53 per cent increase in the immigrant population between 2002 and 2006', and that 'foreign born residents' account for 'more than a quarter of the population in large areas of Dublin' (Kelly, 2007), are misleading. According to Gilmartin and Feldman (2007), such claims confuse immigrant numbers with place of birth, they pay little attention to migration history, and, moreover, the map accompanying *The Irish Times* report of these census figures uses the colour red to signify areas of high 'immigrant' concentration, indicating danger, and an illusion of 'immigrant invasion'.

Indeed, close analyses of the census figures show that the majority of migrants come from the EU (275,776, of whom 100,000 are from the EU accession countries – headed by Poland and Lithuania), followed by Asia (25,326), Africa (24,425), the rest of Europe and the Americas (45,549), and many in-migrants are returning Irish citizens (Mac Éinrí, 2003). Moreover, the 2006 census 'ethnic question' – which, according to King-O'Riain (2006), was in fact a 'racial' question – found that nearly 95 per cent of the population are 'white', and just 1.3 per cent are 'Asians' and 1 per cent 'black'. This means that 'non-Irish nationals' mark a new racialisation of Irishness: whatever these migrants are, they are definitively 'not Irish' (Lentin & McVeigh, 2006: 37); driven by the 'success' of capitalism in Ireland, Irishness became racialised in new ways (McVeigh, 1996; Loyal, 2003).

Theorising Ireland as a 'racial state', as I outline below, is enabled by analysing the state's approach to immigrants, divided between labour migrants deemed essential to the continuing growth of the Irish economy, and asylum seekers, considered illegal and 'bogus', even though they constitute less than 10 per cent of all immigrants (Lentin & McVeigh, 2006: 41). Colin Harvey (2003) posits a clear link between state sovereignty and the insistence by states on determining who is a refugee and who is entitled to enter their territory and become a citizen. Racial states distinguish between 'asylum seekers' and 'refugees' even though this distinction does not exist in the Geneva Convention. The notion of 'asylum seeker' is invented by racial states in order to deny refugee status to many people who say they are refugees and yet are denied recognition as such by states employing their own restricted and limited definition of what constitutes a refugee. According to Harvey, refugee law, with its focus on the award of a status, leaves too much to the state to decide. The purpose is always to 'secure national level protection' (Harvey, 2003: 17).

Irish asylum applications were recorded at 39 in 1992, peaked at 11,632 in 2002 and declined to 4,323 in 2005, and 4,241 in 2006 (www.ORAC.ie). The state's boast that the decline in applications signals the success of Ireland's asylum policy omits to mention that about 4,000 per annum since 2004 have been refused leave to present asylum applications (Kelly, 2005). Throughout Europe, asylum seekers are demonised to conjure up cheat, liar, criminal, sponger; the figure of asylum seeker has become a caricature just as 'Blacks', 'Jews' and 'Gypsies' have been and still are, constituting, according to Schuster (2003), a racist asylum regime. In line with European racialisation of asylum seekers, the former minister in charge of the asylum process, Michael McDowell, showed little regard for the rights of people to apply for asylum in Ireland. In May 2005 in response to a Dáil question about the high cost of deportations, he claimed that asylum seekers tell 'cock and bull stories', stating he 'would prefer to interview these people at the airport, but the UN insists that I go through due process' (Holland, 2005).[3]

Deirdre Coghlan (2003) documents the trajectory from the paternalistic approach towards invited programme refugees, conceived as 'deserving and rights-bearing', by the Department of Foreign Affairs, to the restrictive approach towards asylum seekers, deemed as 'undeserving and fraudulent' by the Department of Justice. She argues that criminalising asylum seekers as undeserving was enabled by the earlier view of refugees as deserving and entitled to help, but also by the dialectic self-glorification of the Irish as generous helpers and donors – another way of juxtaposing entitlements, useful in campaigning for the legalisation of Irish illegals in the US while at the same time excluding illegals in Ireland.

It bears remembering that the history of restrictive refugee policies in Ireland is not new: during the Nazi era Ireland admitted only some 60 Jewish refugees (Keogh, 1998). And, while having supposedly welcomed several groups of programme refugees – Hungarians in the 1950s, Chileans and Vietnamese in the 1970s, Iranian Bahá'is in the 1980s and Bosnians in the 1990s with varying degrees of 'open arms' (Ward, 1999; Fanning, 2002; Halilovic-Pastuovic, 2007), since the 1990s, the Irish State has used governmental technologies of dispersal, direct provision and deportations to control asylum seekers, as I now briefly illustrate.

Although, unlike some other EU States, Ireland does not have a policy of systematically detaining asylum seekers, the 1996 Refugee Act does provide for the detention of asylum seekers in certain circumstances, and asylum seekers are dispersed to direct provision centres[4] and are routinely detained in Irish prisons prior to deportation (Kelly, 2005). Steven Loyal argues that asylum seekers in Ireland 'have the least entitlement to social and material resources… they are marginalised, excluded, poor, and, in many respects, they lack freedom' (Loyal, 2003: 79). Despite the obviously desperate economic conditions asylum seekers are forced to live under, the state frequently complains that asylum seekers 'cost too much'.

Before the enactment of the 1999 Immigration Act, the Minister for Justice's power to deport foreign nationals was based on the 1935 Aliens Act and the 1946 Aliens Order. In 2002 deportations were part of the commitment the coalition partners made in their *Programme for Government,* which vowed to 'maintain the integrity of the asylum policy' (Department of the Taoiseach, 2002), and the amended Refugee Act and the Immigration Act enabled increasing numbers of deportations.[5] Deportations are costly,[6] and they often separate parents from their children, left behind in Ireland as the parents are being deported. Despite this, the language used by the media to report deportations and the 'simplification' of the asylum process makes them sound routine and normal. In real terms, the Irish immigration regime has spawned the Irish Naturalisation and Immigration Service (INIS), a 'one stop shop' for immigration, asylum, visas and citizenship services and 'key linkages with the work permit system' providing, according to the Minister for Justice, 'a strong foundation for better service provision and the *enhancement of enforcement strategies* in these areas' (Mac Cormaic, 2005[emphasis added]).

'Race', racialisation and racism are complex terms. 'Race' must be understood not merely as a 'floating signifier' (Hall, 1997) – a way of reading bodily signs and giving them ethnically hierarchical meanings, but more importantly, as a political idea, used by states to classify people into populations and thus regulate them. 'Races' were fabricated (or socially constructed) categories used to differentiate between members of the nation and their enemies from without but also between 'us' and 'them' within, regardless of differences in appearance (Lentin & McVeigh 2006: 8–9). Racialisation denotes a process of domination and the relationship of power involved in the assigning of inferiority using bodily signifiers (Gilroy 1998; Lentin, 2004: 28). In the current climate, it has been difficult to discuss racism – which Hesse (2001) theorises as a 'political ideology aiming to regulate bodies' – not only because it remains contested and widely disavowed, but also because, in liberal democratic regimes, the vocabulary of racism is addressed through discussions of how to integrate ethnic minorities into the national majority with little consideration for the effects of racialisation (Law & Sayyid, 2007: 529). Crucially to my argument, however, as I discuss below, racism is 'inextricably linked both to the policy instituted by states and to the political climate engendered by governmental leaders playing the proverbial "race card"' even as they disavow it' (Lentin & Lentin, 2006: 2).

To consolidate my argument I now turn to outlining the three-pronged theoretical foundations of this article, viewing Ireland as a 'racial state', and arguing that what we are witnessing is what Agamben terms a 'state of exception', and what Foucault terms a 'biopolitics of care'.

Racial State of Exception

Goldberg (2002) theorises all modern nation-states, each in its own way, as racial states, where race and state are defined in terms of each other, since states' main aim is to construct homogeneity, while appropriating difference through enacting multicultural (or in the Irish context, 'intercultural') policies, the aim of which is coping with what is constructed as the 'problem' of ethnoracial diversity. The racial state is a state of power, asserting control over those within the state and excluding others from entering the state. Through routinised technologies of governmentality such as constitutions, border controls, the law, policy making, bureaucracy, census categorisations, and also invented histories and traditions, ceremonies and cultural imaginings, modern states are defined by their power to exclude (and include) in racially ordered terms, to categorise hierarchically, and to differentiate. The modern state aims to keep racialised others out while also legislating against the so-called degeneracy of indigenous minorities (which explains the persistence of antisemitism and anti-nomadism and, more recently, Islamophobia).

Goldberg outlines two traditions of thinking about racial states. The first, which he calls naturalism, fixes racially conceived 'natives' as pre-modern, and naturally incapable of progress. The second, which he calls historicism, elevates Europeans over primitive or underdeveloped others as a victory of western progress (Goldberg, 2002: 43).[7] For the racial naturalist the racially subjugated are surplus labour at best, detritus at worst, while for the racial historicist, the racially immature are inserted into a narrative of developmental progress, which is only possible through mimicking the Euro-centre (Goldberg, 2002: 94–96). Understood as the space of white men of property, the racial state's historicist progressivism aims, through amalgamation and assimilation, to assist its racial others to 'undo their uncivilised conditions'. But beneath its liberalism, historicism camouflages racism, and is ultimately about the ordering zeal of modernity (Goldberg, 2002: 92–93). According to Goldberg, the law – as a technology of racial rule – is central to modern state formation, promoting ethnoracial categorisation and identification and shaping national identities through legislating on immigration controls and citizenship rights, shaping race in legal terms, and threading it into the fabric of the social (Goldberg, 2002: 141–147; Gilroy, 1987: 74).

Goldberg's theorisation of all modern nation-states as racial states, while not building explicitly upon it, resonates with Michel Foucault's (1990) argumentation that when natural life becomes included in mechanisms of state power, politics turns into biopolitics, the territorial state becomes a 'state of population', and the nation's biological life becomes a problem of sovereign power, exercising what Foucault terms 'biopower'. Through a series of governmental technologies, biopower creates 'docile bodies' and the population – its welfare, health, longevity and wealth – becomes the goal of government. Foucault charts a shift from the power of pre-modern sovereigns to killing unwanted people to the modern state's biopower which is addressed at living beings, or their mass – as population. Put simply, Foucault charts the difference between the sovereign power of the old territorial state – 'to make die and let live', and modern biopower – 'to make live and let die'. If the old order exerted the right to kill, the new biopower aims to make the care of life the concern of state power, exercised by governmental technologies such as the hospital, the psychiatric clinic, the prison, the concentration camp, and in recent times, also the refugee camp and detention centre. In *Society Must Be Defended* (2003), Foucault uses the concept of biopower to document the birth of state racism. The duty to defend society, or defend the state against its migrant and indigenous others means that the modern state can scarcely function without racism, which he sees as the break 'between what must live and what must die' (Foucault, 2003: 254). Rather than serving one group against another, racism becomes a tool of social conservatism, a racism that society practices against itself, an act of constant purification and normalisation.

In constructing what Goldberg terms homogeneity, the state not only denies its internal heterogeneities, it is also a normalising, regulating biopower state. Foucault's theory of racism is an expression of an ongoing social war nurtured by biopolitical technologies of purification. Thus racism is intrinsic to the nature of all modern states, occurring in varying intensities from social exclusion to mass murder. Biopower conceptualises the state as a 'body',[8] and the use of state power becomes vital to protecting the 'life' of the nation, making genocide an obvious outcome of biopower when 'lives unworthy of living' are removed in order to protect the life of the *volk*, or, put another way, to defend the 'common good'. The Irish State's invocation of the 'common good' in relation to its immigration policies approximate Foucault's 'biopolitics of care', where the state envisages a 'happy balance between social diversity and social cohesion', to cite the former Minister for Justice,[9] which means continuing labour migration needed to maintain Ireland's economic growth while limiting what the state constructs as 'illegal' immigration, and instituting 'colour blind' integration policies which employ Foucauldian strategies of surveillance, regulation and control (Lentin & McVeigh, 2006: 17).

Giorgio Agamben (1995, 2005) draws on the Foucauldian concepts of biopower, biopolitics and its subjects, which he calls 'bare life', to develop an argument about the tendency of modern states to withdraw legal rights and protection from citizens and non-citizens alike. Although like Foucault, he sees biopower peak in the Nazi camps, Agamben updates the concept to the twenty-first century in relation to refugee camps and 'unlawful' combatants in detention camps such as Guantánamo Bay. In each of these spaces 'zones of exception' are formed. Agamben theorises the state of exception, after Carl Schmitt (1985), as state power's immediate response to extreme internal conflicts (Agamben, 2005: 2). Increasingly in states of exception the application of the law is suspended and different categories of people are reduced to what Agamben calls 'bare life', his re-articulation of the Roman category of *homo sacer* – he who can be killed with impunity yet who cannot be sacrificed (Agamben, 1995: 71). My key point is that these categories remain inescapably racialised when applied to humans who fall outside the boundaries of state citizenship, as I argue below.

While the concepts of 'biopower', 'biopolitics' and 'states of exception' are still evolving and remain contested, I want to argue that they meet the core theoretical challenges in understanding contemporary racism and its relationship to the state, as they posit a fundamental connection between racism and nation-state biopolitics, particularly as liberal democratic states move away from blatant racial discrimination to a regime of regulation and control of sub-populations which fall short of full citizenship.

In the wake of the Citizenship Referendum there is no longer any doubt that the Republic of Ireland can be theorised as a racial state of exception, though such theorisation must be firmly embedded in a global context as McVeigh and I argue

(Lentin & McVeigh, 2006). My argument is that Ireland's exponential economic growth since the 1990s has meant its restructuring as an exclusive racist state, where labour migrants, needed to ensure continuing economic growth, are welcome (albeit on differing terms depending on their economic positionalities, Allen & Loyal, 2006), while asylum seekers, seen as superfluous to Ireland's economic growth, are increasingly prevented from landing to present their applications, and where citizenship parameters are being re-defined away from birth right (*jus soli*) to blood right (*jus sanguinis*), as I now go on to discuss.

Citizenship From *Jus Soli* to *Jus Sanguinis*

Exploring the origins of the 1789 French Declaration of the Rights of Man and Citizen (after Arendt, 1979), Giorgio Agamben reminds us that it is precisely bare natural life, or the pure fact of birth, which is the bearer of rights, and that the nation – deriving etymologically from *nascere*, to be born – thus closes the open circle of man's birth (Agamben, 1995: 127–128). Following Foucault's theorisation of the transition from divinely authorised sovereignty to national sovereignty – a process which transmutes 'subject' into 'citizen' – Agamben argues that birth is the immediate bearer of sovereignty. In the passage from subject to citizen, however, birth becomes nation and rights are attributed to man (*sic*) solely to the extent that man becomes citizen. Thus the principle of 'blood and soil' (expressed most terrifyingly in the National Socialist vision of the world) has ancient juridical origins from Roman law through to the French revolution when *jus soli* (soil-based citizenship) develops into *jus sanguinis* (blood-based citizenship) in the transition from 'man' to 'citizen'. Hence the centrality (and ambiguity) of the notion of 'citizenship' in modern political thought; hence, too, the development, since the French Revolution, of regulatory provisions specifying which man was a citizen and which one not. According to Agamben, this is why refugees – who break the continuity between man and citizen, nativity and nationality – represent such a disquieting element in that they put the originary fiction of modern sovereignty in crisis (Agamben, 1995: 130–131).

To illustrate the transition from *jus soli* to *jus sanguinis* through the use of the law in controlling the citizenship rights of migrant populations, I now discuss the relationship between the Irish State and migrant parents of children born in Ireland, who were therefore Irish citizens. As part of the project of redefining ethnoracial populations,[10] the Minister for Justice could claim in September 2003 that citizen children born to migrants parents – who the state re-defined 'Irish born children', racialising them as different from all other children born in Ireland – have *certain, but not absolute* rights to remain resident in Ireland.[11]

Irish *jus soli* access to citizenship, constitutionally granted to anyone who was a citizen of the Irish Free State before the 1937 constitution, and confirmed by the 1956 and 1986 Nationality and Citizenship Act, was re-confirmed in the amended Article 2 of the Irish Constitution, as part of the 1998 Good Friday Agreement (GFA):

> It is the entitlement and birthright of every person born in the island of Ireland, which includes its islands and seas, to be part of the Irish nation. That is also the entitlement of all persons otherwise qualified in accordance with law to be citizens of Ireland. Furthermore, the Irish nation cherishes its special affinity with people of Irish ancestry living abroad who share its cultural identity and heritage (*Bunreacht na hÉireann*, 1998).

While the debates on immigrants' citizenship and residency rights occasioned by increased in-migration obscured the fact that *jus soli* citizenship right was not merely a consequence of the GFA, the GFA amendment did mean, as was ruled in the 1990 Fajujonu Supreme Court case, that migrant parents of children born in Ireland, who were thus Irish citizens, had a claim to residency in Ireland to provide 'care and company' to their citizen child. This process, which resulted in several thousands migrant parents gaining residency rights, was overturned in January 2003 when the Supreme Court ruled in the Lobe and Osayande appeal, that 'non-national' parents no longer had a strong case to be allowed to remain in Ireland to bring up their child (Maddock & Mallon, 2003). The Lobe and Osayande case involved two families of Czech Roma and Nigerian origin respectively against whom deportation orders were made. While the parents claimed that their decision to remain resident was in their children's best interest, the Supreme Court ruling privileged the state's right to deport, and the 'integrity of the asylum process' over these citizen children's rights. The media debates following the January 2003 Supreme Court ruling exposed a contradiction between nationality and citizenship. The *jus sanguinis*-based rights to Irish citizenship allows up to third generation Irish emigrants to claim Irish citizenship, while at the same time, the state was contesting the *jus soli* citizenship rights accorded to children of migrants and consolidated by the GFA insertion of Article 2 into the Constitution.

The Lobe and Osayande court's ruling illustrates several of my theoretical points. First, it illustrates the centrality of the law as a governmental technology employed by the racial state. Arguably upholding 'control in the face of the anarchic, of order in the face of disorder' (Goldberg, 2002: 94), Chief Justice Ronan Keane was able to rule that the state 'was entitled to take the view that the orderly system of dealing with immigration and asylum applications should not be undermined by persons seeking to take advantage' of the system. According to Siobhán Mullally (2003), the ruling proves that 'the protection of a child's claim to reside within a state (is) made dependent on the legal status and behaviour of her or his parents … in place of a concern with the child's best interests, the state substitutes its own interest in immigration control'. Second, the ruling illustrates Agamben's argument that refugees (or in this instance migrant parents of Irish citizen children) form an unstable category between 'man' and 'citizen' causing,

> the secret presupposition of the political domain – bare life – to appear for an instant within that domain. In this sense, the refugee (or the migrant parent) is truly the 'man of rights' … the first and only real appearance of rights outside

> the fiction of the citizen that always covers them over. Yet this is precisely what makes the figure of the refugee so hard to define politically. (Agamben, 1995: 131)

In the wake of the ruling, on 19 February 2003, the Minister for Justice removed the process whereby an immigrant parent could seek permission to remain in Ireland solely on the grounds of having a child citizen. The abolition of the process resulted in 11,500 migrant parents of Irish citizens becoming candidates for deportation as of July 2003. For almost two years the Minister declared his unwillingness to reverse his decision and recognise en masse migrant parents of Irish citizens who had lawfully applied for residency. Among the 341 people deported between 2002 and February 2005 there were at least 20 Irish citizen children.[12] As late as November 2004 the Minister said in reply to a Dáil question that any amnesty for migrant parents of so-called 'Irish born children' would cause 'chaos' (O'Brien, 2004).

However, rhetoric aside, on 15 January 2005, six months after the state won the Citizenship Referendum with a four to one majority, the decision was reversed and the Department of Justice, Equality and Law Reform announced a new application process for migrant parents of Irish citizen children born before 1 January 2005. Of the 18,000 applications, 16,693 were granted (DJLR, 2006), although the residency rights won were temporary and contingent upon successful applicants not seeking family reunification rights (Lentin & McVeigh, 2006: 54).

Robbie McVeigh and I argue that the Citizenship Referendum represented an act of political brutality disguised as upholding the 'common good'. Like the Nuremberg laws in Nazi Germany, the Jim Crow laws in the American south and the Apartheid laws in South Africa, it 'denationalised' people, stripping people of rights and citizenship. In doing this, the Referendum created a bizarre new category of people who remain 'part of the Irish nation' (the amended article 2 of the Constitution was left untouched), yet have their citizenship removed, deemed to have insufficient connection to the island of Ireland to qualify for citizenship. Ireland has thus created its own version of Agamben's *homo sacer* – people reduced to 'bare life', stripped of all legal and civil rights (Agamben, 1995; Lentin & McVeigh, 2006: 55).

It is worthwhile noting that persuasive as Agamben's theorisation is, and bearing in mind the indelible link he makes between birth and nation, Agamben does not explicitly engender the meanings of the shift from *jus soli* to *jus sanguinis* citizenship entitlements. As the producers or future generations, and the symbolic tropes of nations (Yuval-Davis & Anthias, 1989), women are marked and controlled differently from men, despite universal claims to gender equality. As the nation-state makes nativity the foundation of its sovereignty, when they step outside ethnonational or moral boundaries, (and because they are the producers of future generations of 'racially undesirable' others), women are often banned as impure and transgressive (Yuval-Davis, 1997).

Contextualising the arrival of asylum seekers in Ireland in global restructuring, global capital accumulation and global wars, Eithne Luibhéid (2004) argues that racial states, including Ireland, need asylum seekers in order to 'redraw racial and national boundaries that have become destabilised in the contemporary era'. More specifically, Luibhéid argues that discourses and practices that target childbearing women asylum seekers provided the Irish government with a way of reconstituting the Republic as a sovereign space, while also generating new modes of racialisation and racial hierarchies within Ireland. Put simply, Luibhéid argues that childbearing asylum seeking women 're-nationalise the nation'. To further link the changing parameters of citizenship in the Republic, the racialisation of 'illegal' asylum seekers and migrant parents, and the campaign to grant citizenship to Irish illegals in the US, I now shift the discussion to theorise Ireland as 'diaspora nation'.

Diaspora Nation

The racial state conceptualises migrants as either economically useful – in the case of labour migration (Allen & Loyal, 2006; Lentin & McVeigh, 2006: 58–76), or as problematically surplus – in the case of asylum seekers and migrant parents of Irish citizen children. Such conceptualisation, I want to argue, owes above all to the discursive shift to an unbounded view of the 'Irish nation' as including a bloodline diaspora, and has arguably led to the 2004 Citizenship Referendum. This process was explicitly initiated by former president Mary Robinson, and supported by several social and political commentators including *Irish Times* columnists Fintan O'Toole and John Waters (Moriarty, 2007).

Alice Feldman theorises Ireland as the ultimate 'diaspora nation' in terms of the extent to which 'fluidity and movement of people are defining features of the nation, from the early arrival of Vikings and Normans ... to the unprecedented increase in immigration during the past decade' (Feldman, 2006: 102). Feldman concentrates on the identity construction of her informants, whom she describes as belonging to Ireland's 'majority ethnicity', and whose collective memory, she argues, is underpinned by trauma and loss as well as by opportunities and successes brought about through multiple migrations.

While Feldman provides a sophisticated analysis of the centrality of diaspora to her respondents' self-understanding, based on 'identity narratives and tales of not/belonging to re-present the "psychic maps" according to which the Other is navigated and scripted' (Feldman, 2006: 103), her analysis does not take on board the normative meaning of diaspora for the discursive constructions of Irishness and otherness by the state.

Breda Gray argues (1999, 2002) that one means of bringing together discourses of *em*igration and *im*migration into engagement with each other is through the term 'diaspora', a concept which, in the Irish case, encapsulates discourses of historic trauma in relation to the Famine and associated emigration, allowing emigrants to keep in contact with their country of origin, and self-produce a transnational identity. Gray (1999) cites former President Mary Robinson's speech to a joint session of the Houses of the Oireachtas entitled 'Cherishing the diaspora' as an example of the wish to extend the remit of Irishness to include the diaspora in enriching terms: '[O]ur relation with the diaspora beyond our shores is one which can instruct our society in the values of diversity, tolerance, and fair-mindedness. The men and women of our diaspora represent not simply a series of departures and loss ...' (Robinson, 1995).

Like Robinson, *Irish Times* columnist Fintan O'Toole presented the expansion of Irishness beyond a territorially bounded nation, claiming, that '[e]migration means, quite simply, that the people and the land are no longer coterminous' (1994: 18). However, far from simply expanding the notion of Irishness beyond the national borders, Elaine Moriarty (2007) argues that this discursive shift from boundedness to a territorially unbounded Irishness had the unintended outcome of enabling the Citizenship Referendum. I want to further develop this by arguing that the Referendum's roots in the expanding diaspora nation mean that, at the same time as the state racialises and excludes its unwanted racial others, it can continue to campaign for the rights of its own (illegal) diaspora in the US – conceptualised, as are descendants of Irish American emigrants, in bloodline terms – as I now go on to discuss.

Illegalising Asylum Seekers, Legalising Irish Illegals

> 'In the last months of 2005 and the early months of 2006, the Irish state as a whole responded magnificently to the plight of illegal immigrants. While other governments were taking a hard line, insisting that immigration laws had to be applied with unbending rigour, the Irish government reacted with passion and compassion. In October 2005, both houses of the Oireachtas passed unanimously a resolution expressing deep concern for illegal migrants, acknowledging their great contribution to society, the pointless cruelty of laws that cut them off from their families back home, and the urgent need to give them a proper status. The undocumented migrants in question are, of course, Irish-born people living in the United States. Throughout all of this period, the government continued to deport 'failed' asylum seekers from Ireland' (O'Toole, 2006: i).

The history of political leaders in the Republic of Ireland looking after the interest of Ireland's exiled sons and daughters precedes President Robinson; in fact it dates back to the so-called 'father of the nation' Arthur Griffith, who, already in 1904, during the boycott of the Jews in Limerick, wrote in *The United Irishman:* 'No thoughtful Irishman or woman can view without apprehension the continuous influx of Jews into Ireland and the continuous efflux of the native population. The stalwart men and bright-eyed women of our race pass from our land in a never-ending stream, and in their place we are getting strange people alien to us in sympathy, from Russia, Poland, Germany and Austria – people who come to live amongst us, but who never become of us' (*United Irishman,* 23 April 1904, cited in Keogh, 1998: 42).

'Looking after our own' is a powerful political discourse, particularly when it relates to Ireland's emigrants. Thus, in October 1987, with emigrants leaving Ireland at the rate of 46,000 per year throughout the 1980s and with unemployment around 15 per cent, the then Minister for Foreign Affairs Brian Lenihan could justify emigration as a contemporary 'Irish solution' to a contemporary 'Irish problem': 'I don't look on the type of emigration we have today as being of the same category as the terrible emigration of the last century. What we have now is a very literate emigrant who thinks nothing of coming to the United States and going back to Ireland and maybe on to Germany and back to Ireland again. ... It (emigration) is not a defeat because the Irish hone their skills and talents in another environment; the more they develop a work ethic in a country like Germany or the US, the better it can be applied in Ireland when they return. *After all, we can't all live on a small island*' (cited in Gray, 2003: 31[emphasis added]).

Ironically, around the same time, the then US House Speaker Senator Tip O'Neill explained that he voted 20 years earlier, in 1965, for a comprehensive Immigration Bill that arguably killed emigration from Ireland, because he was asked by the Irish government to prevent a brain drain, even though people in his neighbourhood were asking him to enable their cousins and relatives to come to the US (O'Dowd, 2006). According to Niall O'Dowd, editor of *The Irish Voice* and founder and chairman of the Irish Lobby for Immigration Reform, while this did not end the brain drain from Ireland, it did ensure that successive generations of Irish people who did come to America ran 'smack into the illegal alien issue'.

Although most of the US 11–12 million illegal immigrants are from Mexico and Central America, about 50,000 Irish people are among the 3 million illegal immigrants from countries outside Latin America. Speaking about their plight, Celine Kenneally, executive director for the Irish Immigration Pastoral Center in San Francisco, an advice and referral service sponsored by the Irish Catholic Conference of Bishops, told the *San Francisco Chronicle:* 'They are in as dire straits as any other ethnic group. They cannot get driver's licenses, it's harder to open bank accounts, they cannot travel home and return again. ... The relationship between Ireland and America is so long and fantastic, but it's in danger now' (Hendricks, 2006).

Although most Irish immigrants reside in the United States legally, in recent decades, most arrivals from Ireland have overstayed their visas and become illegal immigrants, because the US government is issuing fewer work visas. A 1991 programme offered legal permanent residence to about 16,000 undocumented Irish, but there has been no legalisation plan since then.

I am interested here primarily in how the very real difficulties faced by Irish illegals in post-9/11 USA have become another way of strengthening bloodline Irishness, particularly when compared to the very real difficulties faced by asylum seekers in today's Ireland. Thus, in defence of legalising Irish illegal immigrants in the US, Niall O'Dowd wrote in February 2006, echoing Ministers McDowell and Ahern, that 'Ireland has one of the most liberal immigration systems of any country', although he highlights the 'relative difficulty for Americans to emigrate there'. O'Dowd suggests that this difficulty (for American migrants in Ireland) be sorted through a bilateral agreement between the two states, focusing on legalising Irish illegals in the US (yet ignoring the plight of non-American illegal immigrants in Ireland). The reasons cited by O'Dowd in singling out Irish illegals in post-9/11 America all play the tune of Irish exceptionalism: 'If a deal is not reached, the footprints of the Irish in America will be elided ... within a generation, the ties between

Ireland and Irish America will begin to fray as the direct links between both countries begin to fade... In the short term the Irish undocumented are managing a very difficult situation well. It has been a crushing few years for them as the aftermath of 9/11 has eroded their lifestyles to the point where they are living in constant fear' (O'Dowd, 2006).

It is hard to imagine a similar tone in the debate evoked by the Cathedral hunger strike. Not even the most ardent supporters of asylum seekers in Ireland would argue that 'if a deal is not reached ... the footprints of the Afghans (or Nigerians, or Romanians, or Somalis) in Ireland will be elided ...' or that 'in the short term asylum seekers in Ireland had a crushing few years ... as the aftermath of 9/11 has eroded their lifestyle to the point where they are living in constant fear'.

In the run-up to the 2008 US presidential elections, the campaign to legalise Irish illegals was hotting up already in spring 2007, as (Irish-linked) Democratic senator Ted Kennedy and (Irish-linked) Republican senator John McCain were planning to introduce legislation that would allow most of the estimated 11 million illegal immigrants in the US to remain in the country. Addressing a rally of some 2,500 undocumented Irish immigrants in March 2007, senator Kennedy said the issue was about 'defining our humanity', while New York senator Chuck Schumer thanked the crowd for 'a great warm Irish welcome on a snowy Washington day' before shouting '*Tiocfaidh Ár Lá*' (the slogan adopted by the IRA, meaning 'Our Time Will Come') (Staunton, 2007).

I want to suggest that legalising Irish illegals in the US is a vital link in the diaspora nation chain: expanding the conceptual boundaries of Irishness beyond Irish soil to accord second and third generation emigrants Irish citizenship while narrowing such access to humans born on Irish soil is a new stage in the racialisation of Irishness. While the majority of Irish illegals seeking legalisation in the US are white, the majority of illegal immigrants seeking legalisation in Ireland are racialised as non-white (or not quite white). It is also a logical lead up to the demand, by Taoiseach Bertie Ahern on his annual St Patrick's Day visits to Washington, for rights for undocumented Irish migrants in the US. However, as Fintan O'Toole reminds us, 'the appeal is not for undocumented migrants in the United States to be given a proper status. It is for *Irish* undocumented migrants in the US to be given a proper status' (O'Toole, 2006: i), a further expansion of the diaspora nation in both directions.

To complete my argument, I now turn to discussing the Americanisation of the Republic's immigration regime.

Diaspora Nation Between Boston and Berlin?

In 2000, the then Tanaiste Mary Harney expressed her opposition to further European integration, saying it would be against the interest of Ireland, which, she said, was spiritually 'a lot closer to Boston than Berlin'. The debate about the two models – one favouring low taxes and low welfare provisions, the other favouring the reverse – was sharpened by statements about Ireland's relationship with the US and its attractiveness to American business.[13] It is worth noting that, like the US, Ireland's 'Celtic Tiger' economy is also characterised by the polarisation of wealth – international statistics have shown consistently that the Irish Republic represents the most unequal society in the western world (Coulter, 2003: 22).

The US model extends to the Irish State's approach to immigration, despite state-actors' claims to transparency and openness. The hegemonic view of Irishness as correlated with whiteness and Catholicism has come into conflict with the labour market imperatives of the increasingly global Irish economy. However, the need for immigrant labour, as Loyal (2003) reminds us, is underpinned by the racialisation of that labour, as is obvious from the state's treatment of those immigrants and asylum seekers it does not deem economically necessary.

The Irish migration regime received further reinforcement with the proposal, in September 2006, of a new Immigration, Residence and Protection Bill by the former Minister for Justice, Equality and Law Reform. In the spirit of the post-9/11 'global civil war' (Agamben, 2005), the bill, if enacted, will require all non-EEA nationals in Ireland to carry biometric identity cards, known as residence permits, identifying carriers as either asylum seekers, short-term residents, or long-term residents (including those with refugee status). According to this draconian proposed legislation, non-EEA nationals who commit a range of offences, including traffic offences, will face summary deportation. Other provisions are a prohibition on foreign nationals to change their names, except where authorised, and to marry without first notifying the Minister. A marriage performed in breach of this condition will be void. The Minister may refuse to allow the marriage for a variety of reasons, including public security and public policy. Asylum seekers and holders of non-renewable residence permits may not marry at all. Persons who take part in such marriages or officiate at them or 'facilitate' them will be guilty of an offence. It is also expressly stated that marriage confers no right of residence (Mac Éinrí, 2006).

Announcing the bill, the minister also announced the incorporation of the Office of the Refugee Application Commissioner into a broader body dealing with all immigration and refugee matters – further centralising the control exercised by the racial state on its immigrant others.[14] At the same time, policies are being developed across government departments aimed at encouraging people with sought-after qualifications, skills and entrepreneurial abilities to consider Ireland. While such people will qualify for 'long term resident status', their children, even if born in Ireland, will not enjoy *jus soli* citizenship rights.

My argument is that reconceptualising Ireland as a diaspora nation whose off-shore (emigrant) children are granted citizenship access in preference to its on-shore (immigrant) children, pushes Ireland closer to Agamben's 'state of exception', where the line between democracy and absolutism is getting thinner. In a state of exception, legal/illegal instruments such as the US Patriot Act and the proposed Irish Immigration, Residence and Protection Bill allow the state to erase the individual's legal status at will. Although it has its juridical roots in extreme internal conflicts, Agamben charts the development of the state of exception not merely in totalitarian regimes, but also, alarmingly, in contemporary democracies which often erode the legislative powers of parliaments (today often limited to ratifying measures that the executive issues through decrees having the force of law, as we saw in the lead up to the Iraq war [Agamben, 2005: 7]). Highlighting security and the Foucauldian imperative that 'society must be defended' from its racial others allows racial states, each in its own way, to extend the state of exception in order to defend the 'common good', leaving those outside their protection in a liminal zone between legality and illegality. As Agamben puts it, 'at once excluding bare life and capturing it within the political order, the state of exception actually constituted, in its very separateness, the hidden foundation on which the entire political system rested' (1995: 9).

As the Irish racial state talks the intercultural talk and walks the diversity walk (Lentin & McVeigh, 2006), the Cathedral hunger strikers, understandably reluctant to return to war-torn Afghanistan, continue to live in a liminal twilight zone between legality and illegality, bare life at the mercy of the sovereign power of the Irish diaspora nation. With inequalities of wealth and differential treatment of immigrants, far from offering a real alternative to US neo-liberalism, Irish State practices, including becoming a net importer of people, and differentiating between those useful to the economy and those superfluous to Celtic capitalism, represent, according to Allen (2003), political methods intended to advance the project of privatisation, deregulation and redistribution in favour of the wealthy, and at the same time upholding diasporic bloodline links with Irish illegals in the US–far more akin to Boston than to Berlin.

Conclusion

This article used several strands of social and political theory to link the Republic of Ireland's policy towards people it considers illegal immigrants with its support for Irish illegal immigrants in the United States. Theorising Ireland as a racial state was facilitated by a survey of its immigration regime which favours labour migrants as useful economic commodities over asylum seekers and migrant parents of Irish citizen children, whose entitlement to remain resident in Ireland was upturned by the 2004 Citizenship Referendum, which reversed the historical soil based citizenship with blood based entitlement. The article further posited Giorgio Agamben's theorisation of those people who fall outside the remit of Irish citizenship entitlement as 'bare life', and suggested that in striving for both social diversity and social cohesion, the state is implementing a Foucauldian biopolitics of care, where immigrants are managed, regulated and controlled.

The article then built on the conceptualisation of Ireland as 'diaspora nation', explicitly introduced in the 1990s, to argue that while members of the Irish diaspora are accorded citizenship rights, regardless of residence in Ireland's territorial boundaries, new diasporas in Ireland are denied citizenship, which, in post-Referendum Ireland, is no longer based on birth on the Irish soil. To exemplify my argument, the article juxtaposed the 2006 hunger strike by Afghan asylum seekers, deemed by the state as 'illegal immigrants' entitled to neither residence nor citizenship, with its support for the demand of Irish illegal immigrants in the US to be legalised. I concluded by arguing that Ireland is following the US not only in its economic policies, but also in its immigration regime.

Notes

I am grateful to Dr Elaine Moriarty, Dr Robbie McVeigh and to the editors for their helpful comments on earlier drafts.

1. Kundnani (2007: 95) reports that some 20,000 Afghans sought asylum in Britain in the 1990s, many fleeing the brutality of the Taliban. While these asylum seekers were initially recognised as genuine – in 1999, 800 out of 805 cases were granted leave to remain in Britain – the Home Office then began treating Afghanistan as a safe country, leading to three-quarters of Afghan asylum seekers to be rejected in 2000; yet in 2001 the bombing of Afghanistan by US and UK forces was justified by the need to remove an oppressive regime. Due to its Common Travel Area with Britain, Ireland is clearly following British policies in this regard.
2. A euphemism for non-EU/EEA migrants.
3. It is not surprising that this disdain for the principle of protecting refugees leads to making the actual process of decision making far from transparent, despite claims to the contrary: of the 63,399 applications between 1995 and 2004, only 6,304 were recognised as refugees (Ruhs, 2005: 3).
4. At the end of March 2005, there were 7,280 asylum seekers in 68 direct provision centres (four reception and 64 accommodation centres) of whom 1,678 asylum seekers (21 per cent) had been residing in direct provision for over two years. A quarter (2,094) of those living in direct provision centres, are under the age of four. In addition to basic accommodation and meals, each asylum seeker receives €19.10 per adult and €9.60 per child per week, not raised since the allowances were first introduced in 2000. Asylum seekers in Ireland are also excluded from social welfare provisions and asylum seekers with children, who arrived in the country after 1 May 2004, do not receive child benefit (www.irishrefugeecouncil.ie/stats).
5. Between 1999 and 2005, 2,268 deportations were carried out, and 2,299 were 'voluntarily repatriated' by July 2004 (www.irishrefugeecouncil.ie). Top countries of origin of recipients of deportation orders were and continue to be Romania, Nigeria, China and Moldova.
6. In May 2005 the Minister for Justice admitted in the Dáil to spending 50,200 deporting just one person (Holland, 2005).
7. See Lentin and McVeigh (2006: 11) and Ní Shuinéar (2002) for a discussion of racial naturalism and historicism in the Irish context.
8. Interesting here is Burleigh and Wipperman's (1999) theorisation of the Nazi state as the ideal type racial state, where the object was the *protection of the body* of the volk.
9. Speaking at the 2005 McGill Summer School, cited in Lentin and McVeigh (2006: 17).
10. Also applied to Travellers, whom the Minister for Justice denied the status of an ethnic group (see Lentin & McVeigh, 2006).
11. Written answer to Dáil question no. 1235 by Minister of Justice, Equality and Law Reform, Michael McDowell to Sinn Féin Dáil deputy Aengus Ó Snodaigh, 30 September 2003.
12. Dáil question, 16 February 2005.
13. In Harney's words: 'it is remarkable that a country with just 1 per cent of Europe's population accounts for 27 per cent of US Greenfield investment in Europe' (Brennock, 2000).
14. Coming into office in May 2006, the new Minister for Justice, Brian Lenihan, expressed his support for McDowell's proposed bill, committing to present it to the Oireachtas in Autumn 2007.

References

Agamben, G. (1995) *Homo Sacer: Sovereign Power and Bare Life* (Stanford, CA: Stanford University Press).

Agamben, G. (2005) *State of Exception* (Chicago, IL, and London: University of Chicago Press).

Allen, K. (2003) Neither Boston nor Berlin: Class Polarisation and Neo-liberalism in the Irish Republic, in: C. Coulter & S. Coleman (Eds) *The End of Irish History? Critical Reflections on the Celtic Tiger,* pp. 56–73 (Manchester: Manchester University Press).

Allen, K. & Loyal, S. (2006) Rethinking Immigration and the State in Ireland, in: A. Lentin & R. Lentin (Eds) *Race and State,* pp. 209–228 (Newcastle: Cambridge Scholars Press).

Arendt, H. (1979) *The Origins of Totalitarianism* (New York: Harcourt Brace Jovanovich).

Balibar, E. (1991) Racism and Crisis, in: E. Balibar & I. Wallerstein, *Race, Nation, Class: Ambiguous Identities* (London: Verso).

Brennock, M. (2000) Harney Opposes Closer Integration of Europe, *The Irish Times,* 22 July.

Bunreacht na hÉireann (1998)Nineteenth Amendment of the Constitution Act, (Dublin: Government Publications Office).

Burleigh, M. & Wipperman, W. (1999) The Racial State', in: M. Bulmer & J. Solomos (Eds) *Racis,* pp. 277–287 (Oxford: Oxford University Press).

Coghlan, D. (2003) The (un)Deserving Refugee/Asylum Seeker? Racism and the Irish State, MPhil dissertation in Ethnic and Racial Studies, Department of Sociology, TCD.

Coulter, C. (2003) The End of Irish History? An Introduction to the Book, in: C. Coulter & S. Coleman (Eds) *The End of Irish History? Critical Reflections on the Celtic Tiger,* pp. 1–33 (Manchester: Manchester University Press).

Department of Justice, Equality & Law Reform (DJELR) (2006) Minister McDowell Publishes Outcome Details of Irish Born Child Scheme. 1 May, available online at: http://www.justice.ie

Department of the Taoiseach (2002) An Agreed Programme for Government Between Fianna Fáil and the Progressive Democrats', available online at: http://taoiseach.gov.ie/index.asp?docID=794

Fanning, B. (2002) *Racism and Social Change in the Republic of Ireland* (Manchester: Manchester University Press).

Feldman, A. (2006) Alterity and Belonging in Diaspora Space: Changing Irish Identities and 'Race' Making in the 'Age of Migration', in: N. Yuval-Davis, K. Kannabiran & U. M. Vieten (Eds) *Situating Contemporary Politics of Belonging,* pp. 100–112 (London: Sage).

Foucault, M. (1990) *The History of Sexuality, Vol. 1* (London: Allen Lane).

Foucault, M. (2003) *Society Must be Defended: Lectures at the College de France, 1975–76* (London: Allen Lane).

Gartland, F. & Reid, L. (2006) Asylum Seekers on Hunger Strike Threaten Protest 'to the Death', *The Irish Times,* 16 May.

Gilmartin, M. & Feldman, A. (2007) Census Figures and Immigration, Letter to the Editor, *The Irish Times,* 10 August.

Gilroy, P. (1987) *There Ain't No Black in the Union Jack* (London: Hutchinson).

Gilroy, P. (1998) Race Ends Here, *Ethnic and Racial Studies,* 21(5), pp. 838–847.

Goldberg, D. T. (2002) *The Racial State* (Oxford: Blackwell).

Gray, B. (1999) Steering a Course Somewhere Between Hegemonic Discourses of Irishness, in: R. Lentin (Ed.) *The Expanding Nation: Towards a Multi-Ethnic Ireland* (Dublin: MPhil in Ethnic and Racial Studies, TCD), available online at: http://www.ethnicracialstudies.net/images/docs/expanding_nation, pp. 60–72.

Gray, B. (2002) The Irish Diaspora, Globalised Belonging(s), *Irish Journal of Sociology,* 11(2), pp. 123–144.

Gray, B. (2003) *Women and the Irish Diaspora* (London: Routledge).

Halilovic-Pastuovic, M. (2007) The 'Bosnian Project' in Ireland: A 'Vision of Divisions', in: B. Fanning (Ed.) *Immigration and Social Change in the Republic of Ireland,* pp. 153–167 (Manchester: Manchester University Press).

Hall, S. (1997) Race, the Floating Signifier (Video, Media Education Foundation, London).

Harvey, C. (2003) Refugees, Asylum Seekers and International Human Rights Protection, in: U. Fraser & C. Harvey (Eds) *Sanctuary in Ireland: Perspectives on Asylum Law and Policy,* pp. 6–17 (Dublin: IPA).

Hendricks, T. (2006) Bay Area: Irish Join Battle Over Illegal Immigration, *San Francisco Chronicle*, 15 March.
Hesse, B. (2001) Post-Macpherson: Narrating Narratives of Racism, Paper presented at The Politics of Race and Urban Unrest Workshop, University of Salford, 5 September.
Holland, K. (2005) 50,200 Spent to Deport One Person Last Year', *The Irish Times*, 19 May.
Kelly, M. (2005) *Immigration-related Detention in Ireland: A Research Report for the Irish Refugee Council, Irish Penal Reform Trust and Immigrant Council of Ireland.* (Dublin: Human Rights Consultants).
Kelly, O. (2007) Census Shows Dramatic Rise in Non-Irish Population, *The Irish Times*, 8 August.
Keogh, D. (1998) *Jews in Twentieth Century Ireland: Refugees, Anti-Semitism and the Holocaust* (Cork: Cork University Press).
King-O'Riain, R. C. (2006) Re-racialising the Irish State Through the Census, Citizenship, and Language, in: A. Lentin & R. Lentin (Eds) *Race and State*, pp. 274–291 (Newcastle: Cambridge Scholars Press).
Kirby, P. (2002) *The Celtic Tiger in Distress: Growth with Inequality in Ireland* (Basingstoke: Palgrave).
Kundnani, A. (2007) *The End of Tolerance: Racism in 21st Century Britain* (London: Pluto Press).
Lally, C. (2006) McDowell Says Immigration Policy One of the Fairest in Europe, *The Irish Times*, 22 May.
Law, I. & Sayyid, S. (2007) Racist Futures: Themes and Prospects, *Ethnic and Racial Studies*, 30(4): 527–533.
Lentin, A. (2004) *Racism and Antiracism in Europe* (London: Pluto Press).
Lentin, A. & Lentin, R. (2006) Introduction: Speaking of racism, in: Alana Lentin and Ronit Lentin (Eds) *Race and Stat*, pp. 1-14 (Newcastle: Cambridge Scholars Press).
Lentin, R. & McVeigh, R. (2006) *After Optimism? Ireland, Racism and Globalisation* (Dublin: Metro Eireann Publications).
Loyal, S. (2003) Welcome to the Celtic Tiger: Racism, Immigration and the State, in: C. Coulter & S. Coleman (Eds) *The End of Irish History? Critical Reflections on the Celtic Tiger*, pp. 74–94 (Manchester: Manchester University Press).
Luibhéid, E. (2004) Childbearing Against the State? Asylum Seeker Women in the Irish Republic, *Women's Studies International Forum*, 27(4), pp. 335–350.
Mac Cormaic, R. (2005) Year Total of Asylum Seekers is Lowest Since 1989, *The Irish Times*, 31 December.
Mac Éinrí, P. (2003) *Labour Migration into Ireland* (Dublin: Immigration Council of Ireland).
Mac Éinrí, P. (2006) Scheme for an Immigration, Residence and Protection Bill: Some Preliminary Comments, Integrating Ireland, 21 October, available online at: http://www.integratingireland.ie
Maddock, J. & Mallon, C. (2003) 10,000 Parents of Irish Babies to be Deported, *The Evening Herald*, 23 January.
McVeigh, R. (1996) *The Racialization of Irishness* (Belfast: Centre for Research and Documentation).
Moriarty, E. (2007) *Ireland and Race: Ideas, Intellectuals and Identities* PhD dissertation, Department of Sociology, Trinity College Dublin.
Mullally, S. (2003) Defining the Limits of Citizenship: Children, Family Life and the *jus solis* Principle in Irish Law, unpublished paper, distributed by CADIC, October.
Ní Shuinéar, S. (2002) Othering the Irish (Traveller), in: R. Lentin & R. McVeigh (Eds) *Racism and Anti-Racism in Ireland*, pp. 177–191 (Belfast: Beyond the Pale Publications).
O'Brien, C. (2004) McDowell Rules out Residency Amnesty, *The Irish Times*, 17 November.
O'Brien, C. (2007) One in 10 is From Abroad, Twice the Number in 2002, *The Irish Times*, 30 March.
O'Dowd, N. (2006) Time Running Out for Irish Illegals, *The Irish Times*, 13 February.
O'Toole, F. (1994) *Black Hole, Green Card: The Disappearance of Ireland* (Dublin: New Island Books).
O'Toole, F. (2006) Foreword, in R. Lentin & R. McVeigh, *After Optimism? Ireland, Racism and Globalisation*, pp. i–iii (Dublin: Metro Eireann Publications).
Robinson, M. (1995) Cherishing the Irish Diaspora, Address to the Houses of the Oireachtas, Dublin, 2 February.

Ruhs, M. (2005) *Managing the Immigration and Employment of Non-EU Nationals in Ireland* (Dublin: The Policy Institute, Trinity College Dublin).
Schmitt, C. (1985) *Political Theology* (Cambridge, MA: MIT Press).
Schuster, L. (2003) Common Sense or Racism? The Treatment of Asylum Seekers in Europe, *Patterns of Prejudice,* 37(3), pp. 233–256.
Staunton, D. (2006) Plight of Illegal Irish in US Not Same as Afghans Here – Ahern, *The Irish Times,* 25 May.
Staunton, D. (2007) 2,500 Irish Lobby Congress for Right to Stay in US, *The Irish Times,* 8 March.
Ward, É. (1999) Ireland and Refugees/Asylum Seekers 1922–1966, in: R. Lentin (Ed.) *The Expanding Nation: Towards a Multi-ethnic Ireland,* pp. 41–48 (Dublin: MPhil in Ethnic and Racial Studies).
Yuval-Davis, N. (1997) *Gender and Nation* (London: Sage).
Yuval-Davis, N. and Anthias, F. (1989) *Woman–Nation–State* (London: Macmillan).

Democratic Autonomy, Women's Interests and Institutional Context

IAN O'FLYNN

Introduction

Under the terms of the Belfast Agreement (*Agreement*, 1998), Northern Ireland has sought to address its political problems by building democratic institutions that enable British unionists and Irish nationalists to share power. Although power sharing marks a significant shift away from the more usual majoritarian model of democracy, the thinking behind this shift is easy to appreciate. The fairness of the majoritarian model depends in large measure on the assumption that majority rule will not result in permanent majorities and permanent minorities – since majorities and minorities can be expected to alternate over the course of time, no group need fear being permanently excluded from the government (Jones, 1983: 168). Yet no such assumption can be expected to hold in the context of a deeply divided society such as Northern Ireland – since ethnic groups tend to line up squarely behind their own political parties, voting patterns tend to be relatively stable or unchanging. Consequently, deeply divided societies must opt for power sharing over majoritarianism so that minority ethnic groups will have at least some opportunity to participate in the government (but see Barry, 1975: 405).

The democratic institutions established under the terms of the Agreement not only enable unionists and nationalists to share power, but, in so doing, place unionist and nationalist interests firmly at the heart of Northern Irish politics (O'Leary, 1999: 76). Yet although many people in Northern Ireland care a great deal about the future of the union with Great Britain or about the prospects for a united Ireland, many people also care a great deal about political issues that do not, or at least need not, have anything to do with unionism or nationalism. The question remains, however, as to whether a political system that is built principally around the need to recognise and accommodate the interests of two conflicting ethnic groups can also leave sufficient space for the recognition and accommodation of other kinds of political interests within its decision procedures. In this article, I take up this question with respect to women's interests, such as they might be. More specifically, I ask whether the power-sharing institutions established under the terms of the Agreement treat those interests fairly or whether they discount those interests in ways that should give democrats cause for concern.

Now, at first sight, one might think that the answer to this question is obvious: since the Agreement recognises and accommodates the interests of two ethnic groups, and since all ethnic groups are patriarchal, the Agreement must inevitably fail to provide sufficient space for the recognition and accommodation of women's interests (Okin, 1997; Yuval-Davis 1998). Of course, it would be hard to deny that ethnic groups tend to be patriarchal to one extent or another. Yet it still need not follow that the Agreement treats women's interests unfairly, since much will depend on how ethnic interests are actually framed and institutionalised within its decision procedures (Kymlicka, 1997: 30). At a more philosophical level, we cannot simply say that the Agreement treats women's interests unfairly until we have first decided which democratic standards ought properly to apply in making evaluative judgements of this sort.

In this article, then, I will proceed as follows. First, I will argue that women's interests are best understood in relational rather than essentialist terms. However, a relational understanding brings problems of its own, since there are always limits to the number of interests that can be recognised and accommodated within any given set of decision procedures. Secondly, I will argue that although the circumstances of politics are such that interests must inevitably be prioritised, that prioritisation should not be arbitrary from the moral point of view. Instead, it should be directed by clearly defined and soundly justified democratic standards. To this end, I defend a particular reading of the principle of personal autonomy and suggest different ways in which women might put that principle into practice. Finally, in light of this treatment of the principle of personal autonomy, I evaluate a number of the core institutions established under the terms of the Belfast Agreement (the electoral system and parliamentary decision rules). I conclude that, as far as the recognition and accommodation of women's interests in Northern Ireland is concerned, the evidence is mixed.

Before proceeding, two points are worth noting. First, although this article is concerned with questions of institutional design, it is not explicitly concerned with offering positive proposals for remedying the problems that it identifies. Feminists have already offered a range of proposals of this of this latter sort, highlighting the important role that might be played by instruments and mechanisms such as candidate quotas, reserved seats, equality legislation and bills of rights (Young, 1990; Phillips, 1995; Williams, 1998; Mansbridge, 1999). Yet the fact remains that the appropriateness and utility of those instruments and mechanisms depends on prior normative and empirical assessments of the space for women's interests within particular institutional designs. Secondly, although this article is concerned with the recognition and accommodation of different and sometimes competing interests, not all interests on a par. In particular, a democratic government can have little truck with interests that are inimical to democracy or injurious to its members, no matter whose interests they are or why it is they hold them. For the purposes of this article, I will simply assume that interests of this injurious sort are not at issue.

Conceptualising Women's Interests

Naturally, it is important to begin by explaining how women's interests should be understood, since different explanations can have different implications for our assessment of the fairness or otherwise of any given set of democratic decision procedures. Here, in this section, I consider two possible explanations: essentialist and relational. I argue that the essentialist understanding is both ontologically flawed and democratically suspect. By contrast, I argue that a relational understanding offers a much more ontologically defensible conceptualisation of women's interests, although, as we will also see, it poses a number of difficult democratic questions of its own.

On an essentialist reading, women's interests are traced to an underlying nature in which all women, simply because they are women, share. For example, Carol Gilligan suggests that women's interests can be grounded in their natural capacity for nurturing (Gilligan, 1982). Yet, as most contemporary feminists openly accept, the trouble with essentialist approaches of this sort is that many women simply do not fit the proposed accounts of what it is to be a woman (Phillips, 1995: 68). Some women may see themselves as nurturers, and hence have strong feelings of connectedness to and sense of responsibility for others. In turn, those feelings may colour the interests that they hold more generally. But other women may feel nothing of the sort: their fundamental sense of what it means to be a woman may be very different, bound up with very different life experiences and reflected in very different interests and concerns.

Insofar as different women's interests cannot be traced to a single underlying nature, an essentialist understanding of those interests must be considered ontologically flawed: it does not provide a coherent account of the lived social reality of women in general. Of course, it might be responded that although essentialism might be ontologically flawed, it nevertheless captures the way in which many women actually *perceive* their interests: although there may be no such thing as an underlying nature to which each and every interest can be traced, some women believe that such a nature exists. Such claims are democratically suspect, however. Among other things, democracy entails the view that no one has the right to have their demands met or their interests satisfied without first justifying those interests in ways that others can understand and in principle accept. But if the essential nature to which you point has no meaning for me, it is hard to see why I should be persuaded by the claims that you make on both of us (Barry, 2006: 22–23). To insist on those interests nonetheless, simply because you think that they have arisen from some natural, pre-political source, is to fail to treat me as your equal.

Thus, the decisive factor that counts against essentialist approaches is that many women simply cannot think about their interests in such reductive terms (Young, 1997: 387). Nor, from a democratic point of view, should they be required to do so. By contrast, I want to suggest that a relational understanding provides a far more plausible way of conceptualising women's interests. But as I will also suggest, although essentialist claims are democratically suspect, a relational understanding poses democratic problems of its own.

On a relational understanding, we cannot make sense of the idea that the members of group *A* have a distinct interest in a given issue except in relation to how the members of an opposing group, *B*, see that issue (in the absence of group *B*, the members of group *A* might not even be aware that they have a distinct interest in the issue). Accordingly, when women qua women say that they have a distinct interest in issues such as childbearing, domestic violence or occupational mobility, this should not be understood as a claim about the centrality of those interests to their nature as women, but simply as a claim about how their experiences of childbearing, domestic violence and employment differ from those of men. Admittedly, some women do not have children or suffer domestic abuse, and we know that some women make it to the top of their profession. But since those women have their own particular experiences and perspectives, their interests should be understood not just in relation to those of men but also in relation to those of other women (Young, 1997: 389; Young, 2000: 99; Phillips, 1995: 67–68).

Ontologically, the beauty of a relational approach is that it allows us to account for the different interests that different groups of women may or may not have, if and when they have them. Unlike an essentialist understanding, which is ontologically rigid, a relational understanding is inherently flexible. It treats membership in a social group not as a matter of satisfying some purportedly objective criteria, but, in Iris Young's words, as a matter 'of a subjective affirmation of affinity with that group, the affirmation of that affinity by other members of the group, and the attribution of membership in that group by persons identifying with other groups' (Young, 1990: 172). In other words, on a relational conceptualisation, groups are composed of people who see the world in a similar way and who feel a certain affinity for one another because (among other things) they hold certain interests in common. Of course, our sense of affinity with those others can, and often will, wax and wane over time – as we change as people, our sense of what is of concern to us in life will change also, along with the relations in which we stand to others. There is nothing unusual about this shifting social process. But, as far as democratic decision making is concerned, it can make the recognition and accommodation of women's interests a highly complex affair.

If our interests are those things that we take to be of particular concern to us, then women have many different, and sometimes competing, interests. In the kinds of deeply divided societies with which this article is concerned, women will often oppose one another along ethnic or national lines – for instance, women qua unionists and women qua nationalists disagree fundamentally on the issue of the constitutional status of Northern Ireland. But those same women may simultaneously view themselves as sharing certain affinities that cut across the ethnic divide. They may share a distinct gendered interest in the kinds of issues that I mentioned above (childbearing, domestic violence, occupational mobility and so forth). But they may also share a distinct gendered interest in being able to challenge dominant interpretations of ethnicity from within, especially in those cases where dominant interpretations are highly patriarchal or where they create unwanted expectations about how women ought to behave or what their proper role ought to be (Appiah, 1994: 160–163).

Now, if an essentialist understanding tends to reduce the number of women's interests, a relational approach tends to multiply them (and perhaps multiply them exponentially). In this sense, a relational understanding magnifies the basic challenge that all democracies must confront, namely to design a fair procedure for deciding which interests will find their way into public policy and which will not. This challenge has both normative and empirical dimensions (Habermas, 1994: 124–125). In order to know whether a democratic decision procedure is fair or unfair, we must first have some appreciation of the values and standards against which that decision procedure should measured. But we must also know something about the political context in which that procedure has to operate, since conditions on the ground must also inform our evaluation of it (Goodin & Pettit, 1993: 1). After all, it makes no sense to say we ought to do something unless we can actually do it: ought implies can, as every philosopher knows.

No doubt the need to balance normative and empirical consideration can be extremely difficult in practice. This is especially so in deeply divided societies, where larger democratic goals and purposes will often have to give way in the face of harsh realities – ethnic interests may simply have to come first, not because they have the best arguments on their side, but because the alternatives might be unthinkable (O'Leary, 2005: 9). And yet normative standards continue to have a vitally important role to play.

No democracy is perfect; far from it. But since democracies are not static, the hope is always that they can be socially, politically and even morally improved. In this vein, it is often said that democracy is best understood as an ongoing learning process through which we come to see that democratic standards are better satisfied if, for example, women have the vote or hitherto marginalised ethnic groups are brought in from the cold (Young, 1990: 190; Habermas, 2001: 774–775). But, in order to know that democratic standards are better satisfied, we must, in the first instance, have some appreciation of what those standards are, how they are grounded and why they are worth pursuing. In the next section of this article, I focus on one such standard, namely the principle of personal autonomy. As we will see, this principle has much to tell us about the political recognition and accommodation of women's interests. I begin the section, though, by briefly considering how this principle relates to democracy more generally.

Democratic Autonomy and Women's Interests

From the outset of this article, I have traded on the assumption that a democratic system should allow sufficient space for the recognition of women's interests, or, perhaps more accurately, that a democratic system should not simply discount those interest as being of lesser *a priori* value or importance than ethnic interests. But how is this assumption grounded?

On the face of it, we might be tempted to think that this assumption flows naturally from a relational understanding of group interests: the idea that group interests need to be understood in relation to one another seems to preclude the idea that some interests are antecedently privileged. Yet the difficulty here is that ontological claims only tell us about the way the world is, not about the way the world ought to be – although our ontological commitments may colour the normative claims that we make, they need not determine them (Taylor, 1995: 182–185).[1] Accordingly, in order to move from a relational understanding of women's interests to the normative assumption that a democratic decision procedure should not discount those interests in advance, we must appeal to some intervening moral standard (see Jones, 1983: 165–166).

As I define it, democracy is a procedure for making decisions in which all of those who are bound by the decisions have the right to participate equally in their making. As this definition makes clear, political equality is the central value of democracy: since men and women are bound by the decisions that democratic governments make, men and women should have an equal say in those decisions. And so it follows that if men are entitled and empowered to shape their own relation to the polity (which, as an empirical matter, they generally are), then women must have the same general entitlement. Anything less is undemocratic.

Of course, the value of political equality has been interpreted to mean different things in different contexts. But for many contemporary democrats, the interpretation that is most relevant to the democratic process is expressed in the principle of equal consideration of interests. That principle 'supposes that the weaker members of a democratic association are entitled to the same concern and respect of their government as the more powerful members have secured for themselves' (Dworkin, 2006: 297). Even so, democrats worry that this principle may not be enough, taken on its own, to secure our standing as political equals. After all, it has often been pointed out that a benevolent and informed despotism could claim not only to know what was in your best interests, but also that it could be trusted to advance your interests as if they were its own (Dahl, 1989: 87–88).

In response, some democratic theorists argue that any convincing account of democracy must also involve a principle of personal autonomy which, in its most familiar formulation, supposes that each person should be treated as the best judges of his or her own interests (e.g. Mill, 1991 [1861]: 245–248; Dahl, 1989: 99). There are good prudential reasons for adopting a principle of this sort. Although democratic governments always claim to treat the interests of minority groups with equal consideration, and in many instances are actuated by a sincere desire to do so, the historical record nevertheless suggests that, as John Stuart Mill put it, 'the rights and interests of every or any person are only secure from being disregarded when the person interested is himself able, and habitually disposed, to stand up for them' (Mill, 1991 [1861: 245). Indeed, those who advocate power sharing in deeply divided societies take this reasoning one step further, arguing that unless representatives from the weaker ethnic groups are actually included, as of right, in the government, there is a very real danger that their interests will be depreciated or ignored (e.g. Lijphart, 1977, 2004; Horowitz, 1985, 1991).

Thus, there are good prudential grounds for thinking that the value of political equality should be spelled out not just in terms of a principle of equal consideration but also in terms of a principle of personal autonomy. Of course, it might be objected that the principle of personal autonomy is far more suited to private decisions than to democratic decisions, since our views about our own interests can never be decisive in the public realm in the way that they can be in the private realm. But, as Robert Goodin enables us to see, this objection overlooks an important point, namely that statements of interest entail claims, not just demands:

> To say 'I want *x*' is a demand: we do not need to know why, only that you want *x*, to fully comprehend the nature of the proposition and (if we are in the business of want-satisfaction) to act upon it. To say 'it is in my interests that I should have *x*' is to say something about the *reasonableness* of a want. It explains, rationalises, justifies a want in the way that a statement of brute longing does not. (Goodin, 1990: 184)

On this understanding, when a woman says that her experiences as a woman have led her to have a distinct interest in *x*, she is not simply saying that those experiences are proof enough that her interest in *x* should be satisfied (but see Hartsock, 1983). Rather, what she is saying is that there is something about those experiences, and hence about the interest-claims to which they give rise, that we should find rationally compelling (for example, that they are the product of unjust social hierarchies created and maintained by men to the unfair advantage of their gender). Of course, we might decide on due reflection that other claims are more compelling. But the general point remains that, insofar as we are willing to treat people as the best judges of their own interests, we will not discount their interests in advance.

Clearly, this characterisation of the principle of personal autonomy implies a very particular vision of democracy, one in which decision making proceeds in the first instance by rational discussion and deliberation rather than by bargaining or voting. Since I have written elsewhere on the subject of deliberative democracy in deeply divided societies, I will say no more about that subject here (O'Flynn, 2006, 2007).

Instead, I wish to spell out in more detail what I take this characterisation of the principle of personal autonomy to mean for the recognition of women's interests.

The principle of personal autonomy calls for a democratic decision procedure which affords women an equal say in the decisions that result. More specifically, it calls for a decision process that is flexible enough to allow women to freely shape their own relation to the polity, consistent with a similar freedom for all. In practical terms, there are two general dimensions along which this freedom (or autonomy) might be realised. First, some women might view themselves as having an exclusively gendered interest in some given policy issue, for example, equal pay. They might therefore decide to join a women's politically party in order to pursue that interest. Of course, party members might disagree internally with one another about how exactly they should proceed. But when it comes to engaging externally with other political parties, they will, along this first dimension, see that engagement primarily as a challenge to patriarchal norms.[2] Secondly, some women might think of themselves as having interests in common with men. For example, they might see themselves as sharing a concern for the environment. Those women might therefore decide to join a green political party in order to bring a gendered perspective to bear on that concern. When it comes to internal policy debates, those women may understand their interests in relation to those of male members. But, regardless of whether or not their interests as women shape a particular policy outcome, they will, along this second dimension, act first and foremost as environmentalist when it comes to engaging externally with other political parties.[3]

Now, on one level, these two general dimensions along which the principle of personal autonomy can be put into practice pertain just as much to deeply divided societies as they do to more normal democratic societies. For example, some women born into the unionist (or nationalist) community in Northern Ireland might think about their interests in wholly gendered terms and hence as independent of the concerns of unionism. By contrast, some unionist women might think of themselves as unionists in the first instance and women in the second. In relation to the male members of the unionist community, those women might challenge the development of party policy on, say, grounds of gender equality. But when it comes to engaging externally with nationalist parties, they will typically prioritise their ethnic allegiances to unionism.

On another level, however, it must be remembered that the members of a divided society tend not to think about social issues such as the environment in the same way as ethnic issues. The reason why is obvious: given the legacy of protracted violent conflict, ethnic interests will resonate uniquely for them. But then it seems that, as far as women's interests are concerned, there are good grounds for thinking about the principle of personal autonomy in terms of three general dimensions of autonomous democratic engagement rather than two – as women in their own right (dimension 1), as women with a gendered interest in social (or non-ethnic) issues (dimension 2) or as women with a gendered perspective on ethnicity (dimension 3). In the following section, I consider whether or to what extent women in Northern

Ireland can meaningfully choose to exercise their personal autonomy along each of these three dimensions.

Women's Autonomy in Context: Power-Sharing in Northern Ireland

In what follows, I focus on the electoral system and Assembly decision rules established under the terms of the Agreement. Admittedly, a more complete analysis would need to consider a much broader range of issues, including human rights, justice and security provisions, along with their implications for cross-border relations (Fearon & Rebouché, 2006: 283–287). Yet insofar as democracy is normally thought of in the first instance as a decision procedure, it seems natural to begin by focusing on the two institutional features to which I now turn.

The Electoral System

Northern Ireland uses the single transferable vote (STV) form of proportional representation (PR) to elect representatives to its 108-member parliamentary Assembly. Like all PR systems, STV tends to reduce disproportionate vote-to-seat ratios. It also tends to increase electoral choice, not just because its ballot structure allows voters to vote for any mix of candidates they prefer, for whatever reason they prefer them, but also because its low threshold for election encourages new political parties or independent candidates to run for election (Taagepera & Shugart, 1989: 24–28).

In theory, there is reason to think that STV might serve women well along all three dimensions that I identified above. Since STV operates with a low threshold for election, it can encourage women to stand as independent candidates, to create their own parties or to join social parties that might have little chance of success under some alternative electoral system (dimensions 1 and 2). And since STV tends to increase electoral choice and hence electoral competition, it can also encourage ethnic parties to pay greater attention to women's interests – for example by including gender issues in their party platforms or by fielding a greater number of female candidates at election time (dimension 3). Nevertheless, it might well be objected that matters are no way near as straightforward in practice as they appear to be in theory. Although STV might encourage new political parties and independent candidates, some of whom might seek to promote women's interests, it might just as easily encourage ethnic parties that aim to represent the more extreme ends of the political spectrum. Insofar as those parties polarise society, electoral choice will be reduced rather than increased.

Critics of the Agreement claim that this is precisely what has happened in Northern Ireland (e.g. Horowitz, 2001; Wilson & Wilford, 2003; Taylor, 2006). In particular, they blame STV for the spectacular rise of the two main hard-line parties, Sinn Féin (SF) and the Democratic Unionist Party (DUP), and the equally spectacular decline of the two main moderate parties, the Social and Democratic Labour Party (SDLP) and the Ulster Unionist Party (UUP). More generally, they blame STV for what they see as an unhealthy darkening of ethnicity in Northern Irish political life and, alongside that, an unhealthy narrowing of the space for cross-cutting social interests. Thus, as Robin Wilson and Rick Wilford conclude, 'elections have become entirely communalised affairs, rewarding intra-ethnic outbidding as the only competition' (Wilson & Wilford, 2003: 7).

Those same critics argue that Northern Ireland would fare much better under the alternative vote (AV) electoral system. Like STV, AV also enables voters to rank candidates in order of their preference. But unlike STV, which operates with a relatively low threshold for election, AV operates with a majority threshold. In highly mixed constituencies, a threshold of this latter sort may mean that electoral results will turn heavily on vote transfers, which may in turn encourage candidates to take the broader view. This would be good for women, were it not for the fact that there is a fatal flaw. It is very hard to see why hard-liners, whose inclusion in the negotiations is generally crucial to the success of any peace agreement, should agree to sign up to an electoral system that is explicitly designed to reduce their future chances at the polls (McGarry & O'Leary, 2004: 30–31).

If the critics are misguided on this score, then it may well be that they are also misguided in their criticisms of STV. So let us consider the evidence.[4] The critics suggest that the rise of SF and the DUP has constricted the space for non-ethnic social parties. If this were the case, then we would be right to worry about the space for women to exercise their democratic autonomy along dimension 2. But the facts tell a different story. Social parties such as the Alliance Party of Northern Ireland (APNI) or the Green Party are not doing badly under STV. On the contrary, the Green party won its first seat in the 2007 Assembly elections. In those same elections, the APNI increased its number of seats from six to seven, and its number of female Assembly members from one to two. Of particular note in the present context is the fact that the APNI's new female Assembly member, Anna Lo, is the first member of the Chinese community to win an Assembly seat, which nicely illustrates the ability of STV to capture a wide diversity of social interests, gendered and non-gendered, beyond unionism and nationalism.

Turning to dimension 1, there might be some initial cause for concern. In particular, it is tempting to blame the demise of the Northern Ireland Women's Coalition on the electoral system. But as I have just suggested, STV seems to serve small parties reasonably well. Indeed, the demise of the NIWC may simply indicate that its former supporters have decided that their interests as women are better represented by other parties in other ways. In other words, it may not be a question of the electoral system failing women along dimension 1, but possibly of an electoral system which has successfully provided women with a range of more attractive political options along dimension 2. This is not a wholly speculative thought, since the constituency seat that Anna Lo now holds (South Belfast) is the same seat that Monica McWilliams, the former leader of the NIWC, held until 2003.

The evidence therefore suggests that STV is not making things worse for women along dimensions 1 and 2. Nor, it should be said, is it making things worse for them along dimension 3. For example, the DUP put forward six female candidates in 2007 in comparison to four female candidates in 2003. In both years, it put forward more female candidates than the UUP. SF continues to put forward fewer women candidates than the SDLP. But of the nine female candidates put forward by SF in 2007, eight were elected, which suggests that SF is willing to run female candidates in safe constituencies. Of course, no matter how the statistics are read, women are still grossly under-represented in the Assembly relative to their share of the voting population as a whole. But, as far as dimension 3 is concerned, the argument that STV has made things worse for women does not appear to hold up. At the very least, it would appear that hard-liners are just as sensitive to the interests and concerns of their female supporters as are their more moderate rivals.

Assembly Decision Rules

Assuming, then, that STV allows an acceptable degree of space for the recognition and accommodation of women's interests, judged in terms of our three dimensions of democratic autonomy, does the same hold true of the rules and procedures by which decisions are taken in the Assembly? As we will now see, the picture that emerges is much more mixed.

Take, to begin with, the issue of designation. The Agreement contains strong veto points designed to ensure that key decisions such as budget allocations or changes to standing orders are taken on an inter-ethnic basis. More specifically, all important decisions may be passed under the 'parallel consent' rule, which requires, among those present and voting, an overall majority of Assembly members and a majority of both unionists and nationalist members; or, alternatively, they may be passed under the 'weighted majority' rule, which requires, among those present and voting, at least 60 per cent of all members voting, plus at least 40 per cent of both nationalists and unionist members (*Agreement* (1998), Strand One, para. 5(d); O'Leary, 1999: 70).

Crucially, in order to ascertain whether these requirements have been met, all Assembly members must register upon election as 'unionist', 'nationalist' or 'other' (*Agreement* (1998), Strand One, para. 6). Yet while these measures are intended to ensure that one group cannot dominate or tyrannise the other, the net effect of enforcing vetoes in this way is that it is more rewarding to be a member of one of the two named ethnic groups than of an unaffiliated group such as the APNI or, formerly, the NIWC. In practice, the parallel consent rule implies that once a majority is secured within the Assembly, the 'others' no longer count; at such a point, all that matters is whether or not there is a majority within both ethnic groups. However, by disadvantaging unaffiliated Assembly members in this way, 'the Agreement violates their interest in pursuing politics in their own way on terms of equality with other political actors' (Horowitz, 2002: 195).

Insofar as this analysis is correct, designation favours women who choose to exercise their personal autonomy along ethnic lines (i.e., along dimension 3). But even here matters are not straightforward, since those same women might decide to exercise their autonomy differently on some other occasion (i.e. along dimensions 1 or 2). As I argued earlier in this article, much of the complexity that attaches to our thinking about interests stems from the fact that the same woman can stand in a different relation to others, depending on the issue in question. On one particular issue, a woman might be perfectly happy to prioritise her ethnicity. The *Agreement* will serve her well. But on some other issue, she may see herself as having a stronger sense of affinity with women in general (dimension 1) or with women and men with whom she shares a particular social interest (dimension 2). Yet the trouble is that these choices may not be equally valued, or equally recognised, within the Assembly's decision procedures.

Of course, it is important not to overstate the issue. So long as the policy proposal under discussion is a wholly ethnic issue, it is hard to see why anyone should complain. The issue may simply be of no concern to women who think about their interests as gendered interests plain and simple (dimension 1) or as social issues that cut across the ethnic divide (dimension 2). An example might be a change to the rules governing the flying of flags on public buildings. Or again, it is possible to imagine an issue in which all women thought about their interests solely from an ethnic perspective, under which circumstance they would all be equally protected (dimension 3). For example, a change to Northern Ireland's constitutional status might group women in just such a way. Yet, by the same token, it is also possible to imagine an issue in which no woman thought about her interests in ethnic terms, instead thinking about them in gendered terms plain and simple. Put in relational terms, it may well be the case that, on certain issues, men and women differ, no matter what their ethnic background (see Song, 2005).

For instance, in June 2000, the Assembly debated a motion to prohibit any future proposals to extend the 1967 Abortion Act to Northern Ireland. During the course of the debate, the NIWC tabled an amendment calling for the issue to be referred to the Assembly's Health, Social Services and Public Safety Commitee for further disucssion. The proposed amendment was defeated by 43 votes, and the motion was subsequently passed without further amendment (Fearon & Rebouché, 2006: 292; Hansard, 2001). In the present context, there are two related points about this example that stand out. First, although defeated, the proposed amendment was supported unanimously by all 14 female Assembly members. The fact that they were able to vote as women, independently of their respective official designations, suggests that they were able to act autonomously in their own right (dimension 1). But even so, the fact also remains that their distinct interest in the issue of abortion was trumped by the distinct interest of their male colleauges in that issue. Secondly, most of those who voted against the amendment and in support of the motion 'chose to focus on the so-called rights of the unborn rather than on women's health' (Fearon & Rebouché, 2006: 292–293). But in so doing, they seemingly discounted the fact that a woman's concern for her own well-being gives her not just a distinct interest in abortion, but strong grounds for claiming that her interest in abortion should be appropriately protected.

This last sentence requires comment. In suggesting that her interest in the issue of abortion should be appropriately protected, I am not implying that that interest is grounded in some underlying pre-political essence.[5] As I noted earlier, there is no necessary correlation between the ontological view that one holds and the policies that one advocates. It is, after all, possible to think about interests in relational terms while at the same time advocating policies that rigidly protect those interests. We might, for example, think that unionism and nationalism are most sensibly understood in relational terms, but that unionism and nationalism should nevertheless be expressly protected at the level of the state. Our understanding of the context is everything here, which brings me to a second important point.

As I also noted earlier, women's interests are vast and varied. But since they are so varied, we may want to consider paying special attention to those strikingly unusual cases in which the female members of a deeply divided society speak with one voice. Sometimes, when the members of an ethnic group speak with one voice, we treat this as a sign that their fundamental interests are at stake or that old injustices have resurfaced, and often go to great lengths to protect them, for example, by providing them with vetoes. Naturally, much will depend on the context and in particular on what we know about the treatment meted out to members in the past – whether they have been discriminated against historically, whether they continue to bear the consequences of past injustices, whether equality of opportunity is still a problem, and so forth. But since women also claim that historically they have suffered injustices at the hands of men, there is, as Young has argued, a clear case for claiming that women, too, should have a right of veto on issues that they deem to be of particular concern to them as women (Young, 1990: 184). After all, the principle of equal consideration of interests entails that similar cases should be treated similarly, dissimilar cases dissimilarly.

Of course, the trouble with this particular line of reasoning is that it seems to place us on an extremely slippery slope – insisting that, under some circumstances, women qua women should have the right to veto decisions that are of particular concern to them seems to commit us to the view that, let us say, left-handers should have a similar right to veto decisions that are of particular concern to them. After all, left-handers continue to be discriminated against when it comes, for example, to the design of surgical instruments. Yet it must be obvoius that no functioning democratic system could grant a right of veto to each and every group that claimed that its fundamental interests were at stake or that it is the victim of unfair discrimination (but see Mansbridge, 1999: 635). Insofar as vetoes make groups realise that they must behave fairly towards one another, they can be a friend of democracy but, the greater the number of vetoes, the greater the chances are that decision making will stall.

Indeed, matters are even more complicated than this, since they ultimately pose what Young terms 'a paradox of political origins': who shall decide which groups are to have vetoes and under what conditions shall that decision be made? I agree with Young that there is no determinate answer to questions of this sort (Young, 1990: 190). Or at least there is no determinate answer from within a procedural view of democracy. We are where we are, and so the real challenge is to decide where we should go next. As I have argued in this article, democracy needs to be seen not just as an ongoing learning process, but as an ongoing learning process that is consciously directed in light of sound political principles. Those principles are not a panacea: at best, each case can only be treated on its merits in a rough and ready way, and every decision may well be subject to future challenge or revision. Yet, as I have also argued, although principles such as the principle of personal autonomy can be difficult to interpret and apply, they can nevertheless serve as moral beacons that direct us, albeit imperfectly, in our efforts to build a better, more egalitarian democracy for all.

Conclusion

In this article, I have offered a number of inter-linking arguments. To begin with, I argued that women's interests should not be traced to some underlying nature or essence, but should instead be conceived in relational terms. Yet, as we saw, the problem with a relational understanding is that it multiplies women's interests to such an extent that no democratic system could recognise and accommodate them all. The question, then, is how to choose between them democratically. I have suggested that since choosing inevitably involves making value judgements, we should be clear about which values we are invoking and why, which principles best express those values, and which application is most appropriate in the given context.

As far as the case of Northern Ireland is concerned, I have suggested that the Belfast Agreement is not so bad after all. Its electoral system seems to leave sufficient space both for the recognition of women's interests and for the exercise of their personal autonomy. Its parliamentary structures do not fare quite so well, however. In particular, they raise difficult, if not insoluble, questions not just about the recognition and accommodation of women's interests, but also about the recognition of human interests more generally. That said, I have also stressed the point that no democratic system is perfect. Or, otherwise put, I have stressed the idea that every democratic society needs to learn and grow. Northern Ireland is no different in this respect.

Of course, women face a great many other barriers, besides those that I have considered here, in their efforts to have their interests duly recognised. Those barriers come in many different social, economic and political forms (Reynolds, 1999: 550–557). But in whatever form, the fact remains that no democratic society can ever rise to its full social, political and even moral maturity until they are torn down once and for all. This insight is hardly novel – although John Stuart Mill based certain of his arguments on a questionable assumption about the essential unity of male and female natures, he clearly thought that the full and equal inclusion of women in political life was essential to human improvement generally (Mill, 1991 [1869]: 471, 493–495). And yet, despite the power of this insight, much work remains to be done.

Notes

I wish to thank Jurgen De Wispelaere, Cillian McBride, Shane O'Neill, David Russell and two anonymous referees for this journal for constructive written comments on earlier drafts of this article.

1. Think, for instance, of liberal individualists who nonetheless support the types of holist policies that one might normally associate with the welfare state.
2. In practice, parties of this sort have sometimes used essentialist rhetoric in order to strengthen their political hand; they present themselves as representing all women, not just some particular portion of them (whether or not they actually believe their own rhetoric is, of course, an altogether different matter). But strategies of this sort will often backfire, since essentialist rhetoric can have an alienating effect on many women (Haslanger, 2000: 46). See Little, 2002, for an example from Northern Ireland.
3. Indeed, gender might not even have been the prime motivating factor driving those women to engage in politics; gender may ultimately be of lesser importance to them than the state of the planet.
4. The data presented here are drawn from Queen's University Belfast's Centre for Advancement of Women in Politics website, available online at http://www.qub.ac.uk/cawp/UKhtmls/electionNIMarch07.htm, and from the Northern Ireland Assembly's own website at http://www.niassembly.gov.uk/
5. Nor am I implying that all women think about abortion in the same way. In the example used above, there is no suggestion that the 14 female Assembly members were all pro-choice or all anti-abortion. They all viewed the issue as a healthcare issue, they all wished to talk about the issue further, and they all viewed their interest in the issue in relation to the interest of men. But beyond that, we do not know what they thought or how internally diverse their views actually were. Cf. Phillips (1995: 68) for a nice insight into these types of distinctions.

References

Agreement Reached in the Multiparty Negotiations (1998) (Belfast: The Stationery Office).

Appiah, A. (1994) Identity, Authenticity, Survival: Multicultural Societies and Social Reproduction, in: C. Taylor & A. Gutmann (Eds) *Multiculturalism: Examining the Politics of Recognition*, pp. 149–163 (Princeton, NJ: Princeton University Press).

Barry, B. (1975) The Consociational Model and Its Dangers, *European Journal of Political Research*, 3(4), pp. 393–412.

Barry, B. (2006) Democracy Needs Dialogue and Deliberation, Not Political Blocs, a Commentary on Halef Afshar, in: *Democracy and Islam*, P. Parvan & D. McHugh (Eds), pp. 22–24 (London: Hansard Society).

Dahl, R. (1989) *Democracy and Its Critics* (New Haven, CT: Yale University Press).

Dworkin, R. (1996) Taking Rights Seriously, in: R. Goodin & P. Pettit (Eds) *Contemporary Political Philosophy: An Anthology* (second edition), pp. 289–301 (Oxford: Blackwell).

Fearon, K. & Rebouché, R. (2006) What Happened to the Women?: Promises, Reality and the Northern Ireland Women's Coalition, in: M. Cox, A. Guelke & F. Stephen (Eds) *A Farewell to Arms? Beyond the Good Friday Agreement*, 2nd edn, pp. 280–301 (Manchester: Manchester University Press).

Gilligan, C. (1982) *In a Different Voice: Psychological Theory and Women's Development* (Cambridge: Harvard University Press).

Goodin, R. (1990) Liberalism and the Best-Judge Principle, *Political Studies*, 38(2), pp. 181–195.

Goodin, R. & Pettit, P. (1993) Introduction, in: R. Goodin & P. Pettit (Eds) *A Companion to Contemporary Political Philosophy*, pp. 1–4 (Oxford: Blackwell).

Habermas, J. (1994) Struggles for Recognition in the Democratic Constitutional State, in: C. Taylor & A. Gutmann (Eds) *Multiculturalism: Examining the Politics of Recognition*, pp. 107–148 (Princeton, NJ: Princeton University Press).

Habermas, J. (2001) Constitutional Democracy: A Paradoxical Union of Contradictory Principles?, *Political Theory*, 29(6), pp. 766–781.

Hansard (2001) Official Report of the Northern Ireland Assembly, *Hansard*, 20 June, available online at: http://www.niassembly.gov.uk/record/reports/000620b.htm#2

Hartsock, N. (1983) The Feminist Standpoint: Developing the Ground for a Specifically Feminist Historical Materialism, in: S. Harding & M. Hintikka (Eds) *Discovering Reality: Feminist Perspectives on Epistemology, Metaphysics, Methodology, and Philosophy of Science*, pp. 283–310 (New York: Springer).

Haslanger, S. (2000) Gender and Race: (What) Are They? (What) Do We Want Them to Be?, *Noûs*, 34(1), pp. 31–55.

Horowitz, D. (1985) *Ethnic Groups in Conflict* (Berkeley, CA: University of California Press).

Horowitz, D. (1991) *A Democratic South Africa?: Constitutional Engineering in a Divided Society* (Berkeley, CA: University of California Press).

Horowitz, D. (2001) The Northern Ireland Agreement: Clear, Consociational, and Risky, in: J. McGarry (Ed.) *Northern Ireland and the Divided World: Post-Agreement Northern Ireland in Comparative Perspective*, pp. 89–108 (Oxford: Oxford University Press).

Horowitz, D. (2002) 'Explaining Northern Ireland: The Sources of an Unlikely Constitutional Consensus', *British Journal of Political Science*, 32(2), pp. 193–220.

Jones, P. (1983) Political Equality and Majority Rule, in: D. Miller & L. Siedentop (Eds) *The Nature of Political Theory*, pp. 155–182 (Oxford: Clarendon Press).

Kymlicka, W. (1997) Liberal Complacencies: A Response to Susan Okin's 'Is Multiculturalism Bad for Women?', *Boston Review*, 22(5), pp. 29–30.

Lijphart, A. (1977) *Democracy in Plural Societies: A Comparative Exploration* (New Haven, CT: Yale University Press).

Lijphart, A. (2004) Constitutional Design for Divided Societies, *Journal of Democracy*, 15(2), pp. 96–109.

Little, A. (2002) Feminism and the Politics of Difference in Northern Ireland, *Journal of Political Ideologies*, 7(2), pp. 163–177.

Mansbridge, J. (1999) Should Blacks Represent Blacks and Women Represent Women? A Contingent 'Yes', *The Journal of Politics*, 61(3), pp. 628–657.

McGarry, J. & O'Leary, B. (2004) *The Northern Ireland Conflict: Consociational Engagements* (Oxford: Oxford University Press).

Mill, J. S. (1991 [1869]) The Subjugation of Women, in: J. Gray (Ed.) *John Stuart Mill: On Liberty and Other Essays*, pp. 469–582 (Oxford: Oxford University Press).

Mill, J. S. (1991 [1861]) Considerations on Representative Government, in: J. Gray (Ed.) *Mill: On Liberty and Other Essays*, pp. 203–467 (Oxford: Oxford University Press).

Okin, S. M. (1997) Is Multiculturalism Bad for Women?, *Boston Review*, 22(5), pp. 25–28.

O'Flynn, I. (2006) *Deliberative Democracy and Divided Societies* (Edinburgh and New York: Edinburgh University Press and Palgrave).

O'Flynn, I. (2007) Divided Societies and Deliberative Democracy, *British Journal of Political Science*, 37(4), pp. 731–751.

O'Leary, B. (1999) The Nature of the British-Irish Agreement, *New Left Review*, 233, pp. 66–96.

O'Leary, B. (2005) Debating Consociational Politics: Normative and Explanatory Arguments, in: S. Noel (Ed.) *From Power Sharing to Democracy: Post-Conflict Institutions in Ethnically Divided Societies*, pp. 3–43 (Montreal and Kingston: McGill-Queen's University Press).

Phillips, A. (1995) *The Politics of Presence* (Oxford: Clarendon Press).

Reynolds, A. (1999) Women in the Legislatures and Executives of the World: Knocking at the Highest Glass Ceiling, *World Politics*, 51(4), pp. 547–572.

Song, S. (2005) Majority Norms, Multiculturalism, and Gender Equality, *American Political Science Review*, 99(4), pp. 473–489.

Taagepera, R. & Shugart, M. (1989) *Seats and Votes: The Effects and Determinants of Electoral Systems* (New Haven, CT: Yale University Press).

Taylor, C. (1995) Cross-Purposes: The Liberal-Communitarian Debate, in: C. Taylor, *Philosophical Arguments*, pp. 181—203 (Cambridge: Harvard University Press).

Taylor, R. (2006) The Belfast Agreement and the Politics of Consociationalism: A Critique, *The Political Quarterly*, 77(2), pp. 217–226.

Williams, M. (1998) *Voice, Trust, and Memory: Marginalised Groups and the Failings of Liberal Representation* (Princeton, NJ: Princeton University Press).

Wilson, R. & Wilford, R. (2003) *Northern Ireland: A Route to Stability?* (Birmingham: ESRC).

Young, I. M. (1990) *Justice and the Politics of Difference* (Princeton, NJ: Princeton University Press).

Young, I. M. (1997) Difference as a Resource for Democratic Communication, in: J. Bohman & W. Rehg (Eds) *Deliberative Democracy: Essays on Reason and Politics*, pp. 383–406 (Cambridge: MIT Press).

Young, I. M. (2000) *Inclusion and Democracy* (Oxford: Oxford University Press).

Yuval-Davis, N. (1998) Gender and Nation, in: R. Wilford & R. Miller (Eds) *Women, Ethnicity and Nationalism: The Politics of Divided Societies*, pp. 23–35 (London: Routledge).

Comprehensive Liberalism and Civic Education in the Republic of Ireland

GRAHAM FINLAY

Introduction

Ireland, in 2007, has become an increasingly diverse place. Into this newly diverse society, several proposals have been introduced that set out a curriculum for citizenship education for the Republic of Ireland, to be included in the Leaving Certificate as an extension of the existing Junior Certificate Civic, Social and Political Education Syllabus (CSPE). These proposals pose complex problems regarding the recognition of a diverse set of political and religious viewpoints and the equal treatment of both majority and minority groups in contemporary Ireland. In this paper, I consider the role of civic education in the diverse liberal polity that Ireland is becoming in the light of a robust, 'comprehensive' liberalism, that of John Stuart Mill, and argue that such a liberalism, far from directly attempting to make the citizens adopt the values its liberalism favours, instead supports both a certain kind of critical pedagogical practice and a diversity of institutional forms. Perhaps surprisingly, given Ireland's history of illiberal religious and civic education, Ireland's existing educational institutions can be shown to have a peculiar responsiveness to a liberal society characterised by strong views and diverse groups.[1]

Background: Civic Education in the Republic of Ireland

Although Ireland – with its revolutionary tradition, relative homogeneity and the historic 'special position of the Holy Catholic Apostolic and Roman Church' (removed after a referendum in 1972) (Williams, 1999: 320) – may potentially develop into some form of polity other than a liberal one, its future as a liberal polity is promoted by the claims of its Constitution, its membership in the European Union and its ratification of a number of international human rights covenants. Many of the rights that the Irish state commits itself to in these covenants are relevant to education. As Desmond Clarke very persuasively argues, the right to freedom of thought, enshrined in the European Convention on Human Rights, has far reaching implications for educational practice, especially the traditional practice of civic education in Irish schools (Clarke, 1986). The most important articles of the Irish Constitution for education are Articles 41–42, which complicate the role of civic and moral education considerably. The Constitution grants 'inalienable and imprescriptible rights' to the family to choose schools and to form the morals of their children (Bunreacht na hÉireann 41.1, 42), but also requires the state to take on this role in the absence of the parents, 'always with due regard for the natural and imprescriptible rights of the child.'(Bunreacht na hÉireann 42.5) Further: 'The State shall provide for free primary education and shall endeavour to supplement and give reasonable aid to private and corporate educational initiative, and, when the public good requires it, provide other educational facilities or institutions with due regard, however, for the rights of parents, especially in the matter of religious and moral formation.'(Bunreacht na hÉireann 42.4) Furthermore, as Kevin Williams has noted, Article 44 (Religion) supports freedom of conscience and non-discrimination 'on the ground of religious profession', including 'the right of any child to attend a school receiving public money without attending religious instruction at that school.'(Bunreacht na hÉireann 44.2.4; Williams, 1999: 321).

Notwithstanding these commitments to parental autonomy and non-discrimination regarding religion, Irish pedagogical practice, particularly with regard to moral, social and civic education has not refrained from inculcating particular moral, political and religious beliefs in children, nor have educational institutions – almost all of which are run by various religious denominations, the vast majority being operated by the Catholic Church – observed liberal neutrality regarding differing faiths and political commitments. Until the 1990s, the official position of the Catholic Church and the government was that religious education and civic education were inseparable, and indeed that religious education should permeate every sort of teaching. As *The Primary School Curriculum: Teacher's Handbook* says: 'The integration of the curriculum may be seen ... in the religious and civic spirit which animates all its parts'(cited in Williams, 1999: 324). This combination of religious instruction and 'civics' was even more pronounced in the secondary school curriculum (Williams, 1999: 325–326; Clarke, 1986: 294–296).

The relation between religious and civic education has undergone considerable change recently, at least in terms of official documents. During the 1990s, a series of government papers, culminating in the Education Act of 1998, increasingly emphasised liberal toleration and 'the diversity of values, beliefs, languages and traditions in Irish society' (cited in Williams, 1999: 328). The blending of religious and civic education from sectarian motives is now absent from the guidelines for teachers published by the Department of Education. For example, the Syllabus for Leaving Certificate Religious Education emphasises that: 'The emphasis in the syllabus on the value of religious belief and on diversity and mutual respect is of particular relevance for national and global citizenship'(Department of Education and Science, 2005: 4). Similarly, the CSPE Syllabus for the Junior Certificate emphasises the 'practice of tolerance' as one of the 'attitudes and values' that students are encouraged to 'recognise and develop' (Department of Education and Science, 2006: 6). Finally, the background paper for the future Leaving Certificate civic education syllabus emphasises 'civic self-restraint', 'an openness to deliberative argument, which includes a willingness to challenge authority where appropriate', 'tolerance of diverse positions, cultures and understandings' and aims 'to provide students with the critical thinking and imaginative skills, and the knowledge and values in relation to their political and social contexts that will enable them to be thoughtful and responsible actors in their world' (Tormey, 2006: 3). As Roland Tormey notes in this background paper, the commitment of the State to interculturalism goes beyond tolerating diverse positions to celebrating them. As the National Council for Curriculum and Assessment puts it, 'intercultural education' is 'education which respects, celebrates and recognises the normality of diversity in all areas of human life' (cited in Tormey, 2006: 9). Nevertheless, and with the important exception of the colleges of the Vocational Educational Committee, the organisation of Irish educational institutions remains denominational: although schools can preserve the 'ethos' of the school, they 'must balance this right of schools and their students against the rights to education of students of different denominations or none and the rights of teachers to earn a livelihood'(Government of Ireland, 1995, cited in Williams, 1999: 238). As Williams notes, 'The [Education] Act also imposes on the Minister for Education an obligation to "have regard to the characteristic spirit of a school or class of school in exercising his or her functions"'(Government of Ireland, 1998, cited in Williams, 1999: 328). Only very recently has the notion of the State-run primary school been introduced, in the form of an experimental school in Diswellstown, Co. Dublin, scheduled to open in September 2008, and even this school will have the Catholic Church as a sponsor. All previous schools have been run by some private body, normally denominations, but also community groups and non-profit companies such as Educate Together, which sponsors multi-denominational schools. Speaking of the new school at Diswellstown, Minister for Education, Mary Hanafin, indicated that 'it was her intention to ensure that it would cater for the diversity of religious faiths represented in the area served by the school'. More importantly, this development was welcomed by the Catholic hierarchy (all references to this development are to McGarry, 2007). We can see, then, a remarkable move in recent years towards some kind of liberal conception both of Irish society and of the role of civic education. We should now consider what kind of liberalism best articulates the demands of this liberal conception and the consequences for the civic education of students and for the ethos of schools.

Liberalism and the Teaching of Values

Almost all philosophers have concerned themselves with education as a crucial aspect of political society and as an activity capable of doing great good as well as great harm. In what follows, I will focus on some of the internal debates of liberalism, ignoring other possible approaches such as conservative and civic republican views. Many of the debates of contemporary liberalism revolve around the distinction between 'comprehensive' and 'political' liberalisms, particularly debates surrounding civic education (Callan, 1997; Macedo, 1995). The distinction between 'political' and 'comprehensive' liberals is that of John Rawls, who drew it in response to concerns about the adequacy and, especially, the stability of his great original contribution to liberal theory, *A Theory of Justice* (1971). This distinction is found in his later work, *Political Liberalism* (Rawls, 1996), where he distinguishes between liberalisms that provide a complete solution to the problems of human life – solutions that depend on controversial claims about human nature – and liberalisms that develop 'political' conceptions of the self and justice that rest on no such controversial foundation. As examples of the former, Rawls singles out the liberalisms of Kant and Mill, and he proposes a version of the latter as the best attempt to secure a consensus regarding the claims of his own theory of justice for a society divided by deep religious, cultural and philosophical disagreement. In a later publication and in response to further criticism, Rawls pushes his 'political' liberalism still further towards avoiding the claims of a particular view. In 'The Idea of Public Reason Revisited', Rawls claims that 'the content of public reason is given by the principles and values of a family of liberal political conceptions of justice' (Rawls, 1997: 776). According to Rawls, for a state to act on a comprehensive doctrine would require too much use of state coercion, even if that comprehensive doctrine is a liberal one of the classic type. Rawls is concerned about the 'reasonable pluralism' that characterises contemporary society, the fact that individuals can reasonably arrive at different more or less comprehensive doctrines on the basis of their free use of reason, and holds out the very real possibility of the unjustified coercion of minorities by majorities or the loss of self-respect by minorities, should the search for consensus fail (Rawls, 1996: 36–37).

For the purposes of civic education, political and comprehensive liberalisms rest on different answers to two distinct questions:

1. What is the appropriate conception of the citizen for a liberal society; and
2. What is the appropriate conception of society for a liberal society?

Rawls advocates what he calls the 'political conception of the citizen', based on a conception of the person appropriate to a 'fair system of cooperation'. Persons, so conceived, have two capacities, the capacity for a sense of justice and for a conception of the good (Rawls, 1996: 19). Citizens 'are free in that ... [they have] the moral power to have a conception of the good' and are capable of revising this conception of the good (Rawls, 1996: 30). They are also entitled to make claims on their political institutions to advance their conceptions of the good and capable of taking responsibility for their actions and of adjusting their aims in light of what they can reasonably expect from political institutions (Rawls, 1996: 32–34). This conception of the citizen strongly affects Rawls'sunderstanding of the appropriate society for democracies characterised by 'reasonable pluralism'. In a society made up of a number of different comprehensive doctrines that inform individual conceptions of the good, the appropriate goal is to seek a suitably neutral consensus about some basic principles of justice and democracy that can be endorsed by a variety of reasonable comprehensive doctrines on the basis of the commitments of those comprehensive doctrines. Rawls calls this agreement an 'overlapping consensus'.

We can contrast this conception of the person and society with a particular comprehensive doctrine, that of John Stuart Mill. Mill conceives of individuals as potentially capable of individuality or liberal autonomy, and claims that liberal autonomy is the best route to individual happiness, at least happiness of an elevated sort involving the exercise of certain faculties – centrally, choice – and including active participation in society. He does so on the basis of a set of psychological and social scientific premises that conceive of individuals as radically influenced by alterations in their circumstances, of which the most important is their education. In this he is the leading representative of an important strain in political thought, beginning with Plato, but culminating in some of Mill's most important influences: Helvétius, Bentham and, his father, James Mill (Garforth, 1980: 1–3). Given this conception of the individual's situation, the problem Mill sees is that society, far from being a potential consensus among differing comprehensive doctrines, is characterised by the continuing tendency to impose one set of beliefs and customs – those of the 'strongest power in society' – upon all the individuals of that society, whether they share that power's beliefs or no. In such a society, the danger is not that individuals' conceptions of the good will be so different that they will destabilise society, but that they will be insufficiently different to give individuals a real chance to consider alternative ways of choosing their life plan. Because of his concern about the potential unfreedom of the individual, Mill is also concerned about the coercion of minorities, through both the laws and the lack of recognition involved in social stigmatisation and censure.

How are we to choose between these two conceptions of the citizen and society? Which alternative we choose may depend upon how we understand our own society, and it may be the case that one theory is better suited to a multicultural society such as Canada and another to (still) relatively homogeneous Ireland or that one theory is suited to a society divided by deeply held religious beliefs and another to a society where children are subjected to huge amounts of advertising in the service of a secular, consumerist culture (Brighouse, 2005).[2] Even in the abstract, however, civic education seems like a crucial test for any liberal theory. Indeed, as Callan notes, civic education is the only concrete example Rawls offers about how comprehensive and political liberalisms differ. Rawls'scharge is that a comprehensive liberalism will attempt to create persons with the values that comprehensive view prizes to an extent that goes beyond the limits that a reasonable pluralism morally and practically permits (Callan, 1997: 16, citing Rawls, 1996: 199–200). If civic education is a crucial test for a particular liberalism, any conception of liberalism should, in turn, help to illuminate difficult practical issues in the area of civic education. In considering civic education, tough choices must be made: about curricula, neutrality in the classroom, the dangers of excessive patriotism or sectarianism, and the costs, in terms of self-respect, for groups whose comprehensive doctrines do not receive equal attention in some proposed course of civic education. In what follows, I argue that Rawls is just as concerned as the comprehensive liberal to promote certain kinds of values, and thus to create a certain kind of individual, but that he requires a certain kind of society to result, whereas a Millian comprehensive liberal is content to let the society that results from the education of a particular generation of students depend on the choices of empowered individuals, including students and their parents.

Much of the philosophical literature on civic education focuses on the American context and revolves around two US cases, *Wisconsin* v *Yoder* (406 US 205, (1972)) and *Mozert* v *Hawkins County Public Schools* (827 F.2d 1058(1987)). In the former case, the Supreme Court found in favour of Yoder, one of several Amish parents who wanted to take their children out of school before they had finished their compulsory schooling. The Amish parents claimed that high school education violated their rights to the free exercise of their religion, by exposing their children to values and perspectives that would undermine the Amish's religious beliefs and way of life. In the latter case, the Sixth Circuit Court of Appeals found against the plaintiffs, Protestant fundamentalists who wanted to take their children out of a reading programme because its positive presentation of other religions, its emphasis on the imagination, and its depiction of certain activities, such as boys enjoying cooking, contradicted their values and so infringed upon their free exercise of religion. In the former case, the court upheld the complete withdrawal of the children from school; in the latter, the court ruled that certain items on the curriculum, in which skills were taught but which did not require the students to adopt any values, could be made compulsory. These are two responses to both the pressures that schools put on parents who want to communicate their values to their children and that parents put on the curricula and ethos of public schools. In what follows, I will argue that a Millian comprehensive liberalism can reconcile these two responses and that the normative conclusions of these two court decisions can be made part of a coherent approach to civic education in public schools. This is despite the fact that every aspect of teaching in a public school commits society to a particular conception of the person. For example, 'student-centred' pedagogies emphasise critical reflection, active participation and, in their use of role-playing and group work, expose children to diverse ways of living (Coleman, 1998). I bring up these American cases, then, not because I think that they should influence the Irish case, but to show the kind of pressures that are put on civic education and the idea of the 'common school' (Callan, 1997: chs 7–8). Indeed, I will argue that the different formation of educational institutions in Ireland means that a different and more responsive accommodation of these pressures is possible.

I argue that when it comes to these crucial issues of education, Rawls reveals himself to be as much of an advocate of state intervention as any comprehensive liberal and that, in contrast, Mill develops a complex structure of institutions that guards liberty against the dangers of an overweening homogeneity – including domination by comprehensive liberals of Mill's sort. Thinking of the *Yoder* and *Mozert* cases, Rawls says of the two approaches to civic education:

> The liberalisms of Kant and Mill may lead to requirements designed to foster the values of autonomy and individuality as ideals to govern much if not all of life. But political liberalism has a different aim and requires far less. It will ask that children's education include such things as knowledge of their constitutional and civic rights so that, for example, they know that liberty of conscience exists in their society and that apostasy is not a legal crime, all this to insure that their continued membership when they come of age is not based simply on ignorance of their basic rights or fear of punishment for offenses that do not exist. Moreover, their education should also prepare them to be fully cooperating members of society and enable them to be self-supporting; it should also encourage the political virtues so that they want to honor the fair terms of social cooperation in their relations with the rest of society. (Rawls, 1996: 199)

Although Rawls accuses comprehensive liberals of directly imposing their values on unwilling groups, it is clear, even from this passage, that Rawls is very much interested in encouraging the 'political virtues' necessary for them to 'want to honor the fair terms of social cooperation in their relations with the rest of society'. Far from being a special case, this concern with the direct promotion of values is central to Rawls's project. As I have noted, Rawls makes the viability of a just society, and accordingly of his theory of justice, depend on the stability of that society (including adherence to an overlapping consensus surrounding his two principles of justice, or, in the later version, a family of conceptions of justice). But problems of stability quickly require Rawls to advocate remarkably non-neutral appeals, on the part of the state, to some more comprehensive conception of the citizen and to the use of formative – i.e. educational – state powers to secure the allegiance of citizens to this overlapping consensus. Rawls admits that, when confronted with people who are not reasonable, 'we may eventually have to assert at least certain aspects of our own comprehensive religious or philosophical doctrine' to the extent that we have one (Rawls, 1996: 152–153; Callan, 1997: ch. 2). Clearly the goal is a society with relatively little conflict and, indeed, Rawls makes the test of stability turn on the allegiance of individuals *brought up in such a society* to the consensus surrounding the principles of justice. If people whose moral and political outlook is entirely informed by being raised in Rawls's just society give their allegiance to that society,

Rawls holds it to be stable (Rawls, 1996: 141–143). This characterisation of Rawls's view may seem unfair, but such a test of stability *requires* a more homogeneous society to result from the raising of a generation under just institutions and engages the government in the task of the direct inculcation of particular 'political' values. If the vast majority of individuals who have grown up under 'just basic institutions' do not express their allegiance to the consensus surrounding the principles of justice, Rawls would have to hold the resulting society to be unstable and, accordingly, the theory of justice this consensus is supposed to support would have to be held to be non-viable. Even if they do not directly intend to inculcate particular values in individual students, Rawls does seem to directly intend to create a more homogeneous society.

In contrast, although Mill adopts a clear view about individuals' powers and goals, he has a very different notion of the extent to which the state may directly form individuals' allegiances and preferences or to produce a particular form of society. Because individuals are completely the products of their circumstances, society has 'absolute power over them during all the early portion of their existence …The existing generation is master both of the training and the entire circumstances of the generation to come' (Mill, 1991: 91). Although he decries the notion that children belong to their parents – and, accordingly, that parents can do whatever they like in terms of children's education, including not educating them – he is adamantly opposed to State-controlled education. Parents, by bringing children into existence, have a responsibility to educate their children to 'perform [their] part well in life' (Mill, 1991: 117–118). They can be compelled to support their child's education and, if they are unable, the state should subsidise their children's attendance at schools of the parents' choice. But the state should not direct the education system:

> A general State education is a mere contrivance for moulding people to be exactly like one another: and as the mould in which it casts them is that which pleases the predominant power in the government, whether this be a monarch, a priesthood, an aristocracy, or the majority of the existing generation in proportion as it is efficient and successful, it establishes a despotism over the mind, leading by natural tendency to one over the body. (Mill, 1991: 117–118)

Rather 'education established and controlled by the State' should, at most, be 'one among many competing experiments, carried on for the purpose of example and stimulus, to keep the others up to a certain standard of excellence'(Mill, 1991: 118). Mill's whole aim is to encourage diversity of beliefs and, as individual and collective 'experiments in living', of practices, to give individuals options by which they can express the individuality that he prizes. Far from attempting to directly form individuals in a way that leads to some form of consensus, Mill attempts to resist any consensus that is not produced by the most diverse society possible, in part out of the conflicts between these opposing views. Just as Mill's promotion of individuality indirectly promotes utility, so Mill's encouragement of a diverse society is an indirect strategy for the promotion of individuality.

Although there is some flexibility in the views of both Rawls and Mill that might permit them to approach one another in practice, their different orientations towards questions of consensus will lead to different responses to a number of key questions. Take the curriculum of a course of civic education in a liberal society. Most civic education syllabi aim to develop quite specific values and attitudes in students: the Irish one for Junior Certificate includes 'an appreciation of, and respect for, differing viewpoints, ideas and cultures and an ability to empathise with the situation of other individuals and groups', 'a respect for critical thought processes', and 'a commitment to oppose prejudice, discrimination and social injustice at all levels of society' (Department of Education, 2006: 14). In a Rawlsian society, libertarian individuals who attach considerable importance to the right to property will not be able to pledge their allegiance to Rawls's overlapping consensus, since they will not support Rawls's second principle of justice, which requires any inequalities to benefit the 'least advantaged', possibly through the redistribution of resources. Even if we take Rawls's more flexible view of what principles will be the subject of an overlapping consensus, these libertarians will be vulnerable to accusations that they are unwilling 'to honor the fair terms of social cooperation in their relations with the rest of society' (Rawls, 1996: 199). Will their continued presence in the society be deemed a failure of civic education? Will the transformation of their commitment to libertarianism be a goal of the civic education curriculum?

Mill, on the other hand, responds to these concerns by drawing an important distinction, at least as far as curricula and examinations are concerned, between fact and value. Having already preached the benefits of controversy in his discussion of freedom of expression, he applies the lessons learned from that previous account to the question of the subject of education. Mill says, 'All attempts by the State to bias the conclusions of its citizens on disputed subjects, are evil, but it may very properly offer to ascertain and certify that a person possesses the knowledge, requisite to make his conclusions, on any given subject, worth attending to'(Mill, 1991: 119). So the state can examine children, to make sure they have been given a basic education in the facts about both controversial and non-controversial matters. But, to 'prevent the State from exercising, through [public examinations], an improper influence over opinion, the knowledge required for passing an examination … should … be confined to facts and positive science exclusively'(Mill, 1991: 118–119). This is compatible with teaching the various opinions held by various religions, sects or schools of philosophy and the grounds on which those opinions are held, as long as no attempt is made to make students 'profess' them. In its use of this distinction, Mill's position is strikingly similar to Rawls's attempt to account for the response of the Sixth Circuit Court in *Mozert*, noted above. But because Mill opposes any direct attempt to inculcate virtues or values in students, unlike Rawls, he is better able to make such a distinction between fact and value, since he does not require the stability of society to rest on the successful inculcation of certain values.

Adopting a Millian position has important consequences for civic education. Discussions of human rights could properly focus on the difficulties of grounding human rights, or various well-known objections to the notion of human rights, rather than merely attempting to inculcate a respect for human rights in the student. It would also undoubtedly lead to situations that many teachers of civic education would find upsetting. Eamonn Callan describes an example in which students in a civic education class in Alberta, Canada, argued that national solidarity requires that everyone speak the same language and concluded that the millions of francophones in Canada should return to France if they are unwilling to speak English (Callan, 1997: 216–217). We can imagine – if we have not already experienced – Irish students making equally upsetting comments about the Travelling community. Callan argues that the teacher should have challenged these arguments, because 'teachers cannot responsibly embrace an "anything goes" attitude to moral pluralism', but we should, perhaps, not close off the discussion of the proper response to such situations so quickly (Callan, 1997: 216). Even my comparison of Mill and Rawls, above, suggests there are good reasons to suspect that the direct attempt to inculcate values is self-frustrating and has consequences that make it undesirable (see Ward & O'Shea, 2002: 36). Another version of Callan's 'anything goes' charge is the claim that the fact/value distinction leads to emotivism, in which claims about values are seen as subjective expressions of feeling, ungrounded in the agents' beliefs and incapable of contradicting one another (Macintyre, 1981). The crucial distinction is that it only limits the state's expression of a commitment to particular conclusions about values: students can express their conclusions in as full and heartfelt way as they wish, on the basis of their commitment to a particular set of premises. This distinction between the State's expressing a particular set of values and individual citizens doing so, seems to be lost on most of the creators of civic education curricula in Ireland, as seen below.

Conflicts and Curricula: Current and Proposed Civic Education Syllabi in Ireland

If, as both Mill and Rawls agree, the various opinions and grounds of different schools of philosophy and different religious groups are to be taught, should such teaching also note and explore the fact that these groups differ and differ in ways that they can defend with moral, philosophical and theological arguments that are based on their strongly held commitments? Although Mill would favour such a curriculum, his views are very much at odds with the civic education textbooks of Ireland, textbooks that seem to embody Rawls's desire to avoid certain kinds of conflicts, whether between different cultural and religious groups or between the state and its citizens. In these textbooks, there is little sense that citizens may have deep cultural and religious differences or that the Irish government might fail to respect the deeply held beliefs of its citizens. The conflicts that are described are, with a few exceptions, purely 'private' or 'community issues' in which individuals disagree about which values or interests – interests that they all can be reasonably expected to possess – have priority: a property developer wants to develop a piece of land and different community members disagree on what they would like to see there (Quinn *et al.*, 2004: 46–47): a father wants his son to turn down the radio, a farmer confronts a hill-walker, a factory owner who produces life-saving drugs is confronted by a mother who wants clean air (Harrison & Wilson, 2001: 36). Clearly both the mother and the factory owner value life-saving drugs and clean air, but see them as differently related to their individual interests. The closest thing to a domestic religious or cultural conflict in Harrison and Wilson's *Make a Difference!* for example, is a debate over an Orange Order march, safely over the Border (the recent Love Ulster march in Dublin notwithstanding). Similar to this avoidance of cultural and religious conflict, politics as a contact sport is almost completely absent from such a curriculum. Although we are told the names and histories of the political parties of Ireland, students are given no idea why there should be multiple political parties. Perhaps the most obvious case of this is the uncritical presentation of a particularly demagogic candidate's leaflet from *Make a Difference*! in which the candidate suggests that all the local criminals support his opponents (Harrison & Wilson, 2001: 120).

Thus, although one attitude or value to be encouraged by civic education in Ireland at the Junior Certificate level is 'an appreciation of critical awareness and independence of thought', such critical reasoning is not well-served by the existing curriculum (Department of Education, 2006: 14). This is not, I think, a coincidence, since it stems from treating 'critical thinking' as a value or attitude to be directly instilled, rather than the by-product of the experience of a debate between interlocutors committed to the positions they espouse. It is, accordingly, a mistake to see a comprehensive liberal like Mill's emphasis on critical scrutiny of claims and practices as one more value to be added to the consensus. It is, rather, produced by Mill's principled refusal to stipulate what should be taught on 'disputed subjects', since a diverse and potentially conflictual society is the condition under which any subjects that attract the least controversy *can* be taught.[3] Again, this embodies Mill's commitment to a particular conception of human beings as, at least potentially, exercising a rational choice between alternatives, a commitment which defines his notion of a free person and of a free and 'intellectually active people'. It is certainly the case that the existing CSPE curriculum at Junior Certificate is not working: the subject has a low status, teachers are unprepared and most candidates cannot articulate the skills – or, we can assume, the values – that the Action Project, in particular, is supposed to have instilled in them (Clarke, 2002).

Such attempts to achieve 'liberal neutrality' by protecting children from controversy and controversial 'social prejudices' have been rightly criticised by Amy Gutmann as ignoring 'a strong human impulse; the desire [of parents] to pass some of their particular prejudices on to their children.'(Gutmann, 1999: 34) Mill's view is the complete opposite of such a subtly paternalist neutral approach. His educational theory develops institutions that attempt to mitigate or resist the state's inevitable attempts – also noted by Gutmann – to inculcate particular values or attitudes and does so by harnessing parents' inevitable willingness to inculcate their values in their children. We should remember that *On Liberty* is a plea *for* strong values and their active advocacy on the part of individuals, as long as each is free to seek out and practice his or her own 'experiments in living' on the basis of those values. This is how parents are expected and encouraged to choose between competing educational experiments and is the justification for these diverse experiments. Mill says of his recommendations: 'Under this system, the rising generation would be no worse off in regard to all disputed truths, than they are at present; they would be brought up either churchmen or dissenters as they now are, the State merely taking care that they should be instructed churchmen, or instructed dissenters. There would be nothing to hinder them from being taught religion, if their parents chose, at the same schools where they were taught other things' (Mill, 1991: 119). The only educational institutions where examination in religion should be 'entirely voluntary' are universities or other institutes of higher learning, since it 'would be giving too dangerous a power to governments, were they allowed to exclude any one from professions, even from the profession of teacher, for alleged deficiency of qualifications'(Mill, 1991: 119). As far as his statements on education are concerned, Mill envisages a quite radical diversity of educational practices all of which are, if only indirectly through grants to the indigent, potentially subsidised by the State. This attempt to harness the commitments that parents already have is compatible with Mill's emphasis on critical reasoning discussed above. It also requires the freedom for children to disagree with their parents, so far as they are capable of it. Mill is not in favour of a variety of separate educational spheres, never communicating with one another, but instead is in favour of a diverse society, in which people with opposing opinions to one's own can easily be found. It is the stimulating benefit that these people offer to any believer that makes Mill's diverse society the controversial place it is: a society of people who are prepared to offer and even 'obtrude' 'considerations to aid' others' judgment and 'exhortations to strengthen' others' wills, in short, a society of people who vigorously try to persuade and 'remonstrate' with people with different views (Mill, 1991: 85). Mill's society is not, as some liberal multiculturalists envisage, a society in which people's 'freedom of conscience' is not intruded upon by others' views, but one in which people's conscience is tested by the presence of people whose consciences tell them different things.

From a Millian point of view, then, the notion of a strictly neutral, 'ethos-free' school or curriculum is a dangerous and illusory goal for two reasons. The first reason is that any curriculum that pursues the direct inculcation of values obviously possesses an 'ethos' of its own, however sensitive and tolerant. If certain values are to be the subject of examinations by the state that determine access to certain 'qualifications' and 'professions' – as, in fact, the Irish Leaving Certificate examinations are – then, as Mill noted, the government is taking into its hands the effective power to exclude certain people from these qualifications and professions. Making such a curriculum the subject of a final year examination may well have the result of forcing hypocrisy on students who, for whatever reason, dissent from those values. The second reason is that such a project pretends, somehow, that the school is at a radical remove from social and political life. Although schools may have their own ethos, conflicting views can always be found in the diverse society Mill envisages and that increasingly characterises contemporary Ireland. Other groups, the media and the students themselves will necessarily obtrude diverse and conflicting views on classroom discussions. Indeed, permitting this seems to be the only way to reconcile the serious potential conflict between the 'inalienable and imprescriptible rights' of the family (Bunreacht na hÉireann 41.1) to choose the institutions that will engage in the 'religious and moral formation' of their children (Bunreacht na hÉireann 42.4) and the 'natural and imprescriptible rights' of the child (Bunreacht na hÉireann 42.5), including, in the latter case, the right not to attend religious instruction (Bunreacht na hÉireann 44.2.4) and the right to freedom of conscience (Bunreacht na hÉireann 44.2.1). As Clarke has pointed out, 'freedom of thought, conscience and religion' is a right of everyone, including children (Clarke, 1986: 271). Accordingly, in a Millian comprehensive liberal view, based on a particular view of human nature and potential, we can examine students on particular facts and develop particular skills, but we must, because of the truth of that comprehensive view, refrain from inculcating particular values by means of punitive sanctions and permit free discussion and conflict between views in the classroom. Such pedagogy has to walk a bit of a tightrope: it can be based, to some extent, on the values of informed, critical reasoning and active participation, but it must pursue critical reasoning indirectly, by allowing students to explore their own and others' commitments by their own lights.

It should be noted that the most developed proposal for 'Citizenship Studies' in the Leaving Certificate, that of Eilís Ward with the support of Karen O'Shea, avoids most of the problems of the direct inculcation of values. Ward and O'Shea's curricular proposal – which they now, along with the Political Studies Association of Ireland, propose to call 'Politics and Society' (Ward & O'Shea, 2006: 5; Political Studies Association of Ireland, 2006: 1) – emphasises, as previously noted, the dangers involved in the direct inculcation of values and proposes a model of democratic deliberation that involves a minimal commitment to particular values. It does so by using only those norms implied by democratic deliberation itself and to the extent necessary for democratic deliberation: the interdependence of deliberators, equality of individuals, respect for difference, reciprocity, openness and transparency of dialogue and resolution of conflicts by non-violent means. (Ward, 2002) This is explicitly because of concerns about the rights and freedoms of students as agents. In Ward's words:

> … we rejected the idea that a curriculum devoted to the study of citizenship in a modern, pluralist state would deny the students some of the rights held by all citizens in that state: *viz*: the right to hold contrary views; the right to transgress; the right not to be interested in social change (in other words the right to hold conservative views) and the right to express either reactionary or revolutionary views and so on. (Ward, 2005: 5)

Ward and O'Shea's approach explicitly recommends that students not be prevented from expressing views that may upset others, including 'racist' or 'sexist' views, but notes that not preventing such expression 'does not mean *validating* such opinions.' (Ward, 2002: 38) Controversial remarks can instead be an occasion for developing students' moral views and for promoting awareness of the relevant conflicts in society. Permitting students to exercise their agency, even in ways that might upset other students and the teacher, is part of making the classroom itself a place of democratic deliberation (Ward, 2002: 37–38) All of this does not necessarily require the teacher to adopt a particular view of pedagogy, especially one which comes freighted with values of its own, rather 'teachers are encouraged to use whatever means they find most effective in bringing it home to students that, by their very nature, controversial issues do not admit of easy answers' (Ward, 2002: 67, citing Qualifications and Curriculum Authority, UK, 1998: 60). The same report cited by O'Shea and Ward notes that controversial issues are 'the very essence of what constitutes a worthwhile education' (Qualifications and Curriculum Authority, UK, 1998: 57). Permitting inegalitarian or disrespectful speech, such as racist and sexist speech, shows that Ward and O'Shea's norms of democratic deliberation do not constitute values to be instilled, but the conditions under which controversies can be had. Ward and O'Shea's proposals show that an alternative to the direct approach of inculcating values is possible and can be made the basis of a determinate curriculum and educational practice for a qualification as important as the Irish Leaving Certificate. The use of Ward and O'Shea's curricular proposal at Leaving Certificate level would not only increase the currently low status of CSPE as a Junior Certificate subject, but will, it is to be hoped, encourage the removal of the direct inculcation of values from the syllabus and textbooks for the Junior Certificate.

Experiments in Living: School Ethos and Civic Education in Ireland

Such a minimalist and democratic approach to the teaching of civic education does not remove, however, the difficult problem of school ethos in a society in which there are adherents of a variety of religions, or no religion, and in which individuals' membership in a variety of cultures cuts across those religious persuasions. As such a society develops in Ireland, the peculiar Irish system of combining State support for schools with their operation by various groups makes it more able to respond to increasing diversity and the demand, by parents and children, for schools that represent their values. Although it has been the focus of most debates surrounding civic education, the rigorous division between public schools and religious commitment that characterises education in the United States is the exception. Even in '*laique*' France, the State subsidises the vast majority of private schools, most of these private schools being religious schools (Clarke,1986: 289). It is possible and desirable, however, that the system be made even more responsive to changes in the attitudes of parents and children. The rapid rise in the number of people who want a multidenominational or secular education for their children, as expressed in the strong demand for Educate Together's multidenominational schools, strongly suggests that the state should promote the development of such schools, as acknowledged in Bunreacht na hÉireann 42.4 (Flynn, 2007). This accommodation of parental desires should not be seen as different in kind from the accommodation of other views, including, for example, the provision of more Muslim schools in response to similarly strong demand (Holden, 2006). The responsiveness of the Irish system of establishing primary schools has been emphasised by the Department of Education itself, although it should be noted that it is harder to set up a new secondary school, where most civic education currently occurs and is proposed to occur (Holden, 2007).

Greater responsiveness might mitigate the greatest problem posed by the role that ethos plays in the Irish school system: the giving of priority to children of a particular faith. The school in Diswellstown is a response to the policies of the two existing local schools, both of which gave priority to Catholic children, with the result that 90 children could not get into a school in the Diswellstown catchment area (Raftery, 2007). Such discrimination is clearly at odds with the duty of the government to 'provide for' education for children (Bunreacht na hÉireann 42.4). A Millian approach to education neatly navigates this difficulty, albeit at the cost of maximising diversity in the classroom. The distinction between requiring a student to be informed of something and to profess something clearly forbids requiring students to profess a particular creed to gain entrance to the school. Greater responsiveness on the part of the system should reduce the number of students who have to attend schools whose ethos is not to their liking and should reduce, accordingly, the pressure on schools to take students who do not share their ethos.

Such responsiveness could be promoted even further by extending the primary school model for school establishment to second level and by a number of reforms for both levels, including a buildings and salary fund for which proposed new schools could compete by demonstrating parental demand or a voucher programme by which parental attitudes could be expressed regarding existing schools. Although the issue of vouchers is a very controversial one in the philosophy of education, (Brighouse, 2001; Gutmann, 1999: 64–69), it should be noted that the use of vouchers in Ireland would have the very opposite effect of their use in the United States. Whereas in the United States the use of vouchers could be construed as an illicit subsidy of religious schools, in violation of the constitutional separation of church and state, in Ireland it would have the effect that more State supported schools would be operated on a multidenominational and secular basis (as well as by other unrepresented religious groups). Parents and interested members of the community could also participate in their children's secondary schooling by serving as the elected parental and community representatives to school boards of management, as is now the case for primary schools. Empowered governing boards for individual schools will provide exactly the kind of local institutions that, Mill thought, educate adults to better perform their roles as citizens, both in terms of improved knowledge and in terms of greater public spirit (Mill, 1977: 534–537). The way that the current system rewards parental initiative also supports the civic education of adult citizens.

If this understanding of school ethos is adopted, then it turns out that the Catholic Church's traditional claim that civic education is inseparable from other aspects of the curriculum is largely right: there can be only limited separation of civic education from the ethos of the school or from the other subjects taught in the school. This has been recognised in the Junior Certificate CSPE syllabus in Ireland:

> It is increasingly recognized that the ethos, organization, extra-curricular activities and operational structures of schools also have a significant impact on the pupils' understanding of the civic, social and political dimensions of their lives. Through its 'hidden curriculum', a school provides aspects of Civic, Social and Political Education even where this is not explicit. (Department of Education and Science, 2006: 3)

The civic education syllabus can also be adjusted to the ethos of the school (Department of Education and Science, 2006: 15). Recognising the relation of civic education to all aspects of the curriculum, we are confronted with the tough choices that would be forced upon us by an adoption of a Millian approach to education. It is easy to talk about empowering children, parents and schools, but what if those schools choose to teach sectarianism, Islamism or creationism or any set of beliefs in, an apparently un-Millian, conformist and dogmatic manner? Would such a dogmatic approach be more likely to succeed in a system with a diverse set of institutions based on school ethos? Does a greater diversity of ethos in schools necessarily require more homogeneous classrooms within schools? With its commitment to a society of individuals capable of strong commitments, a Millian approach would be consistently permissive regarding controversial subjects being taught in schools and from the point of view of believers: the only condition it would force upon such schools is requiring the pupils to sit exams in which knowledge of different religious and secular views and different theories be assessed. We should note, however, that Mill thinks the best expositors of these views are committed believers themselves. In the increasingly diverse society that Ireland is becoming, it is becoming easier and easier to find representatives of any different perspective. Having guest speakers from different viewpoints could go a long way to mitigate the homogenising effects of a pluralist approach to school ethos.

Such an understanding of the role of education would help resolve difficult cases, such as the case of a Muslim School in Cabra in which the Taoiseach alerted the Minister of Education about 'disturbing claims' regarding the management of the school (Corcoran *et al.*, 2005). It was alleged that 'too much time was being devoted to teaching of the Koran', that some students refused to play sports with teams from other schools that included girls, 'that some outside religious teachers refuse to go into the staff room if there are women teachers present', that pupils refused to listen to certain kinds of music and that classes are disrupted by some pupils suggesting that others are 'impure' for not performing certain purification activities at school (Corcoran *et al.*, 2005). There were further concerns from the Irish National Teachers' Organisation (INTO) about a lack of library books, computers and 'art and craft materials', as well as 'health and hygiene concerns' (Walshe, 2005). It should be noted that the school contested the allegations, that the

INTO was satisfied that any deficiencies had been corrected and that the allegations regarding religious education, even if true, were within the department's guidelines (Murphy, 2005). Regardless of the facts of the particular case, we can imagine how a Millian approach to education would resolve these potential controversies. Some of these issues are clearly contrary to good pedagogy and to the freedom of the students: taunts of 'impure' that disrupt the school day should not be tolerated. Because such schools are part of a wider society, activities involving women cannot be cancelled to satisfy someone's private convictions. So women teachers should continue using the staff room, and the teachers who refuse to join women teachers there will have to forego whatever benefits the staff room provides. The school should continue to play sports with other schools and students who object to the presence of girls on other teams will have to forego the benefits that participating in sports provides. When it comes to art, there should be more leeway: students may absent themselves from classes in which certain types of music are being played, since a particular type of music is not central to the skills needed by the citizen or the facts needed by the pupil. Curricular choices surrounding art or religion – less representative art and more Arabic – are permissible both because of the importance of the ethos of the school, as acknowledged by the Department of Education, and because a Millian approach permits and encourages a devolved responsibility for implementing the common curriculum. If schools are free to modify this curriculum, subject to the need to teach certain facts and the openness constraints discussed above, they do not offend against a Millian vision of the liberal society in which people are free to explore their own 'experiments in living' as thoroughly as is compatible with other people's experiments and in institutions that are open to the influences of the most diverse society possible. Mill fears curricula imposed by the central state and too close regulation of schools by the dominant power in society more than he fears the excesses of private persons pursuing their good with the assistance of others. Accordingly, the existing consensus-seeking curricula of Irish civic education textbooks need to be open to modification by the teachers who have to teach them and they need to pay more attention to the political context in which civic education is taught.

What should be taught also depends on the nature of the controversy. Mill's distinction between fact and value may, in some cases, privilege certain claims: pupils could be examined on the facts of evolutionary biology, even if their religious views endorse a creationist view of the world. Although pupils would be encouraged to critically examine the theory of evolution, creationism is not a theory of the same sort as evolution, not playing even the same role that phlogiston theory plays in chemistry or geocentric views of the solar system play in astronomy (Mill, 1991: 41–42). Our confidence in the theory of evolution is because people have been free to contest it and it has been contested, not because every single person on earth has been convinced of it. As Mill says: 'Complete liberty of contradicting and disproving our opinion, is the very condition which justifies us in assuming its truth for purposes of action; and on no other terms can a being with human faculties have any rational assurance of being right' (Mill, 1991: 24). (Note the role that Mill's comprehensive conception of the human being is playing in this argument). Among the 'purposes of action' Mill is talking about here, I argue, is the drawing up of the list of facts on which students can be examined. Otherwise, there is no way that Mill can sustain both his commitment to the distinction between facts and values in determining the subject matter of examinations and also his commitment to free discussions of particular claims, including scientific claims. Even in scientific matters, Mill feared direct appeals to the authority of experts. *On Liberty* is full of reminders that the finest thinkers of all ages have believed things that we now laugh at or have persecuted groups for beliefs that we now think are central to our culture. Deference to experts is the chief way people avoid learning the grounds of their own opinions.

Still more dangerous is the extension of the authority of the 'instructed class' over the whole society. It is tremendously important to note that Mill's claims about education for citizenship are inseparable from his notion of citizenship and the extension of the suffrage. Rather notoriously, Mill proposed a system in which people receive the vote upon meeting basic standards of literacy and numeracy and then 'plural votes' on the basis of their level of education or, if like Mill they have not been educated in a school, by their results on examinations that are exactly like the examinations he proposes for children of school age. The educated, however, should not be given so many plural votes that they become the strongest power in society themselves and exercise their own class legislation (Mill, 1977: 476). Mill uses the example of China, however inaccurately, as a warning to the West of the dangers of centralised education. In China, he says, the system of education, excellent though it was, became the sole route to political power and led to bureaucratic rule. As a result, China became overly homogeneous, custom-bound and stationary. In the end, the civic education that Mill recommends for minors is inseparable from the 'educative democracy' he plans for all citizens.[4] In Ireland, this truth is recognised by the recent report of the Taskforce on Active Citizenship, the guiding principles of which include the 'lifelong learning' of citizenship, 'diversity in cultural expression, values and lifestyles' and 'subsidiarity … enabling and empowering decision-making as close to the citizen as possible' (Taskforce on Active Citizenship, 2007: front matter). Although the vision of the taskforce for Irish democracy and society may seem, in places, less contestatory than Mill's, it is committed to principles that, like Irish constitutional and educational practice, lead naturally to a vision of Irish citizenship and civic education of a Millian sort: devolved, diverse and participatory.

Conclusion

The prospect of an approach to school ethos and the teaching of citizenship that is so immediately responsive to the changing attitudes of different groups may alarm many people and excite a newfound enthusiasm for both a more centrally controlled education and for a particular form of civic education. Indeed, the coming experiment in State-operated schooling in Diswellstown may be just such a reaction to the rapidly changing nature of Irish society. I have argued that the existing Irish system may be peculiarly capable of responding to the new diversity in Irish life and to the concerns about power that animate a comprehensive liberalism that promotes diversity in its indirect pursuit of its liberal values. To all those, liberal and otherwise, who are daunted by the challenge Mill's writings on education pose for Irish citizenship today,[5] I would ask a series of questions:

1. Do governments tend to use education as a tool for inculcating a particular ethos, particular skills and attitudes in the interest of promoting a particular kind of society?
2. Do various religious and political groups, and parents who belong to them, strongly desire to pursue their ethos and to inculcate its values in their children?
3. Are human beings' characters, their preferences and their pursuits, to a very considerable extent, the product of their education?

I will not attempt to answer the first two questions, beyond what I have already said. I merely note that the very idea of civic education seems to involve a positive answer to question 3, which is the assumption about human nature that anchors Mill's arguments and gives rise to his fears for the future of liberal society.

Ireland is engaged in a great experiment that deserves attention from a wider audience than just citizens of the Republic. Suddenly experiencing a remarkable diversity, it has the resources, in its institutions, and the official commitment, in its government's commitment to active citizenship on the part of all citizens, to find a new way to develop a diverse, liberal and participatory polity. The prospect of a polity in which people are not simply permitted, but enabled to pursue their own commitments as part of their own individuality, and to pass those commitments on to their children through a robust liberal form of civic education is one which promises an exciting vision of how one country can cope with dramatic social change and can forge a lively and healthy society out of a community of different individuals.

Notes

I would like to thank Iseult Honohan for her kind invitation to give the original version of this paper at the Creating Citizens? conference she organised at University College Dublin and for her very helpful comments, Eilís Ward, for allowing me to cite her own unpublished paper from that conference and for her very helpful comments on my characterisation of her proposal, and Wendy Ross for allowing me to plunder the bibliography she has developed for her own research into civic education.

1. 'Ireland' will hereafter refer to the Republic of Ireland, unless noted. I focus my attention on civic education in the Republic of Ireland because the state of civic education in Northern Ireland is quite different. Although citizenship education is only now being integrated into the Northern Irish curriculum as a specific subject, it is further complicated by the history of conflict, by the need to relate the curriculum to the civic education syllabi of the United Kingdom and by a different history of sectarian educational institutions. See Dunn & Morgan (1999) and Smith (2003). I will also use 'civic education', avoiding 'education for citizenship' which implies the direct development of particular skills and attitudes.

2. For an exceptionally sophisticated articulation of the threat of homogenisation, both in the name of the nation and of the capitalist order, and an exceptionally sensitive response that is, I think, sympathetic to the view of this paper, see Dunne, (2003). Dunne has also noted the dangers of the economic approach to education in another paper (Dunne, 2002: 83).
3. Amy Gutmann seems to come close to making this mistake in Gutmann (1999: 95–97).
4. *Educative Democracy* is the title of Garforth's (1980) compelling study of Mill's educational theory.
5. See Ruth Dudley Edwards' hostility to Muslim schools, (Dudley Edwards, 2006) and Mary Raftery's hostility to religious patronage of schools (Raftery , 2007). It is striking to find both the left and right agreeing about the perils of religion's involvement in school ethos.

References

Brighouse, H. (2005) *On Education* (London: Routledge).

Brighouse, H. (2001) 'School Vouchers, Personal Autonomy, and the Separation of Church and State', in: S. Macedo & Y. Tamir (Eds) *NOMOS, vol. XLIII, Moral and Political Education* (New York: New York University Press).

Callan, E. (1997) *Creating Citizens* (Oxford: Oxford University Press).

Clarke, D. M. (1986) Freedom of Thought in Schools: A Comparative Study, *The International and Comparative Law Quarterly*, 35(2), pp. 271–301.

Clarke, M. (2002) Citizenship Education and Assessment: What Counts as Success?, in: D. Scott & H. Lawson (Eds) *Citizenship Education and the Curriculum* (Westport, CT: Ablex Publishing).

Coleman, J. (1998) Civic Pedagogies and Liberal-Democratic Curricula, *Ethics*, 108, pp. 746–761.

Corcoran, J., Bradley, L. & Walshe, J. (2005) Taoiseach blew the whistle on Muslim School, *The Irish Independent*, 16 October.

Department of Education & Science (2005) *Religious Education – Guidelines for Teachers.* Accessed online at: http://www.education.ie/servlet/blobservlet/lc_religion_guide.pdf?language=EN

Department of Education & Science (2006) *Civic, Social and Political Education – Junior Certificate Syllabus,* accessed online at: http://www.education.ie/servlet/blobservlet/jc_civics_sy.pdf?language=EN

Dudley Edwards, R. (2006) Government Supports Schools for Scandal, *The Irish Independent*, 20 August, accessed online at: http://www.ruthdudleyedwards.co.uk/Journalism06/IrInd06_27.htm

Dunn, S. & Morgan, V. (1999) 'A Fraught Path' – education as a basis for developing improved community relations in Northern Ireland, *Oxford Review of Education*, 2(1–2), pp. 141–153.

Dunne, J. (2002) Citizenship and Education: A Crisis of the Republic?, in: P. Kirby, L. Gibbons & M. Cronin (Eds) *Reinventing Ireland: Culture, Society and the Global Economy* (London: Pluto Press).

Dunne, J. (2003) Between State and Civil Society: European Contexts for Education, in: K. McDonough & W. Feinberg (Eds) *Education and Citizenship in Liberal-Democratic Societies*, pp. 96–120 (Oxford: Oxford University Press).

Flynn, S. (2007) Call for Access to School Programme, *The Irish Times*, 30 March, accessed online at: http://www.ireland.com/newspaper/ireland/2007/0330/1175003486571.html

Garforth, F. W. (1980) *Educative Democracy: John Stuart Mill on Education in Society* (Oxford: Oxford University Press).

Government of Ireland (1995) *Charting Our Education Future: White Paper on Education* (Dublin: The Stationery Office).

Government of Ireland (1998) *Education Act 1998* (Dublin: The Stationery Office).

Gutmann, A. (1999) *Democratic Education* (Princeton, NJ: Princeton University Press).

Harrison, C. & Wilson, M. (2001) *Make a Difference! Civic, Social and Political Education* (Dublin: Folens Publishers).

Holden, L. (2006) Where being Muslim and Irish go together hand in hand, *The Irish Times*, 21 March, accessed online at: http://www.ireland.com/newspaper/features/2006/0321/4054387345EDMAR21MUSLIM.html

Holden, L. (2007) The rise of the gaelscoil – is this the new playground of the elite?, *The Irish Times,* 17 April, accessed online at: http://www.ireland.com/newspaper/education/2007/0417/117645475 8125.html

Macedo, S. (1995) Liberal Civic Education and Religious Fundamentalism: The Case of God vs. John Rawls?, *Ethics,* 105, pp. 468–496.

Macintyre, A. (1981) *After Virtue* (London: Duckworth).

McGarry, P. (2007) Church Puts its Faith in State-run Primary Schools, *The Irish Times,* 20 March, accessed online at: http://www.ireland.com/newspaper/education/2007/0320/1173880582368.html

Mill, J. S. (1977) Considerations on Representative Government, in: J.M. Robson (Ed.) *Collected Works,* Vol. XIX (Toronto: University of Toronto Press).

Mill, J. S. (1991) On Liberty, in: J. Gray (Ed.) *On Liberty and Other Essays* (Oxford: Oxford University Press).

Murphy, C. (2005) Muslim School Defends Iitself, *Village,* 19 October, accessed online at: http:// www.village.ie/Religion/Pope/Muslim_school_defends_itself/

Political Studies Association of Ireland (2006) *Social and Political Education in Senior Cycle: PSAI Response to Consultation Paper,* accessed online at: http://www.psai.ie/news/ PSAI_ResponsePaper.pdf

Qualifications & Curriculum Authority, UK (1998) (The Crick Report) *Education for Citizenship and the Teaching of Democracy in Schools,* accessed online at: http://www.qca.org.uk/downloads/ 6123_crick_report_1998.pdf

Quinn, R., Mistéal, S. & O'Flynn, O. (2004) *Taking Action* (Dublin: C. J. Fallon).

Raftery, M. (2007) State Must be School Patron, *The Irish Times,* 7 June, accessed online at: http:// www.ireland.com/newspaper/opinion/2007/0607/1180721205536.html

Rawls, J. (1971) *A Theory of Justice* (Cambridge, MA: Harvard University Press).

Rawls, J. (1996) *Political Liberalism* (New York: Columbia University Press)

Rawls, J. (1997) The Idea of Public Reason Revisited, *The University of Chicago Law Review,* 64(3), pp. 765–807.

Smith, A. (2003) Citizenship Education in Northern Ireland: Beyond National Identity?, *Cambridge Journal of Education,* 33(1), pp. 15–31.

Taskforce on Active Citizenship (2007) *Report of the Taskforce on Active Citizenship,* accessed online at: http://www.activecitizen.ie/UPLOADEDFILES/Mar07/Taskforce%20Report%20to%20 Government%20(Mar%2007).pdf

Tormey, R. (2006) *Social and Political Education in Senior Cycle* (Dublin: National Council for Curriculum and Assessment), accessed online at: http://www.ncca.ie/uploadedfiles/publications/ social%20&%20pol%20ed.pdf

Walshe, J. (2005) Muslim School in Probe, *The Irish Independent,* 10 October.

Ward, E. (2002) *Citizenship Studies: A Curricular Proposal for Social and Political Education in the Leaving Certificate (Established)* (Dublin: CDVEC Development Unit).

Ward, E. (2005) Human Flourishing in Contested Space: Citizenship Studies *ab Initio,* presented to Creating Citizens?, University College Dublin, 11 November, accessed online at: http:// www.citizenship2005.ie/Documents/Conference/Papers/Eilis%20Ward.pdf

Ward, E. & O'Shea, K. (2006) *Consultation Process on Citizenship Studies: A Report on Findings,* accessed online at: http://www.citizenship2005.ie/Documents/Small%20Grants/CS%20Final%20 Report.pdf

Williams, K. (1999) Faith and the Nation: Education and Religious Identity in the Republic of Ireland, *British Journal of Educational Studies,* 47(4), pp. 317–331.

The Battle(s) over Children's Rights in the Irish Constitution

AOIFE NOLAN

Introduction

The debate surrounding the position of children as right-holders under the Constitution is longstanding. As international and domestic recognition and acceptance of the status of children as rights-bearers have increased, there has been growing awareness of the need to address the perceived shortcomings in the protection afforded to children by the Irish Constitution.

The last 18 months have witnessed a series of battles that have been fought over children's rights under the Irish Constitution. These have taken place in the courts, the political arena and Irish civil society.[1] A number of high profile court cases and the public debate and outcry generated by them culminated in publication of the Twenty-eighth Amendment to the Constitution Bill 2007 by the government in February 2007. This Bill provided for the replacement of Article 42.5 of the Constitution, with a provision explicitly recognising constitutional rights of the child other than those related to primary education. Due to the dissolution of government in May 2007 prior to a general election, the Bill fell. However, in their election manifestos, all of the main parties expressed the intention to amend the constitution to give greater protection to children.

Bearing in mind these recent events and the longstanding criticism of the Constitution's failure to accord adequate protection to children's rights in various contexts, it is timely and appropriate to consider the battle(s) that have been, and are currently being, fought over children's rights under the Irish Constitution. In doing so, I will discuss the implications that the various issues raised and the conceptions of rights have for a consideration of the extent to which the Irish Constitution (or any constitution, in fact) can and should protect the various interests of children.

Tobin has outlined three kinds of constitutional approaches to dealing with children. First, the 'invisible child' constitution, in which children are neither seen nor heard and are accorded no special treatment or recognition. Second, the 'special protection' constitution, under which children are given special recognition within the text because of their vulnerability and need for care and special protection. The principal lens through which the special protection approach views the situation of the child is that of the parents and it is often their rights that are of major concern. Children are perceived as passive objects in need of special protection rather than as active subjects. Finally, there is the 'children's rights' constitution in which the special recognition of children is addressed in terms of children's rights rather than the welfare approach that characterises their treatment under 'special protection' constitutions (Tobin, 2005: 94, 109).

The vast majority of those working on children's rights issues in Ireland – including this author – has argued that it is vital that children's rights be accorded adequate recognition under the Irish Constitution (albeit that there is some disagreement as to how this should be achieved). A key element of this paper will be an assessment of the extent to which the Irish Constitution as it stands qualifies (if at all) as a 'children's rights constitution' and to evaluate whether the proposed constitutional amendment would have succeeded in bringing the Irish Constitution into the 'children's rights' category of constitution.

The Problems with Children as Right-holders

Before considering the extent to which the Constitution does and (had the proposed constitutional amendment been passed) *would have* qualify as a 'children's rights constitution', it is important to consider the controversy surround the issue of children as right-holders. This is because of the implications that such debates will have for the alleged desirability of a 'children's rights constitution' and for assessments of the stated preference of this author and other commentators for this model over one that is more 'protective' in nature.

First, numerous objections to the idea of children as right-holders' claims are premised on concerns about the implications of such rights for the authority of parents or the family unit. Some argue that according rights to children would be harmful due to the negative impact this will have on the parental authority over, and responsibility for, children. An excessive primary focus on family/parent-centric concerns is reflected in both the Irish constitutional framework and the judicial interpretation of that framework. These concerns were also carried through into the proposed constitutional amendment published in February 2007. In this section, however, I wish to focus on objections that are more explicitly focussed on children themselves.

Objections to the notion of children as moral right-holders frequently centre on the implications of the characteristics often associated with children (in particular, dependency, irrationality, a reduced capacity for autonomy and a diminished ability to 'claim' or 'exercise' rights) for general theories of rights such as the 'will/choice' or 'interest' theories of rights (see Federle, 1994).

The will/choice theory with its focus on capacity and autonomy poses clear problems for children as right-holders. It is frequently asserted that children lack the capacity to choose – a key element of a 'will/choice' theory of rights. Indeed, even if one accepts that reports of children's limited capacity for choice are frequently exaggerated, it is clear that there will be some children who, due to age or limited material and emotional development, will be unable to exercise their will. Neil MacCormick has argued persuasively that the presumption underlying the 'will' theory of rights that people are the best judges of what is best for them, should not be extended to young children whose 'rationality' may be questionable (MacCormick, 1976: 316). Indeed, in the view of some commentators, the equal moral worth of children is often best protected by ensuring that they have properly protected positive rights justified in terms of their fundamental interests (Campbell, 1992).

Federle, however, critiques the interest theory of rights for perpetuating 'a caretaker ideology that promotes the powerlessness of children'. In her view, by tying rights-generating interests to children's incapacities, interest theorists suggest that children are incapable of caring for themselves:

> [t]hose interests that warrant protection as rights under interest theory, such as the need to be nurtured and cared for, reaffirm the vulnerability and helplessness of children. Moreover, because the satisfaction of these interests depends upon some other capable being, such as a parent, interest theorists assume that any action taken will benefit the child. (Federle, 1994a: 1590)

In her view, interest theorists are more concerned with the child's protection and with paternalistic justifications for the choices adults make on behalf of children. In contrast, she proposes an empowerment theory of rights, under which children's rights are based on their powerlessness (Federle, 1995).

There are numerous different theories of children's rights, and the aim of this section is not to state an explicit preference for one particular theory. Rather, I seek to highlight the particular problems that children pose to those conceptualising moral rights. This is important due to the fact that, I would argue, legal rights are generally underpinned by, or correspond to, moral rights. Indeed, the constitutionalisation of rights might well be described as the translation of moral rights into legal rights. When – as is the case in Ireland – there is discussion in relation to which rights of children should be legally enshrined, it is crucial that the debate surrounding particular moral (i.e. 'not yet legal') rights of children be explored. Admittedly, much of the debate in Ireland has focused on the extent to which the international legal human rights enshrined in the UN Convention on the Rights of the Child (CRC) should be domestically incorporated. However, these rights, in turn, are reflective of, and seek to guarantee, those outcomes for children that moral theorists claim are required by moral rights. For example, dignity, equality and recognition.

When dealing with children's rights – whether legal or moral – it has to be borne in mind that even where children are accorded rights there will be situations in which they will not be able to assert such rights themselves. In some cases, this is attributable to the legal or political framework which does not recognise children as right-holders or accord children the tools with which to exercise their rights. Such situations can be resolved relatively easily as they merely require a change to the legal framework. However, it is more problematic where children's inability to secure their rights for themselves is a result of their incapacity to make the necessary claims due to their immaturity and lower level of biological development.

Feinberg describes a right as a valid claim and describes such a claim as an assertion of right (Feinberg, 1980: 149) or as being the activity of claiming what is due to one. In his view, having rights makes claiming possible; but it is claiming that gives rights their special moral significance. If one was to regard the ability to claim a right as a precondition of being a rights-bearer, those (generally younger) children who are incapable of articulating or making such a claim arguably do not qualify as right-holders. Feinberg asserts, however, that although very small children cannot claim their rights, adult moral agents can represent them and claim their rights for them. Thus, children are moral right-holders. It has been highlighted in the legal context that this issue of representation of children – in the sense of someone asserting their rights for them – may be problematic. In the Irish Baby Ann case,[2] Justice Hardiman of the Supreme Court noted that, '[a] right conferred on or deemed to inhere in a very young child will in practice fall to be exercised by another on his or her behalf ... *it will actually empower whoever is in a position to assert it and not the child himself or herself* ... The creation or acknowledgement of an entirely independent right in a person or entity personally incapable of exercising that right may have unintended or undesired legal consequences.' Justice Hardiman's concern about children's rights resulting in the empowerment of non-children fails to address the issue that refusing to accord children rights – in the sense of refusing to accord them enforceable claims – will not only fail to empower them but will also almost inevitably result in their disempowerment in a legal or political context.

Ann McGillivray points out that the children's rights movement differs from other rights movements only in that, 'thus far, rights are claimed, fought for and administered primarily by those outside of that group, by adults But all adults were once members of that group and can legitimately claim representation' (McGillivray, 1994: 253–254). The issue of representation cannot be so easily disposed of, however. First of all, there is considerable institutional room for manoeuvre in the rights model with respect to determining who will represent children's rights, and how this function is to be discharged. Should representation be performed by parents, the state, other entities or a combination of these? In addition, it is clear that the representation of children's rights-claims by others is problematic and open to abuse. Is it appropriate to always trust the priority accorded to, or the balance struck between, the various rights or interests of children by those (parents, adults, the state) who purport to represent them? Can we be confident that children's rights will be appropriately represented where they potentially threaten or conflict with those of their representatives? However, while there is no doubt that the representation of children's rights claims by others is far from problem-free, it should be borne in mind that if it is presumed that entities accorded 'representative' status are not capable of adequately representing children's rights claims, then this will require a reassessment of, amongst other things, the presumption that non-children are capable of representing children's rights and interests in democratic decision-making processes that affect those rights and interests. The issues of the effective representation of children's rights claims is not just limited to the legal context.

Another related matter is the question of what practical benefit children will reap from being accorded express rights? Freeman observes that the enactment of legal rights will not be sufficient – a wide range of social institutions must take action to ensure that such rights are implemented (Freeman, 1982: 33–34). Indeed, one must query whether the legal system will be able to 'deliver on' what children's rights advocates hope will be achieved by children's rights. From a legal practise perspective, one must ask whether, even where children can claim their own rights or where parents effectively represent children's rights claims before the courts, it can be assumed that the courts will give effect to these rights so as to benefit children? No doubt this is a valid concern. However, while there is no doubt that one can query whether the courts will correctly prioritise children's rights and interests in cases before them, the fact that children are accorded rights by law will mean that these rights will, at least, be taken into account in and the focus of judicial consideration. As the Irish jurisprudence has demonstrated, this will be highly unlikely if children were not granted the status of right-holders.

In discussing children's rights, Arneil refers to Dworkin's description of rights as 'moral trump cards' and states that '[if] you want to take children's needs and interests seriously, and make claims on their behalf that will compete with any other moral claims, it is necessary to make such claims in the language of rights [as] … any non-rights moral claim simply does not carry the same weight in contemporary moral or political debate' (Arneil, 2002: 70).Thus, where children's needs and interests are invoked against the 'stronger' rights claims of other entities such as parents and the state, they are very unlikely to prevail. Certainly this has been demonstrated in the Irish context, where the constitutional rights of parents and the family have been held to effectively overrule children's individual rights in a range of different contexts. Furthermore, to assert that children are not entitled to the 'superior moral claims' symbolised by rights is essentially to perceive children as inferior, lacking the dignity, respect, and freedom from arbitrary treatment, that different commentators argue that rights signal.[3] Freeman notes that 'if we have rights we are entitled to respect and dignity: no amount of benevolence or compassion can be an adequate substitute' (Freeman, 1991: 29).

In contrast to a special protection constitution model, a children's rights constitution grants recognition and respect to children. By explicitly acknowledging that children are rights-bearers, their equal moral status with other members of society is affirmed. While rights will not single-handedly solve the problems faced by children in contemporary society, they serve as important imperatives for law and policymakers. Rights may not operate as a panacea for all the problems facing children in their day-to-day life. Indeed, rights do not (and are not expected to) serve that purpose for other right-holders in society either. Rights are, however, crucial legal and political tools for children and actors working on their behalf in ensuring the provision for, and protection and participation of children in Irish society.

Children in the Eyes of the Irish Constitution

The Irish Constitution of 1937 predated the international and national children's rights movements and its children's rights provisions (or lack thereof) stand in stark contrast to those in more recent constitutional instruments such as those of South Africa and Timor Leste.[4] Tobin regards the development of 'special protection' constitutions as according with the provisions relating to the treatment of children under the Universal Declaration of Human Rights (1948), the International Covenant on Civil and Political Rights (1966), and the International Covenant on Economic, Social and Cultural Rights (1966) (Tobin, 2005: 88). These instruments emphasise the need for special measures of protection and assistance for children. However, although the Irish Constitution could not have been influenced by the burgeoning post-war human rights movement and does not include any specific enjoinders in relation to child protection or assistance, it is clear that it shares a number of features that Tobin regards as indicative of a 'special protection' constitution. These include: a strong preference for treating children as vulnerable and in need of special protection, rather than as the beneficiaries of rights per se, as well as the delineation of parental rights and duties with regard to the upbringing of their children (Tobin, 2005).

The limited consideration of children (and of children as right-holders, specifically) in the 1937 Constitution is undoubtedly largely attributable to the contemporary societal perception of children as objects of parental rights and duties rather than autonomous right-holders. In the Dáil debates on the draft Constitution we find references to the child as a person 'whose will and mind are not developed, as a matured person' who should not be held 'as responsible for certain actions' as an adult (Dáil Debates, 11 May 1937). While this recognition of the reduced capacity or responsibility of children might be welcomed from a child-rights perspective in some circumstances, it is perturbing that the perceived difference in 'social and physical capacity' and 'social function' (Article 40.1) between children and 'matured person[s]' was expressly presented in the Dáil Debates as a basis for not holding children to be 'equal before the law' (Dáil Debates, 11 May 1937). Indeed, the Supreme Court has indicated that classifications based on age are not presumptively proscribed by Article 40.1, which expressly provides that the State may 'have due regard to differences of capacity, physical and moral, and of social function' in its enactments.[5]

While it is clearly desirable that the law should accommodate the special position of children and acknowledge the lower level of physical and cognitive development of (especially) young children relative to that of adults, this justification for differential treatment may result in children being accorded lesser protection of the law in some circumstances. Admittedly, it is acceptable under a substantive conception of equality that those in different situations should not be treated identically. However, such different treatment must be motivated by the aim of treating people as equals or guaranteeing equality of outcomes or results for different individuals/groups. This will not be the case where legal differential treatment results in children being disadvantaged in terms of enjoyment of their rights relative to adults.

Children's Rights in the 1937 Constitution

According to Tobin, recourse to the discourse of rights and the provision of a dedicated section for children within the constitution is the common theme that unifies so-called 'child rights constitutions' (Tobin, 2005: 112). There is no detailed section of the Irish Constitution that is devoted to children. However, in addition to the personal rights furnished to 'every citizen' by various sections of Articles 40–44 and implied from Article 40.3.1 (see below), there ise a limited number of child-specific rights and duties set out in the Constitution. Due to space constraints, I will not attempt to provide a comprehensive legal–historical discussion of the position of children under Irish constitutional law. Rather I will highlight a couple of key themes.

The rights of the family and education are set out in Articles 41 and 42 of the Constitution. The articles are generally considered to have been inspired by papal encyclicals and by Catholic teaching (Whyte & Hogan, 2003: 1827) . They certainly reflect the priority accorded to the family unit and the designation of gender roles forwarded by the Catholic Church at that time (e.g. Pope Pius XI, 1931). Article 41.1 recognises the family as the 'natural primary and fundamental unit group of society, and as a moral institution possessing inalienable and imprescriptible rights, *antecedent and superior to all positive law*' [emphasis added]. In Article 41.2, the State 'guarantees to protect the Family in its constitution and authority'. This explicit constitutional protection of the family is consistent with a 'special protection' constitution (Tobin, 2005: 106).

Article 42 'acknowledges that the primary and natural educator of the child is the Family and guarantees to respect the *inalienable rights and duty* of parents' [emphasis added] to provide for the education of their children (Article 42.1). Again, this is consistent with the approach of 'special protection constitutions', which tends to provide that parents have the primary obligation to raise and educate their children (Tobin, 2005: 108). The 'education' referred to in the article does not merely deal with scholastic education but corresponds to the 'upbringing' of the child (Shannon, 2005: 3). The provision goes on to outline the broad freedoms enjoyed by parents in relation to educating their children.

The values of parental autonomy and family privacy are strongly enshrined in Article 41. The same is true with regard to the right to education in Article 42. While the child is not *expressly* relegated to the private sphere by the text of the Constitution in the way that women are (see, Article 42.21), children are effectively located there by the dominant position accorded to the family and the clear subjugation of children within that institution. The huge level of power exercised over, and with regard to, children by the family/parents and the very limited role accorded to the State clearly entails a separation of the public power of the state from the private relationships within the family in nearly all circumstances.[6]

According to Article 42.4, the State is obliged to 'provide for' (but not necessarily 'provide') primary education[7] and is 'to endeavour to supplement and give reasonable aid to private and corporate educational initiative, and, when the public good requires it, provide other educational facilities or institutions *with due regard, however, for the rights of parents, especially in the matter of religious and moral formation*' [emphasis added]. Article 42.4 seems a clearly child-specific provision (and indeed has been interpreted by the courts as such).[8] However, Quinn has suggested that the inclusion of the right to education in the Irish Constitution had less to do with giving effect to the substantive right to education per se and more to do with preserving the arrangement between the funders of education (the State) and the providers of education (religious bodies and parents) prevailing at the time at which the Constitution was being drafted (Quinn, 2001: 49).

In general, the Constitution accords the State a supplementary role in relation to the education and upbringing of children. However, it does make provision for the State to perform a default role where parents fail to satisfy their duties under the Constitution. Article 42.5 provides that '[i]n exceptional cases, where the parents for physical and moral reasons fail in their duty towards their children, the State as guardian of the common good, by appropriate means shall endeavour to supply the place of the parents, but always with due regard for the natural and imprescriptible rights of the child'. In contrast to the strident statements in relation to 'parental' and 'family' rights and duties set out in the Constitution, these 'natural and imprescriptible rights' of the child are not outlined anywhere in the document. Article 42.5's focus on parental failure, rather than the needs or welfare of the child, renders the provision highly parent-, rather than child-, centric. The use of the word 'exceptional' clearly indicates the very limited role contemplated for the state.[9]

It is thus clear that the 1937 Constitution accords paramountcy to parental rights[10] and the consequent subordination of children's rights and welfare has often been borne out in judicial interpretations and application of the constitutional rights provisions. This has been particularly evident in cases involving disputes about custody between parents and third parties. A recent case involving a conflict between a child's personal rights and parental/family rights in a parent–stranger custody dispute – the so-called 'Baby Ann' decision – played a key role in the formulation of the proposed constitutional amendment. This case demonstrates the highly vulnerable situation of children as right-holders under the current constitutional framework.

Baby Ann was placed for adoption by her unmarried parents the week of her birth and was taken into custody by her purported adoptive parents at the age of four months (Barnardos, 2007: 5). She lived with them for almost two years and was highly attached to them (ibid). Her parents subsequently married and brought a constitutional action to have her returned to them (ibid). In adjudicating between the conflicting interests of both couples in the case, the primary consideration for the Supreme Court was the constitutional presumption that the welfare of the child is best met within the marital family (Ombudsman for Children, 2006: 10) 'unless the court is satisfied on the evidence that there are compelling reasons why this *cannot* be achieved, or unless the court is satisfied that the evidence establishes an exceptional case where the parents have failed to provide education for the child and to continue to fail to provide education for the child for moral or physical reasons' [emphasis added].[11] Thus, consideration of the position (and rights) of the child was confined to an examination of its right to belong to a marital family and of the marital family's right to provide for the child (Ombudsman for Children, 2006: 10). Indeed, Baby Ann was not even granted separate representation due to the nature of the proceedings. Thus, while the court acknowledged that her rights would be implicated by the decision, she was not granted any practical recognition as a right-holder in the legal process itself. The Supreme Court focused on whether there were 'compelling reasons' and/or 'a physical or moral failure of the parents'. It was held that there were not. Not even the placement of the Ann for adoption and signing all the necessary consent forms by both natural parents constituted such failure.

Despite the lack of express children's rights provided under the Constitution, the courts have proceeded to identify a number of 'unenumerated' children's rights, which are primarily guaranteed under Article 40.3.1 of the Constitution. Arguably, the existence of an extensive range on unenumerated rights for children could serve to transform a constitution that it is not, on the face of it, a children's rights constitution into one that is.

There has been a number of cases in which the courts have stated that children have been accorded certain socio-economic rights that must be vindicated by the state.[12] In recent years, however, the courts have displayed a growing reluctance to recognise and give effect to such rights, even in the face of governmental failure (and sometimes unwillingness) to give effect to previously identified constitutional obligations. This is probably the result of Irish judicial reluctance to become involved in alleged issues of 'distributive justice' and animosity to socio-economic rights per se, rather than of judicial animosity to *children's* socio-economic rights in particular. This reluctance has also been demonstrated by the fact that, in the face of ever-increasing litigation by the parents of children with special needs seeking the provision of education rights-related services and facilities, the Courts have become progressively more restrictive in defining the obligation imposed on the state by Article 42.4 (see, e.g., *O'Carolan v Minister for Education* 2005 IEHC 296). This has been particularly evident in the context of the judicial identification of the level of service provision which the state is constitutionally obliged to provide.

This judicial opposition to giving effect to (and, in some cases, recognising) children's individual constitutional socio-economic rights operable against the state, has clear implications for children's enjoyment of goods and services that are directly linked to their well-being, welfare, physical, moral and social development, and capacity for autonomy. It also has implications for the extent to which the unenumerated rights doctrine can effectively 'transform' the 1937 Constitution into a children's constitution in the broader sense. In Tobin's analysis, a 'children's rights constitution' is simply characterised by recourse to the discourse of children's rights. He makes no claims in relation to which rights such a constitution may/should have other than arguing that rights in such constitutions frequently reflect those in the Convention on the Rights of the Child (CRC). I would go further and argue that a true 'children's rights constitution' – that is one that accords proper respect and recognition to children as right-holders – must expressly or implicitly recognise the range of rights accorded to children and the state obligations imposed by those rights. I would rely on the CRC as a (non-exhaustive) basis for determining what rights should be included. This is due both to the CRC's authoritative international law status and the fact that, as I have previously stated, in my view its provisions reflect the range of moral rights (provision, protection and autonomy) accorded to children.

There is one final, crucial children's rights issue that has been dealt with in the context of unenumerated rights and has major implications for the equality enjoyed by different groups of children. The 'inalienable' rights and duties of parents and the imprescriptible' rights of the marital family set out in Articles 41 and 42 of the Constitution have been construed as applying to marital families and their members *only*, while those of parents and children in non-marital families are considered to be unenumerated rights flowing from Article 40.3.1, which are less absolute in nature.[13] There is thus constitutionally enshrined discrimination between the children of marital families and those of non-marital ones, which may result in the unequal enjoyment of rights by these different groups of children. Such a situation is in direct contrast with that under many other 'special protection' constitutions which enshrine the equal status of non-marital children (Tobin, 2005: 107).

Article 45, which sets out non-justiciable Directive Policies of Social Policy, makes a number of direct references to children. For instance, the State undertakes to endeavour that 'the tender age of children shall not be abused and that citizens shall not be forced by economic necessity to enter avocations unsuited to their sex, age or strength'.

The approach adopted towards children in Article 45 and other sections of the Constitution was founded on the notion that children require special protection both from their parents and the state and are consistent with a 'special protection constitution'. While such protection may serve to satisfy children's rights-related needs, it is premised on disputable presumptions about the vulnerability, incapacity, immaturity and irrationality of children. From a paternalistic perspective, children are less capable, more immature, irrational and vulnerable, than adults, i.e. inferior to adults. Their perceived difference from and inferiority to adults is often used as a ground to invoke special protection for them while simultaneously denying them autonomy and keeping them under adult control. While such protections may well benefit children, the paternalistic ideology that underlies them frequently serves to reinforce the inequality of children (Sheppard, 1992: 204).

I should clarify at this point that I am not arguing that paternalism is always unacceptable in the context of children's rights. Indeed, the inevitability of some degree of paternalist decision-making is expressly recognised in the most celebrated children's rights charter, the CRC, which provides in Article 3(1) that in all actions concerning children, 'whether undertaken by public or private social welfare institutions, courts of law, administrative authorities or legislative bodies', the best interests of the child are to be a primary consideration. The power to determine precisely what the best interests of a child are or entail is generally reserved to parties other than the child. However, the paternalism of Article 3(1) is tempered (at least in part) by the participation rights provided for under the Convention (see, e.g., Article 12, CRC), albeit that the CRC does not provide that children's views will be determinative in decision-making processes concerning them.

It has been pointed out that 'paternalism' in the upbringing of children, in some sense is inevitable and wholly proper, whether imposed by the state in the child's interest or by the parents themselves, and 'that is because there will be some respects at least in which even an older child cannot known his own interest' (Wellman, 1995). The claim that there will be circumstances in which 'an older child' of 17 will not be capable of determining his own interest is open to debate. However, there is no doubt that this is certainly true of younger children. Thus, the main question we are faced with is not whether or not paternalism is ever acceptable. Rather we need to consider the determination and/or the justification of the parameters of acceptable paternalism. I would agree with Freeman's arguments in favour of 'liberal paternalism' (based on a Rawlsian conception of the social contract) which legitimises intervention directed at conduct that is irrational when judged against a neutral theory of the good (Freeman, 1991: 37–39). Relying on the child's capacity for autonomy, rather than actual autonomy, such an approach serves to protect the child's future autonomy while permitting pluralistic visions of the good. It thus maximises the autonomy and equality of the child while shielding him/her from danger. I would add to Freeman's model by arguing that paternalistic constraints on children must be consistent with the right of the child who is capable of forming her own views to express those views freely in all matters affecting him/her and have them given due weight in accordance with the age and maturity of the child.[14] Such a requirement would promote the child's capacity for self-determination and autonomy by requiring consultation and participation in decision-making. However, ultimately it would not require that the child's decision on matters affecting them or their rights should be automatically implemented where this would have negative implications for their future capacity for autonomy.

It should be noted that the paternalistic assumptions that underpin the express and judicially identified rights of children under the Irish Constitution, contrast strongly with the autonomy or capacity basis of some of the traditional civil rights accorded to them and all other citizens as personal rights under Articles 40.3–40.6, such as the rights to liberty, to form associations and unions, to peaceably assemble, and to express freely convictions and opinions. These rights are, however, not child-specific and there have been relatively few opportunities for children to exercise these rights in contemporary Irish society. Furthermore, the adoption of 'protective' stance by the courts has resulted in children being denied equal enjoyment of the constitutional rights accorded to 'every citizen'. For instance, the Supreme Court has held it to be acceptable to limit a child's right to liberty on the basis that this was required by the child's 'welfare'.[15] In addition, the relevant provisions outlining these civil rights are neither as unqualified nor as broadly phrased as the equivalent rights accorded to children under the CRC.

Previous Amendment Proposals and Events Leading up to the Proposed Amendment

There had been a number of reports and studies arguing variously for amendments to, and retention of, the various constitutional articles pertaining to children's rights. since 1937 (Committee on the Constitution (1967); Report of the Second Commission on the Status of Women 1993).[16] However, until relatively recently, these did not focus on the rights of children. In 1993, the Kilkenny Incest Investigation highlighted the fact that 'the very high emphasis on the right of the family in the Constitution may consciously or unconsciously be interpreted as giving a higher value to the rights of parents than to the rights of children' (Kilkenny Incest Investigation, 1993). In its 1996 report, the Constitution Review Group recommended that the Constitution should include an express guarantee of certain rights of the child which 'fall to be interpreted by the courts from the concept of "family life"', as well as an express requirement that, in all actions concerning children, whether by legislative, judicial or administrative authorities, the best interests of the child shall be the paramount consideration (Constitution Review Group, 1996: 336–337). It also recommended that the right to every child of free primary education should be explicitly stated in the Constitution and that this right should be extended to second-level education as may be defined by law (Constitution Review Group, 1996: 353). Despite being seized upon by civil society and being endorsed by the Commission on the Family in 1998, these recommendations were not implemented. In its 2006 report, the All-Party Oireachtas Committee on the Constitution advocated an amendment to be inserted in Article 41 stating that 'All children, irrespective of birth, gender, race or religion, are equal before the law. In all cases where the welfare of the child so requires, regard shall be had to the best interests of that child.' This was at least partially attributable to the large number of organisations who urged the Committee to recommend a constitutional amendment expressly granting rights to children to be protected and represented, although the actual recommendation made was criticised by the Ombudsman for Children for failing to include express provision for the rights of the child (Logan, 2006).

In addition to the 'Baby Ann' case, 2006 witnessed two other high-profile and highly controversial children's rights-related cases. In *CC* v *Ireland*,[17] the Supreme Court found the law governing statutory rape trials[18] to be unconstitutional, as it failed to allow for a defence of mistake as to age in a case of unlawful carnal knowledge of a girl under 15 years.[19] Subsequent legislation making provision for a defence of 'honest mistake' for similar sexual offences has been criticised for potentially exposing child victims to cross-examination in order to establish to whether a mistake was actually made. Following the CC decision, another man applied for an order directing his release from custody on the grounds that his detention was unlawful since the law grounding his conviction had been declared unconstitutional. In refusing to grant the order, the Court found that the application of a principle of absolute retroactivity would be a denial of justice to the victims of crime and offend against fundamental and just interests of society.[20] The Court did not, however, directly address the issue of the rights of the child.

It has been argued that, had children's rights been expressly recognised in the Constitution when these cases were decided, they might have been decided differently in terms of either substance or procedure (Barnardos, 2007: 6). Indeed, there was no reference to children's rights whatsoever in the course of either judgment. The public outcry and concern that followed this decision had a clear influence on the government's decision to tackle the issue of children's rights and child protection in the Constitution. In November, the newly-established Joint Oireachtas Committee on Child Protection recommended a constitutional amendment to allow for an offence with 'absolute liability' in relation to sex with children under a certain age (Joint Committee on Child Protection, 2006: 26).

Finally, there was also international pressure on the state to strengthen protection of children's rights, with the UN Committee on the Rights of the Child urging the constitutional incorporation of the CRC (Committee on the Rights of the Child, 1998). In September 2006, Brian Lenihan, Minister for Children, told the Committee that he had embarked on 'an examination, on an article by article basis, of the provisions of the Constitution as they impact on children' (Minister for Children, 2006). The stage thus seemed to be set for the introduction of a 'children's rights' constitutional amendment.

A Public Mandate for a 'Children's Rights Constitution'?

Prior to the extensive analysis of the proposed amendment in the media earlier this year, there appeared to be much public confusion regarding the extent of children's rights in the Irish Constitution (Barnardos, 2007: 19). A large number of the 1,200 respondents to a survey commissioned by Barnardos in September 2006 were under the impression that children enjoy a wide range of rights under the constitution. While 58 per cent believed that there was a right to education under the Constitution, 35 per cent and 16 per cent of respondents incorrectly thought that there was a right to healthcare and a right to childhood, respectively (Barnardos, 2007: 19). Six per cent said that children have no rights and 24 per cent said that they did not know what rights children had (Barnardos, 2007: 19).

Despite these misapprehensions, the survey demonstrated very strong support for the inclusion of a children's rights provision in the Constitution. Seventy-four per cent of respondent adults felt that there should be an explicit commitment to children's rights in the Constitution, only 4 per cent were in disagreement with the question and 21 per cent were unsure (Barnardos, 2007: 19).

It would seem, therefore, that there was some evidence of general societal agreement that the Constitution should be amended to strengthen the rights of children.

However, as one journalist observed, although almost everyone is instinctively well-disposed to the concept of giving children greater protection, '[t]urning this instinctive support into a majority Yes vote for a specific constitutional change is an entirely different task. There is a long political road to travel before such a referendum can be assured of success' (Whelan, 2006).

The Battle over the Content of the Proposed Amendment

The first public statement by the government that a referendum would take place to 'put the rights of children in a central place in [the] Constitution' was by the Taoiseach on 3 November 2006. This was followed by a consultation between the Minister for Children, Brian Lenihan, a representative of the non-governmental sector, government and opposition politicians, and constitutional experts, to agree the government's formulation of wording for a constitutional amendment. The Non-Governmental sector was represented by the umbrella organisation, the Children's Rights Alliance (CRA), which is made up of a range of different organisations working on child-related issues.

In the run-up to the publication of the draft amendment, a number of those working in the children's rights sector made proposals expressing support for the inclusion of an explicit list of children's rights within the constitution. These recommendations were explicitly child-centric and were greatly influenced by international child rights law, particularly the CRC (Children's Rights Alliance, 2007; 2006: 4). Both the CRA and the Ombudsman recommended the adoption of a provision similar to section 28 of the South African Constitution, which enumerates a wide range of child-specific rights and enshrines the best interest principle. Barnardos – who work particularly on children protection issues – had previously proposed a draft amendment that was essentially 'protective' in nature. It focused on the duty of the state in relation to the welfare of the child, providing parents 'with a basis from which to defend their children's rights if they think these rights are not being honoured' (Barnardos, 2007: 22–23). However, Barnardos explicitly acknowledged that the inclusion of express rights into the Constitution would place children's welfare at the heart of Irish laws. There was thus a clear preference on the part of many of the most prominent actors in the children's rights sector for a 'children's rights constitution'.

There appeared to be tacit acceptance amongst children's rights campaigners that, while the position of children needed to be strengthened under the Constitution, this would not be at the expense of the family. None of the proposals published by civil society during this most recent debate on children's rights directly suggested significant restructuring of Articles 41 and 42, other than those of the Ombudsman (Ombudsman for Children, 2006: 4). This was probably largely a strategic decision in light of perceived public and political support for retention of the position of the family in the constitutional framework. In addition, at the outset of the consultation process, it was made clear by the Minister that a change to Article 41, in particular the interpretation of 'family' as being based on marriage, was not under consideration. However, it meant that those proposals made were necessarily piecemeal, failing to fully address those features of the Constitution that had resulted in the historical sidelining of children's rights and interests.

The Proposed Constitutional Amendment

In his speech on the day of the publication of the proposed amendment, Bertie Ahern emphasised that all of the elements of the draft constitutional provision 42A would protect the rights of children and, significantly, none of them would undermine the role of parents or the constitutional safeguards for the family. He concluded his speech by saying '[w]e will change the Constitution to protect [the children of the future]. We will value and defend childhood to an extent never before attempted, and we will do it in a way that enhances the position of families and defends the rights of parents' (An Taoiseach, 2007). According to the Táiniste and Minister for Justice, '[t]his amendment to the Constitution is, quite simply, about protecting our children' (An Tánaiste, 2007). It is clear from these statements that the 'special protection' and paternalistic attitude exhibited towards children in the 1937 Constitution is not a thing of the past. The Minister for Children adopted a slightly different approach, noting that: 'In general, our Constitution strikes balances between personal rights, the status of the family, the rights and duties of parents, and the powers of the State as guardian of the common good. The aim of the Government is simply to include children in this equation' (Minister for Children, 2007).

He proceeded to say that strengthening the position of children had to be balanced with other constitutional principles such as the duty of parents and position of the family which are '*as important* in protecting and safeguarding children' [emphasis added].

It is obvious that the government did not intend a dramatic rebalancing exercise between the priority accorded to the rights and duties of parents/families and the rights of the child. Nor did it attempt to alter the definition of the 'family' to apply to non-marital families.

There was criticism from the press and from members of the opposition and civil society about both the apparent 'rush' to a referendum prior to the General Election and the delay in publishing the word of the proposed amendment (O'Brien, 2007a). Fine Gael and Labour expressed their preference for dealing with children's rights and the 'child abuse' and 'soft information' separately, with the 'children's rights' issue to be dealt with in second amendment after the election (Hennessy, 2007). In contrast, some civil society members expressed concern that if the referendum was postponed, this could result in it being put off to a date far in the future (O'Brien, 2007b). Other groups, who were dissatisfied with the level of protection accorded to children's rights by the proposed amendment, expressed opposition to the amendment being held at all due to its failure to adequately ensure the protection of children's rights.

As stated earlier due to the dissolution of government prior to the May general election the Bill fell. However, each of the main parties' mainfestos contained a commitment on holding a constitutional referendum on children's rights. Following the election, in its Programme for Government, the recently elected coalition stated that it would 'establish an all-party Committee to examine the proposed constitutional amendment with a view to deepening consensus on this matter' (Programme for Government, 2007). This was presumably a reaction to the fact that the government had failed to secure all-party agreement on the amendment prior to the general election.

In August 2007, the newly appointed Minister for Children announced that he would approach Opposition parties in the coming weeks in order to establish an All-Party Oireachtas Committee that would examine the wording for a change to the Constitution (O'Brien, 2007c). According to media reports, the proposed wording for a referendum published by the government earlier this year (2007) will be the basis upon which talks with Opposition parties will take place (O'Brien, 2007c). It remains to be seen what the final wording (if any) will be put to the electorate. However, bearing in mind the fact that the current draft is the foundation on which the Committee will work, it is reasonable to take it as strongly indicative of the approach that will finally be adopted – especially in light of the new Minister's statement that any adapted wording would not in any way affect the rights of parents (O'Brien, 2007d).

Bearing in mind that there will almost certainly be changes made to the proposed amendment, I will merely focus on a number of issues that arise in it. The first, crucial, issue is that the proposed amendment does not contain an explicit list of rights for children – a fact that gave rise to much criticism of Article 42(A)1. Instead, it provides that '[t]he State acknowledges and affirms the natural and imprescriptible rights of all children'. There is thus explicit acknowledgement that children bear individual rights that are not tied to those of the family. According to the Taoiseach, to try to list exhaustively what the rights of children are to be would be counter-productive, for it would have the effect of excluding all the rights which are not listed (An Taoiseach, 2007). This claim is easily disproved as it would have been quite possible to phrase the amendment so as to provide a list of children's rights and to indicate that this list was non-exhaustive. Indeed, it seems bizarre that a 'children's rights' constitutional amendment should not expressly enumerate any children's rights!

Under the draft Article, only the judiciary would be able to specify additional or existing constitutional rights in the absence of a constitutional amendment providing for their express inclusion. The Ombudsman and the Irish Council for Civil Liberties (ICCL) heavily criticised the language of the provision, stating that 'natural and imprescriptible' is unclear and, in the absence of any further guidance, would present interpretative problems for the courts (ICCL, 2007a: 7). In its review of the amendment, the ICCL expressed the view that the unenumerated rights identified under Article 40 are incoherent and insufficient to protect children's rights (ICCL, 2007a; 2007b: 6). This author agrees. There are other clear problems with leaving the identification of children's rights to judges. First, the Supreme Court's recent reluctance to acknowledge or ensure the enforcement of children's economic and social rights means that a large number of rights that are of crucial importance to children might be sidelined. In addition, it seems inappropriate that a 'children's rights' amendment to the constitution which is to passed by 'the people' should reserve the power to determine what such rights *are* to the judiciary as opposed to the electorate.

There was also no comprehensive effort to amend the constitutional protection of the family in Articles 41 and 42. Children's rights would thus remain subordinate to those of parents and the family unit. In addition, the retention of the 'special position' of the marital family means that non-marital children of the non-marital family would still be disadvantaged under the proposed constitutional framework. (ICCL, 2007a: 17). The very high threshold of proof required to trigger state intervention by the old Article 42.5 would remain – albeit that that duty currently owed by the State under Article 42.5 would be extended to 'any child' (rather than merely children of marital families). According to the ICCL, in reality, this proposal would mean that children of non-marital families would be 'equally disadvantaged'.

The CRA, Ombudsman and the ICCL recommended that the term 'proportionate' be inserted after the word 'appropriate' (e.g. 'the State as guardian of the common good, by appropriate *and proportionate* means shall endeavour to supply the place of the parents'), which would result in the expansion of the obligation imposed on the state in terms of support and assistance to the family. A similar view was expressed by the Special Rapporteur to the Oireachtas on Child Protection (Shannon, 2007). He argued that there is a clear need to tackle poverty and inequality and specifically to strengthen supports to children and families where a child is at risk of being, or has been, taken into care. He argued that the insertion of 'proportionate' would place an obligation on the State to ensure that the first point of State intervention would be family support, unless exceptional circumstances made this inappropriate. The battle for resources to address the needs, and fulfil the rights, of disadvantaged children has raged between civil society and the state over the past 20 years, with the government proving reluctant to pass rights-based legislation enshrining socio-economic rights and entitlements for children. The proposed amendment would be unlikely to provide a weapon which could be used either to coerce the state to resource children in need or as a basis for litigation by, or on behalf of, children who are impoverished and marginalised (Browne 2007). Thus, it would be unlikely to advance at least one key aspect of ensuring social justice for children. Bearing in mind the fact that the courts have proved unwilling in recent years to recognise or ensure the effective implementation of the limited socio-economic rights accorded to children under the constitution, this is a key failing in the amendment.

The proposed amendment contained a number of changes in relation to adoption. According to the proposed amendment, the Oireachtas would be able to make provision for the adoption of marital children, where parents have failed in their duty towards their child for a set period or time, and where the best interests of the child so require. It would also enable the Oireachtas to make provision for parents in marital families to voluntarily place their children for adoption. Finally, draft

Article 42(A)4 states that, 'provision may be made by law that in proceedings before any court concerning the adoption, guardianship or custody of, or access to, any child, the court shall endeavour to secure the best interests of the child'. The permissive language of the provisions, which would grant the State discretion as to how and when to implement the principles set out therein, were highly criticised. The failure to directly enshrine the best interests principle into the law and to integrate it into *all* legislation applicable to children was another source of discontent with the proposed wording, as was the failure to explicitly address to constitutional presumption that the best interests of the child are found within its family (ICCL 2007a; Ombudsman, 2007).

Arguably, the provisions of Section 5 have greater implications for the rights of non-children than they do for those of children – specifically the right to fair trial and privacy rights of adults accused or suspected of sexual exploitation or abuse. Section 5 is undoubtedly primarily 'protective' in nature. However, the debates surrounding the issues raised in that provision have demonstrated that, despite the lack of express reference to children's rights therein, Section 5 could have strong ramifications for the enjoyment of rights of various groups of children and, therefore, are key to our consideration of whether the proposed amendment would have resulted in a 'children's rights constitution'.

Sections 5(2) and (3) would, amongst other things, empower the Oireachtas to create absolute or strict liability offices 'committed against or in connection with a child under 18 years of age'. They were the subject of great debate. The Ombudsman and the Children's Rights Alliance criticised these provisions for their very wide scope, in not being limited to sexual offences (Ombudsman, 2007: 12; Van Turnhout, 2007). Indeed, one commentator asked whether the phrase 'in connection with a child' could even cover cases in which the child was an accused (Carolan, 2007). The ICCL and the Ombudsman also expressed concern about the impact of strict liability offences on children and older teenagers — the group most likely to be involved in sexual activities with children under 16 (ICCL, 2007b: 9). Thus, it was suggested, a measure that was intended to protect children could have a serious impact on the rights of other 'offending' children.

As it stands, Section 5 could lead to the clear potential conflict between the rights of 'defendant' and 'victim' children being ignored or overlooked. Indeed, by failing to outline the rights of the child defendant in the way that the CRC and the South African Constitution do, in practice, the proposed amendment would seem likely to result in the inevitable subordination of the rights of one group of children to those of the other. While conflicts of the rights will certainly arise where one has a children's rights constitution and children perpetrate crimes against other children, the conflict will be acknowledged (and may be addressed) in a way that would not be possible under the simple paternalism of the protection model, which section 5(2) seems to embody.

But would the proposed amendment have resulted in the 1937 Constitution qualifying as a 'children's rights' constitution? According to Tobin, recourse to the discourse of rights and the provision of a dedicated section for children within the constitution are the common theme that unifies so-called 'child rights constitutions'

(Tobin, 2005: 112). Both of these elements appear to be provided by the proposed amendment – at least to some extent. However, before arriving at any firm answer to the question being asked, it is important to consider the discrete elements of the proposed amendment.

Using Tobin's framework, Section 1 of the proposed amendment, in which '[t]he State acknowledges and affirms the natural and imprescriptible rights of all children' would seem to move the Irish Constitution some way towards being a 'children's rights' constitution. Although the indeterminacy of these 'natural and imprescriptible rights' means that is it is not clear whether this would be the case in practice. Furthermore, bearing in mind the fact that the unenumerated rights of children that have been identified so far by the courts have largely been premised on 'children being passive objects in need of special protection rather than as active subjects bearing rights' (Tobin, 2005: 88), it is not clear that this reference to rights would actually result in the courts adopting a 'child rights-based approach'. The proposed test for state intervention in the family is firmly centred on the 'special protection of children'. The same is true of Section 42(A)(2)2o which would empower the Oireachtas to make provision for the adoption of a child in the case of prescribed parental failure, although it includes a reference to the best interests of the child, has implications for children but is not expressly premised on either the rights or the welfare of the child. Although the 'best interests principle' enshrined in section 4 (and referred to in section 2(2)) is child-centric, ultimately this principle is primarily paternalistic and thus can be seen as protective rather than rights-based (albeit that it is a feature of the CRC and a number of constitutions identified by Tobin as 'child rights' in nature and must be interpreted and applied in light of the rights accorded to children under those instruments).

In conclusion, it would seem that the proposed amendment would not have resulted in the transformation of the 1937 constitution into a strong 'children's rights constitution' in the way that the provision of an explicit list of rights for children would have done. It would, however, have empowered courts to accord greater weight to the rights and interests of children that are directly and indirectly implicated in the cases before them and would enable them (to quote Minister Lenihan) 'to include children in the equation' (Minister for children, 2007).

Conclusion

According to Tobin, written Constitutions have been described as 'at a minimum "important indicators of a state's legal and political culture", and, by implication, have something, but certainly not everything to say about the status of children within a given society'.[21] If the government and Irish society are serious about improving the status of children in Ireland then it is crucial that the Constitution serves as a framework for that commitment. This cannot occur in the absence of according recognition to children as rights-bearers through the effective transformation of that instrument into a children's rights Constitution. Any future proposals for constitutional amendment must reflect this.

Notes

1. Another key children's rights issue in recent years has been the extent of the constitutional rights enjoyed by citizen children whose parents are non-nationals. Due to space constraints, and the fact that the proposed constitutional amendment does not expressly address the position of such child right-holders, this paper will not focus on this matter. For more on this issue see Brazil (2007).
2. *N* v. *Health Service Executive* [2006] IESC 60.
3. Adapted from (Minow, 1995: 296).
4. See, e.g., Constitution of the Republic of South Africa, Section 28; Constitution of the Democratic Republic of East Timor 2002, Section 18(2).
5. See the dissenting judgment of Justice Denham in *DG* v *Eastern Health Board* [1997] 3 IR 511, cited in (Whyte & Hogan, 2003: 1348).
6. Language adapted from Mullally (1998: 148).
7. For more on this, see *Crowley* v *Ireland* [1980] IR 102, at 122.
8. See *Sinnott* v *Minister for Education* [2001] IESC 39.
9. See, e.g., *North Western Health Board* v *W. (H.)* [2001] IESC 90, ('*NWH* case'). *Per* Denham J in *NWH* case at para 184.
10. For more on this, see Duncan (1996: 612) and Lynch (1998: 323–323).
11. In *Re J. H.* [1985] IR 375.
12. See, e.g., *G* v *An Bord Uchtála* [1980] IR 32 and *FN* v. *Minister for Education* [1995] 1 IR 409.
13. See, e.g., *G* v *An Bord Uchtála*, *per* Walsh J.
14. Article 12 CRC.
15. *D. G.* v *Eastern Health Board & Ors.* [1997] 3 IR 511.
16. For a discussion of the various reports, see Murphy (1998). For more a more recent example, see Law Society (2005).
17. [2006] IESC 33.
18. Section 1.1 of the Criminal Law (Amendment) Act 1935.
19. Children's Rights Alliance, *Briefing Note on the 28th Amendment Bill* (March 2007).
20. *A .v. The Governor of Arbour Hill Prison* [2006] IESC 45, per Murray C. J. and McGuinness J.
21. Tobin (2005: 88) citing Ted McDorman & Margot Young, *Constitutional Structures and Human Rights in South-East Asia: Cambodia, Indonesia, Thailand and Vietnam* (1998) University of New Brunswick LJ 85, p. 87.

References

An Tánaiste, McDowell M. (2007) Speech by An Tánaiste at the launch of the 28th Amendment of the Constitution Bill Referendum on Protection of Children, 19 February.

An Taoiseach, Ahern, B. (2007) Speech on publication of 28th Amendment of the Constitution Bill 2007, 19 February.

Arneil, B. (2002) Becoming Versus Being: A Critical Analysis of the Child in Liberal Theory, in: D. Archard and C. Macleod (Eds) *The Moral and Political Status of Children*, pp. 70–94 (Oxford: Oxford University Press).

Barnardos (2007) *The Case for Constitutional Change* (Dublin: Barnardos).

Brazil, P. (2007) The Rights of Irish Children Born to Non-National Parents, unpublished paper presented at conference on The Constitution at 70, Trinity College Dublin, 8–9 June.

Brown, D. (2007) Government Goals on Childcare Law Unclear, *Irish Times*, 24 February.

Carolan, E. (2007) Bill's Fatal Ambiguities must be Addressed, *Irish Times*, 21 February.

Campbell, T. (1992) The Rights of the Minor: As Person, As Child, As Juvenile, As Future Adult, *International Journal of Law, Policy and the Family*, 6, pp. 1–23.

Children's Rights Alliance (2007) The Constitution and Children: Position Paper on the Proposed Referendum on Children's Rights.

Committee on the Constitution (1967) *Report of the Committee on the Constitution.* (Dublin: Stationery Office).

Committee on the Rights of the Child (1998) Concluding observations of the Committee on the Rights of the Child: Ireland, 04/02/98. CRC/C/15/Add.85.

Constitution Review Group (1996) *Report of the Constitution Review Group* (Dublin: Stationery Office).

Dail Debates (1937) *Dail Debates,* Vol. 67, 11 May.

Dail Debates (1937) *Dail Debates,* Vol. 67,3 June.

Duncan, W. (1996) The Constitutional Protection of Parental Rights, in: Constitution Review Group (Ed.) *Report of the Constitution Review Group,* p.612 (Dublin: Stationery Office).

Federle, K. (1995) Looking for Rights in All the Wrong Places: Resolving Custody Disputes in Divorce Proceedings, *Cardozo Law Review,* 15, pp. 1523–1566.

Federle, K. (1994) Rights Flow Downhill, *International Journal of Children's Rights,* 2, pp. 343–368.

Feinberg, J. (1980) *Rights, Justice and the Boundaries of Liberty: Essays in Social Philosophy* (Princeton, NJ: Princeton University Press).

Freeman, M. (1982) *The Rights and Wrongs of Children* (London: Frances Pinter).

Freeman, M. (1991) The Limits of Children's Rights, in: M. Freeman and P. Veerman (Eds) *The Ideologies of Children's Rights,* pp. 29–46 (Dordrecht: Martinus Nijhoff Publishers).

Freeman, M. (1992) Taking Children's Rights More Seriously, in: P. Alston, S. Parker and J. Seymour (Eds) *Children, Rights and the Law,* pp. 52–71 (Oxford: Clarendon Press).

Hennessy, M. (2007) Dáil Referendum Debate Delayed, *Irish Times,* 21 February.

Irish Council for Civil Liberties (2007a) *ICCL Response to The Twenty-Eighth Amendment of the Constitution Bill 2007 – Commentary on the Proposed New Article 42A, Sub-articles 1–4 on Children* (unpublished).

Irish Council for Civil Liberties (2007b) *ICCL Response to The Twenty-Eighth Amendment of the Constitution Bill 2007 – Commentary on the Proposed New Article 42A, Sub-article 5 on Children* (unpublished).

Joint Committee on Child Protection (2006) *Report on Child Protection.*

Kilkenny Incest Investigation (1993) Report Presented to My Brendan Howlin TD, Minister for Health by South Eastern Health Board (Dublin: Stationary Office).

Law Society (2005) *Rights-based Child Law: The Case for Reform – Part 1* (Law Society: Dublin).

Lindley, R. (1989) Teenagers and Other Children, in: Geoffrey Scarre (Ed.) *Children, Parents and Politics* (Cambridge: Cambridge University Press).

Logan, E. (2006) Retrograde Step for Children's Rights, *Equality News,* Spring pp. 4–6.

Lynch, K. (1998) The Status of Children and Young Persons: Educational and Related Issues, in: S. Healy and B. Reynolds (Eds) *Social Policy in Ireland,* pp. 321–353 (Dublin: Liffey Press).

MacCormick, N. (1976) Children's Rights: A Test-Case for Theories of Rights, *Archiv für Rechts und Sozialphilosophie,* 62, pp. 305–317.

McGillivray, A. (1994) Why Children Do Have Equal Rights: In Reply to Laura Purdy, *International Journal of Children's Rights,* 2, pp. 244–258.

Minister for Children, Lenihan, B. TD (2006) Statement at the Examination of Ireland's Second Periodic Report to the UN Committee on the Rights of the Child, 20 September.

Minister for Children, Lenihan, B. (2007) Speech by Minister for Children on Publication of the Bill to Amend the Constitution in Relation to the Rights of Children, 19 February.

Minow, M. (1995) Whatever Happened to Children's Rights?, *Minnesota Law Review,* 80, pp. 267–298.

Mullally, S. (1998) The Equality Guarantees in Irish Constitutional Law – the Myth of Constitutionalism and the 'Neutral State', in: T. Murphy and P.k Twomey (Eds) *Ireland's Evolving Constitution,* pp. 146 162 (Oxford. Oxford University Press).

Murphy, T. (1998) The Family in the Constitution – Principle and Practice, in: T. Murphy and P. Twomey (Eds) *Ireland's Evolving Constitution,* pp. 79–95 (Oxford: Oxford University Press).

O'Brien, C. (2007a) Government Warned not to Rush Referendum on Child Pprotection, *Irish Times,* 15 February.

O'Brien, C. (2007b) Wording Opens 'Wide Range' of Interpretation, *Irish Times,* 22 February.

O'Brien, C. (2007c) Plan to Hold Vote on Child Protection Next Year, *Irish Times*, 13 August.

O'Brien, C. (2007d) Plan to hold vote on child protection next year, *Irish Times*, 13 August.

Ombudsman for Children (2006) *Advice of the Ombudsman for Children on the Proposed Referendum on Children's Rights.*

Ombudsman for Children (2007) *Report to the Oireachtas on the Twenty-Eighth Amendment of the Constitution Bill 2006.*

Pope Pius XI (1931) *Quadragesimo Anno – The Encyclical of Pope Pius IX on Reconstruction of the Social Order.*

Programme for Government (2007) 12 June.

Purdy, L. (1994) Why Children Shouldn't Have Equal Rights, *International Journal of Children's Rights*, 2, pp. 223–241.

Quinn, G. (2001) Rethinking the Nature of Economic, Social and Cultural Rights in the Irish Legal Order, in: C. Costello (Ed.) *Fundamental Social Rights: Current European Legal Protection and the Challenge of the EU Charter on Fundamental Rights*, pp. 35–54 (Dublin: Trinity College).

Shannon, G. (2005) *Child Law* (Dublin: Thompson, Roundhall).

Shannon, G. (2007) Constitutional Change is Vital for Children, *Irish Times*, 7 March.

Sheppard, C. (1992) Children's Rights to Equality: Protection Versus Paternalism, *Annals of Health Care*, 1, pp. 197–211.

Tobin, J. (2005) Increasingly Seen and Heard: The Constitutional Recognition of Children's Rights, *South African Journal on Human Rights*, 21, pp. 86–126.

Van Turnhout, J. (2007) Children's Rights – A View from the NGO Sector, unpublished paper presented at *Children's Rights and the Constitution*, Trinity College Dublin, 21 February.

Wellman, C. (1995) *Real Rights* (New York: Oxford University Press).

Whelan, N. (2006) Children's Rights Should be Handled Gently, *Irish Times*, 11 November.

Whyte, G. & Hogan, G. (2003) *J. M. Kelly: The Irish Constitution*, 4th edn (Dublin: Butterworths).

Disability Rights in Ireland: Chronicle of a Missed Opportunity

JURGEN DE WISPELAERE & JUDY WALSH

Introduction

In July 2005 the Irish Parliament passed the Disability Act 2005, which forms the legislative centrepiece of a wider strategy regulating access to public services for disabled people in Ireland.[1] The Act is the result of a protracted legislative and consultative process, following the popular defeat of proposed disability legislation in 2001. It is hailed by its supporters as one of the most progressive pieces of legislation in Europe (*Irish Times*, 2004a). At first blush, the government's disability strategy seems to confirm Ireland's reputation as a frontrunner in the international battle for the inclusion and recognition of disabled people, witnessed most recently in its proactive role in promoting the United Nations Convention on the Rights of Persons with Disabilities and its Optional Protocol, adopted on 13 December 2006 in New York (Doyle, 2003; Quinn & Bruce, 2003; Toolan, 2003a; Quinn, 2007). Yet the Disability Act 2005 remains highly contested by many disability groups in Ireland, who lament its content and feel sidelined despite the extensive process of consultation that preceded its enactment.

The purpose of this paper is to offer a critical evaluation of the Disability Act 2005, and in particular to assess what remains the largest bone of contention: its rights-based grounding. Ireland is an interesting case in that both the government and the disability sector continue to affirm the importance of rights-based disability policy. But they adopt opposing positions on whether the current legislation is genuinely rights-based. An important source of disagreement appears to be the involvement of the legal system in securing disability rights, with the government claiming strict justiciability amounts to *rights essentialism*, the view that involvement of courts is the only way to secure rights, whereas the disability sector insists that legal remedies are crucial for ensuring disabled people's rights are properly safeguarded. For critics, the absence of a substantive role for the legal system demonstrates that the Act is not rights-based.

While this disagreement about the role of courts and legal remedies is no doubt partly the result of the prevailing policy context and partly driven by purely political considerations, a third reason for persistent political disagreement might be related to genuine uncertainty about the nature of disability rights. A common conception of disability rights does not emerge from the wealth of political statements, policy briefings and expert submissions that have informed the Irish disability debate. In short, despite ample discussion of the needs of disabled people and of the inequalities they face, which rightly engender demands for redress and rectification, significant disagreement remains about the precise form and nature of disability rights. There appear no agreed foundational benchmarks that specify what rights must be protected at what level, and how this protection must be enshrined in policy and law for disability legislation to count as genuinely rights-based. In our view serious conceptual and normative ground still needs to be covered before we can ascertain whether the Disability Act 2005 satisfies the criteria of rights-based disability legislation.

This article extends the debate on disability rights in two ways. First, in contrast to the approach of the Irish government, we do not privilege a single focal point at which rights to disability services ought to be institutionalised and where political commitment to protecting such rights is subsequently evaluated. Specifically, whereas the government's perspective privileges needs assessment, we maintain that a robust model of disability rights ought to provide for substantial evaluation of the political commitment to both needs assessment *and* service delivery. Second, to accommodate these dual focal points within a single model of disability rights, we propose to shift from a substantive model to one that safeguards fair procedures in decisions pertaining to both needs assessment and service delivery. In this respect our position diverges from that of the disability sector. However, we also argue that the specific model we propose – based on a disabled person's *right to challenge* key decisions regarding needs assessment and service delivery – does not merely represent a version of empty formalism but produces substantial outcomes in terms of services delivered as well as the manner in which key decisions are made.

This paper proceeds as follows. The next two sections sketch the development of disability legislation in Ireland to provide some background to the subsequent discussion and review the prevailing conceptions of disability rights in the current Irish debate. We then propose our alternative model by rethinking the core of the rights-based approach to disability services in terms of a justiciable right to challenge. Having established a firm conceptual and normative grounding for understanding disability rights we then turn our attention to the Disability Act 2005 and assess its alleged rights-based status. We identify features of the current legislation that fail to ensure disability rights as conceived in this article and conclude that recent developments represent a missed opportunity for safeguarding the rights of disabled citizens in the Republic.

Disability Rights in Ireland: A Brief Overview

Ireland's engagement with the disability sector is complex and ambiguous. While forged by a history of disability charity driven by Catholic institutions, contemporary policy is framed by a neo-liberal economic agenda but also by a public commitment to mainstreaming equality of opportunity, social inclusion and human rights norms (Allen, 2003; Doyle, 2003; Toolan, 2003a; Quinn, 2000; Quinn & Bruce, 2003). To understand the legal status of disability rights in the Republic of Ireland we need to appreciate that attempts to compel government action through litigation have been largely unsuccessful. Claims to various forms of services for disabled people have been hampered by the absence of a substantive equality guarantee and a conservative Supreme Court stance on socio-economic rights (De Blacam, 2002; O'Mahony, 2002, 2006; Whyte, 2002, 2006; Quinn, 2000; Walsh, 2006). In the absence of entrenched constitutional rights to disability services, the impetus very much lies with elected representatives and government initiatives in the field.

December 2001 witnessed the publication of a bill which, according to the government, would deliver on key recommendations of the Commission on the Status of People with Disabilities (1996).[2] However, the Disability Bill 2001 was withdrawn in February 2002 following opposition from disability groups and disability rights campaigners. It could be argued that the series of public protests and meetings that greeted the draft law heralded the arrival of a disabled people's civil rights movement in Ireland. The Supreme Court judgment in Sinnott,[3] which had been issued the previous summer, cemented political mobilisation and attracted media attention and public support, rivalled only by the notorious High Court decision on reproductive rights in X.[4] These events perhaps demonstrate how adverse litigation outcomes may in fact propel a social movement forward (Hunt, 1990).

The key stumbling block was Section 47, which in effect provided that no element of the legislation could be enforced before a court. 'The Disability Bill appeared to be an attempt to restrict the use of the courts system to vindicate rights where agreed actions were not forthcoming' (Toolan, 2003a: 180). Following a protest meeting held outside Dublin's Mansion House, the Cabinet first announced its intention to revise the draft legislation, then decided to jettison it entirely.[5] Human Rights Commissioner Gerard Quinn (2003: 3) rightly commented that '[t]he question of legal remedies has become a test of whether proposed legislation is rights-based or not'.

The collapse of the 2001 Bill put disability rights firmly on the political agenda: the Disability Legislation Consultation Group (DLCG), a body established from representatives of eight umbrella disability organisations working in close association with the National Disability Authority (NDA), undertook a nation-wide consultation process. In February 2003 the Group's recommendations were published in the form of a report entitled *Equal Citizens: Proposals for Core Elements of Disability Legislation.* This report explicitly adopts a rights-based approach:

> The DLCG consider that the right to independent needs assessment should result in services that are made available *as a right* for people with disabilities. These services should be identified to meet the needs set out in the Statement of Need. In the event of services not being available a programme of measures should be put in place in order to realise these services within an established timeframe. [emphasis added] (DLCG, 2003: 18).

September 2004 witnessed the launch of the government's National Disability Strategy with a revived draft Disability Bill at its core.[6] While most disability groups acknowledged improvements on its predecessor, the 2004 Bill was generally not well received. Within weeks of its publication the DLCG produced a document outlining fundamental flaws in the proposed legislation, reflecting the disillusionment felt throughout the Irish disability sector.[7] While most disability groups acknowledged improvements on its predecessor, the 2004 Bill was generally not well recieved (Irish Times, 2004b). On 8 February 2005 an alliance of 12 disability groups held a public meeting attended by over 700 people and chaired by the President of the Irish Human Rights Commission (IHRC), which sought ten key changes to the draft legislation (*Irish Times*, 2005).

The fact that the proposed legislation did not really secure access to legal remedies was again a chief cause of concern. During the Dáil debates, the government's response to this criticism was to the effect that legal rights would divert resources allocated for service provision into the pockets of lawyers. Taoiseach, Bertie Ahern, famously quipped that the Disability Bill was meant to be 'rights-based but not lawyer-led'.[8] Arguing that litigation is an inevitable feature of any rights-based model, the contention was that disability rights are better served by introducing robust policy measures but without providing for review by courts.[9] This view underlies the government's disability strategy as expounded in the Disability Act 2005, which was signed into law on 8 July 2005 and is being progressively implemented.[10] In essence, the Act confers a right on disabled Irish citizens to have their needs assessed, but no enforceable right to any of the services that may flow from such an assessment. Further, although provision is made for several internal appeal mechanisms, there is no recourse to legal remedies in case of substantial disagreement between clients and providers about the interpretation of needs or service provision.

If it is the case, as we suggested in the introduction, that political disagreement about the role of courts in part masks a deeper uncertainty about the nature and form of disability rights, a better understanding of the latter might offer a first step towards resolving or at least clarifying the conflict between the different parties. This means we now must turn our attention to a conceptual and normative discussion of disability rights.

Disability Rights: Needs Assessment and Service Delivery

As part of a broader strategy of combating oppression and improving social and political participation, disability theorists and advocates in recent years have increasingly invoked the notion of *disability rights* (Barnes & Oliver, 1995; Charlton, 1998; Clements & Read, 2003). A rights-based approach contrasts with the prevailing social welfare model, in which goods and services are granted to disabled people by public authorities (Waddington & Diller, 2002).[11] The disability rights perspective is meant to enshrine disabled people's entitlements in law, allowing individuals to actively claim their rights through a set of legal remedies. Advocates of the rights-based approach maintain that the social welfare model fails to safeguard and promote the moral standing of disabled individuals in society in large part because the voice of disabled individuals has too little weight in the decision-making process. As Jenny Morris (1997: 54) points out, '[e]mpowerment means choice and control'. Failure to employ a rights-based approach not only jeopardises the adequate delivery of much-needed goods and services but in essence affirms the second-tier citizenship status of disabled people in modern society. It is no surprise, then, that disability movements are often referred to as the 'last civil rights movement' (Driedger, 1989).

Justiciable disability rights have not only permeated the discourse of theorists and advocates; in recent years they have become the mainstay of political and legislative initiatives pertaining to various aspects of disability policy. The least contested legally enforceable right, that of protection from discriminatory treatment, is now standard across the European Union Member States, and in comparable polities including Australia, Canada, New Zealand and the USA (Jolls, 2001; Breslin & Yee, 2002; EU Network of Independent Experts on Disability Discrimination, 2004; Lawson & Gooding, 2005). And developments within nation states are mirrored by increased recognition of disabled people's rights at supranational level (Degener & Quinn, 2002) culminating in the recent adoption of the United Nations Convention on the Rights of Persons with Disabilities.

The Irish government's commitment to the idea of disability rights appears to align with the developing situation in theoretical discourse and international practice, but there remains confusion what the idea itself refers to. In its appraisal of the draft law, the Irish Human Rights Commission (IHRC: 2004) applied international human rights benchmarks to highlight procedural and substantive areas of concern, but the complex question of how various universal norms are given effect in specific contexts allow divergent understandings of compliance with disability rights to co-exist (Galligan & Sandler, 2004). Two very different interpretations or models of disability rights have come to dominate the Irish debate. We outline each in turn and then suggest how their perceived deficits offer useful insight into a third model.

In the Disability Act 2005, disability rights boil down to a statutory entitlement to an assessment of health and education needs.[12] The ensuing Assessment Report includes a statement about the nature and extent of a person's disability (if any), the health and education needs arising from such a disability, and the services deemed appropriate to meet those needs as well as an indication of the timescale for delivery. The Assessment Report is then translated into a Service Statement which includes information regarding the practicability of providing the required services and the financial resources available. The view of the government, both implied in the Act and made explicit when commenting on the disability strategy, is that the new legislation is rights-based precisely because it *guarantees,* by means of a statutory entitlement, that each and every disabled individual in Ireland is entitled to a process of having his or her needs assessed.[13]

Several assumptions underpin this perspective. On the one hand, there is an assumption that without a systematic process of needs assessment, it is impossible for a disability policy to deliver adequate services. A system of 'categorical' service delivery – that is, service delivery based on the *type* of disability, without taking into account personal circumstances – produces both false positives and false negatives: some disabled individuals will receive services they neither need nor want, while others fail to get hold of the services they require (Toolan, 2003b). An individualised needs assessment procedure would ensure that needs are evaluated on a personal basis, targeting service delivery to those who effectively require it.

However, the latter point is critically dependent on the further assumption that, once the right to needs assessment is properly institutionalised, adequate service delivery will follow. This assumption has been challenged by the disability sector as being both simplistic and lacking in credibility (Forum of People with Disabilities, 2004; National Parents' and Siblings' Alliance, 2005). There is considerable concern amongst disability advocates that there are too many bottlenecks obstructing a fluid transmission of needs assessment into service delivery. Having a right to needs assessment is still a long way from having a guaranteed right to the services this assessment calls for.

There are at least two obvious ways in which needs assessment may fail to generate adequate service delivery. First, the needs assessment itself may not be accurate or at least contested by the disabled person being assessed. Second, even if an assessment appropriately indicates a particular service is needed, local contingencies – notably, resource limitations – may intervene such that the disabled person fails to receive a service despite having his statutory right to a needs assessment fully respected. In particular, as Mike Oliver (1996: 71) observes, a 'fundamental problem with needs-assessment is that it is going to take place in the context of fixed budgets'. To foreshadow the analysis below, the fact that the Disability Act 2005 makes a formal distinction between Assessment Reports and Service Statements, which contain qualifications as to practicability and resource availability, clearly demonstrates the contingent nature of the assessment impacting on actual service delivery. For the disability sector, needs assessment is simply too weak a focal point to enshrine a robust set of disability rights; consequently, the government's interpretation of a rights-based policy as framed through needs assessment remains contested.

In their critique of the Irish government's stance, the disability sector typically advances a more expansive version of disability rights. The acid test of rights-based legislation is whether a disabled person has a (statutory) right to have her needs met, effectively shifting the rights focus from needs assessment directly onto service delivery. For proponents of this expansive interpretation a disability policy is rights-based if (and only if) it safeguards that disabled people's needs are *effectively met*, not merely assessed. This interpretation has been criticised by the Irish government as well as by a number of researchers who believe it to be both confused in principle and counter-productive in practice.

The main problem is that a right to effective service delivery is potentially open-ended, which in turns gives rise to two concerns. First, such rights are potentially *economically infeasible* because they could conceivably entail ever-expanding demands on limited resources. The problem many opponents of open-ended rights see is the following: rights depend on resources but both the number of rights and the amount of available resources are variable; as proliferation sets in more rights require protection, which in turn demands more resources being diverted to rights protection. Stephen Holmes and Cass Sunstein (1999: 94) emphasise that '[t]aking rights seriously means taking scarcity seriously'. Consequently, either we make do with the available resources by economising on the rights we effectively ensure, or the levels at which we protect a set of rights; alternatively, we divert resources spent elsewhere to securing disability rights. The former is not an option under the expansive rights view, while the latter is possible but runs into the further objection that 'overstatement [of the absoluteness of rights] can create problems too, and an insistence that rights are absolute may lead to the over-protection of some rights to the detriment of others that have an even greater claim' (Holmes & Sunstein, 1999: 103). This raises questions of justice or fairness regarding competing claims on rights-protection.

Second, guaranteed service delivery might be considered *undemocratic* if the goal of ensuring disability rights conflicts with other values that a democratic community holds dear, including the power of legislators to set social and economic policy. The democratic objection is especially forceful when introducing *legally enforceable* rights to a range of disability services, which it is argued implies a shift of political control from the legislator to the courts because such disability services can no longer be revoked or revised by the democratic majority (Nolan, 2003; O'Donnell, 2003; more generally Waldron, 1999).[14]

The previous discussion suggests that even where both parties genuinely agree that disabled Irish citizens are entitled to have access to services as a matter of right, the precise nature and content of disability rights remain disputed. The Irish government adopts a perspective that proceeds by instituting a statutory right to needs assessment, but at the same time allowing service delivery to depend on the availability of resources and organisational capacity (both of which are assumed to be relatively fixed and determined prior to needs assessment). The disability sector asserts that an assessment of needs must also imply the right to have those needs met. This in turn implies that a government that formally endorses disability rights ought to commit to providing a level of resources sufficient to delivering needed services.[15] Each model privileges a single focal point – needs assessment and service delivery, respectively – and suggests that the ultimate judgement as to whether disability policy is genuinely rights-based depends on how well it enshrines and protects rights at the respective point. Given the normative and practical concerns raised with respect to each model, it is hard to see how we can objectively opt between one or the other. One solution would be to give up on disability rights altogether and return to the much-maligned social welfare model. Instead, we propose a model of disability rights as the right to challenge decisions in relation to needs assessment and service delivery (the 'right to challenge'' for short). In the next section we outline its main advantages compared to the previous models. The following section then evaluates the Disability Act 2005 from the perspective of the right to challenge.

Disability Rights as the Right to Challenge

To accommodate the problems identified with the two models of disability rights that feature in the Irish debate we propose an alternative model organised around a robust and justiciable *right to challenge*, which we argue is capable of meeting the main concerns of both the government and the disability sector. In this section we outline our model by discussing in turn what the right to challenge implies, the main properties that have to be met when institutionalising the right to challenge and, above all, why we believe the right to challenge is preferable to the other models.

What Does the Right to Challenge Imply?

The first question to address is what aspect of disability policy the right to challenge is meant to contest. Although there are many points at which decisions are made that affect a disabled person's access to public services, the right to challenge primarily addresses the two focal points identified in the previous section, namely the assessment of needs and the delivery of services.

To elaborate, in the first place a disabled person (or her advocate) should be able to challenge the process of needs assessment. Needs assessment is a crucial gateway for access to services, as explained above, and forms a natural point for challenging key decisions regarding services. Having the ability and power to directly contest the administrative evaluation of the extent of disablement, the needs incurred by the disability and the services required to remedy those needs, in effect puts the perspectives of the disabled service user and the person conducting the assessment on a more equal footing. Moreover, the right to challenge thus affirms the view that the assessment of an individual's needs is not an objective enterprise, but instead unavoidably reflects a measure of subjectivity grounded in a person's particular context, history and overall lived experience (but see Doyal & Gough, 1991 for reservations about needs subjectivity).

The right and ability to challenge the process of needs assessment also affirms the fact that neither party necessarily has a superior outlook on what constitutes an appropriate set of services for a particular person, and that the final assessment ideally represents the informed perspectives of both service user and assessment officer. This last claim may be controversial to radical disability advocates, who typically favour the user's perspective as the decisive voice in assessment of needs and required services, but also to the establishment of expert health care and education practitioners, who regard needs assessment a matter of objective measurement. However, in our view needs assessment requires both the perspective of the lived experience and that of the disembodied expert who offers a more general outlook based on statistics and aggregate data across different persons and lives, and the right to challenge is designed to balance both perspectives.[16]

In addition, disabled people should be entitled to challenge the process of service delivery. Specifically, they should have the right to challenge the quality of service, the timeframe for delivery in accordance with the needs assessment, the level of resources committed to a particular service scheme and, arguably, even future commitments by service providers (including local and national government) pertaining to resource inputs and effective delivery capacity. At this level, the disabled service user engages head-on with the supply side of service delivery by challenging any failure to provide services in accordance with the agreed needs assessment. Note that the right to challenge does not in itself ensure a right to service delivery, but instead offers the service user a mechanism to contest the grounds upon which service provision has been (partially) refused and in turn assert her own reasons for insisting upon them. This exchange of reasons is a crucial component of a contestatory mechanism like the right to challenge. We return to this point below.

By allowing service users to challenge both needs assessment and service delivery our proposed model avoids tying the notion of a disability right to either focal point. Instead, the model vindicates the importance of service user involvement at *any* juncture at which decisions are made that affect access to services. The model also explicitly endorses the view that a rights-based disability policy must reflect a form of public agreement – or at least an agreement that reflects conditions of public reason (see below) – across the whole process of decision-making, from assessing needs to delivering services. On this view, participation of service users in some robust form is a *conditio sine qua non* for a rights-based policy on disability services.

What Are the Central Properties of a Right to Challenge?

There are a number of ways in which a robust right to challenge could be institutionalised. This variation is a strength when we consider questions of political feasibility and implementation, so we are hesitant to offer a particularly restrictive institutional model. Nonetheless it is worth noting that the regular court system need not be the primary forum of redress: for instance, various forms of tribunals have been established to resolve disputes throughout common law jurisdictions (Richardson & Genn, 2007). In the Irish context the Ombudsman system[17] and the various employment rights bodies, most notably the Equality Tribunal, offer interesting templates for relatively expedient and inexpensive resolution of grievances. Whatever form is employed, in our view there is a number of properties that must be present for the right to challenge to deliver on its intended goals. These are: individual mechanisms for contestation, justiciability, and fair proceduralism.

One key feature of the right to challenge is that it entails an *individual* right, allowing a disabled service user or her advocate to challenge decisions in a private capacity. In his work on contestatory democracy Philip Pettit (1997; 1999; 2000) has argued that, in a democracy, mechanisms of collective decision-making must always be complemented by some means by which individual citizens can contest policy. Acknowledging the importance of collective action for influencing political decision-making or the presence of major coordination benefits when addressing concerns about disabled people as a group does not invalidate the notion that these collective mechanisms cannot fully capture the features of an individualised right to challenge. In the first place, as is evident from observing diversity within the disability movement itself, representation only captures part of the specific reality faced by a disabled service user.[18] Second, groups and organisations are subject to political dynamics that might effectively curtail an individual's capacity to contest a particular decision. In the Irish case, consultation for policy-making is highly coordinated and regulated through the inclusion of select representative groups in social partnerships. As has been argued by several scholars, such a mechanism produces exclusion and silences perspectives through the very process that is aimed at embracing broader perspectives and diverse opinions (Baker *et al.*, 2004: 91–95, 111–113; Murphy, 2006). An individual right to challenge is a necessary and useful democratic complement to any corporatist scheme, including social partnership mechanisms. Finally, an individual right to challenge produces symbolic value of a sort that can never be fully substituted by a collective mechanism: a disabled service user being able to express her particular viewpoint in a case of disagreement with a needs assessment or service delivery is a key feature of what it is to have a right. We return to this point briefly below.

Second, we argue that the right to challenge requires robust *access to the legal system*. The main reason for making the right to challenge justiciable is to ensure that grievances can be heard in a properly independent forum. As we show in the next section, the Disability Act 2005 fails in this respect. But justiciability as conceived under the right to challenge is of a different character to the justiciability of substantive disability rights, and objections to the latter, if sustainable, do not apply in the same way to the former.[19] A justiciable right to challenge is not undemocratic since it does not impose substantive policies that might run counter to the policy agreed by the democratic majority. Instead, the right to challenge asserts a legally protected power for disabled service users to enquire into the reasons for not delivering on the services sought; the validity of these reasons in turn are assessed against the views of the democratic community as expressed in constitutional or legislative documents, policy statements and political debates. Recent work on deliberative democracy emphasises the importance of reasons, in particular public reasons, as a core component of a democratic process of decision-making (Gutmann & Thompson, 1996), and the right to challenge should be regarded as a mechanism that extends deliberation into policy-making with respect to disability services.

Nor is the right to challenge subject to the charge of inefficiency because it does not automatically endorse or promote rights expansion. While it is true that the right to challenge may end up contesting current resource priorities – both within the field of disability services and as between larger social projects – this does not imply an inefficient arrangement. The right to challenge might even allow for a more efficient prioritisation within a particular budget constraint, simply because it offers a mechanism for service users and service delivery agencies to coordinate priorities across services. Why not treat challenges to needs assessment or service delivery as a source of relevant policy information, allowing the various stakeholders to adapt to each other's positions, thus coordinating the development of resource priorities and organisational capacities across time to accommodate the rapidly changing situation on the ground? Looked at this way, the right to challenge is an important instrument for *enhancing* efficiency in disability policy.

Of course one key objection to justiciable rights is that it eats into the available resources by diverting them from actual policy delivery to defraying legal expenses. As the Irish government was eager to point out, it is important that resources are spent on providing disabled citizens with services, not on subsidising the legal establishment. There are several replies to this objection. In the first place, it remains to be seen whether a justiciable right to challenge will indeed lead to a litigation culture; it is equally plausible to assume that the right to challenge will produce a select number of high-profile cases with subsequent impact on the way administrators assess needs or organise service delivery as well as on the expectations of disabled people. If anything, current practice in Ireland supports our supposition rather than the nightmare scenario advanced by the government. The vast proportion of discrimination complaints referred to the Equality Tribunal, for instance, are resolved at that level with few filtering into the regular court system.[20] If the right to challenge operates largely because of the possibility of using the legal system, the legal costs incurred are neither prohibitive nor unjustified. Further, it is not unreasonable to think that disabled people themselves might prefer to divert a part of the resources to embedding the right to challenge in disability policy if this provides them with a robust means to participate into the relevant decision-making processes (see also the point about dignity below).

A third key feature of the right to challenge is its commitment to what we term *fair proceduralism.*[21] Fair proceduralism sets itself apart from substantive fairness in that decisions are considered fair when arrived at through a procedure that itself is considered fair; that is to say, outcomes are fair because the procedure is fair, not because of some intrinsic properties of the outcome itself.[22] However, the procedures at hand must satisfy a set of substantive conditions. Procedures that merely legitimise a particular outcome because there is *a* procedure in place constitute a fetishistic form of empty formalism. Although intuitively plausible and a mainstay of modern democratic thought, fair proceduralism nevertheless raises important questions when applied to the context of disability services.

To begin with, the right to challenge, as we envisage it, is procedurally fair insofar as it substitutes a right to a particular service with the right to hear and contest the reasons for a particular needs assessment or service delivery decision. But why should this be deemed an acceptable arrangement, since it might lead to a decision being challenged, resources being spent on advocacy, tribunal or even court proceedings, and in the end make no real difference in terms of a disabled citizen's access to services? There are several replies to this objection. One could point out that even this process expresses an important value, namely that of recognition of disabled service users as key participants in the process of deciding on appropriate service delivery and the dignity associated with it.

However, thinking through the dynamics of the right to challenge offers a more powerful reply. While there are some concerns that the proposed system might fail to secure the fulfilment of even the most urgent needs, there are reasons to believe that the proposed right to challenge when robustly instituted will actually deliver a core content of disability rights as required under international human rights law (see further below). In the first place, the outcomes of individually exercised rights to challenge serve as important precedents informing both future legal and even bureaucratic decision-making. Given that such precedents act as a binding framework, individual claimants, respondents, and their advocates or legal representatives, will put a lot of stock in the body of legal decisions already in place. Bureaucratic decision-makers likewise will try to pre-empt challenges and adapt their decisions partly on the basis of the cases already under review. A process of continuing mutual engagement between the various stakeholders effectively establishes a cumulative perspective on what is to count as justified reasons or legitimate complaints, respectively, when deliberating on a failure in service provision.[23]

Further, the right to challenge invites all parties to present the reasons for their particular views, but the assessment of those reasons will undoubtedly be heavily influenced by pre-existing legislation, policy and even political debates. Thus the right to challenge does not operate in a moral, legal or policy vacuum, but is informed by the evolving standards promoted by domestic and supranational institutions such as the Council of Europe and the United Nations. Norms that enjoy a binding legal status will have a direct purchase within the review process. Finally, we must not underestimate the importance of ensuring that administrative agencies offer genuine reasons for making decisions in terms of promoting accountability and overall responsiveness of policy-makers to the democratic will as expressed in law and policy. Failure to offer reasons that are publicly deemed acceptable is likely to trigger popular indignation and anticipating this response offers an important administrative (and political) incentive to take the needs and views of disabled service users much more seriously. In short, the right to challenge may not offer a simple indication of what substantive rights will be secured, but in our view it nevertheless becomes an important mechanism for ensuring that governments take their responsibilities towards their disabled citizens seriously when considering access to public services.

Fair proceduralism requires that certain conditions are met to ensure procedures remain fair throughout.[24] Applied to the present context we believe there are two that must be firmly put in place. On the one hand, the right to challenge requires a system of disability advocates to ensure that all disabled citizens have not merely the formal right but also the effective opportunity to challenge decisions (Clements & Read, 2003: 41–46). On the other hand, the right to challenge requires *independent* redress processes if it is to become an effective and fair mechanism for balancing reasons. Independence here must be ensured by formally separating the process of challenge from the processes that determine needs assessment and service delivery. We will return to this point in the next section. Independence must also be substantially ensured in that the process of challenge must take a principled unbiased attitude to the different parties in the dispute, although not to the *reasons* brought forward as explained above in relation to the role of legal and policy precedents.

There is understandable scepticism about the capacity of legal action to bring about change (Engel & Munger, 2003; Roulstone, 2003; Runswick-Cole, 2007), but in our view this concern does not invalidate the right to challenge as such; rather it sets conditions for its effective implementation. If properly implemented along the lines suggested here, a right to challenge may become a powerful tool in the arsenal of those concerned with securing fair access to disability services.

Why Advocate a Right to Challenge Model?

Having outlined the key features of the right to challenge, we can now turn to its justification. One possible justification is pragmatic: the right to challenge takes an intermediary position between the oppositional models discussed in the previous section, with increased scope for political compromise for future disability policy reform. Because the right to challenge offers a substantial measure of empowerment to disabled service users and their advocates we might expect the disability movement to endorse this model; similarly because it falls foul of demanding substantive service provisions as a matter of right, we suggest many of the government's concerns about expansive disability rights do not apply and one might expect their resistance to be equally mollified.

Nevertheless, the main reason for adopting this model is not to do with its prospects for political compromise but with a particular understanding of what fairness and social justice in relation to access to public services requires. The right to challenge does not offer disabled individuals the sort of expansive right to a particular service delivery sought by radical disability advocates. Instead, it acknowledges explicitly that there may be legitimate reasons to deny that a particular disability implies a need that generates a duty for the state to meet at all costs. Most importantly, it acknowledges that legitimate reasons may exist that override the entitlement to a particular service *even where a genuine need has been identified.* This follows from the fact that a right to challenge invites both parties to submit reasons for their respective position in the disagreement, which then requires adjudication in favour of one or the other. But it also insists that, as a matter of respect and recognition of moral and political status, the disabled person who is denied such a delivery is entitled to hear the reasons against meeting her needs. In this regard, the right to challenge again moves considerably beyond the right to needs assessment; it could even be argued that in terms of recognition, the right to challenge performs at least as well as an expansive right to service delivery without running into similar problems.

The philosophical foundation behind this position is familiar in political theory. Most recently it has been developed in Philip Pettit's republican ideal of *contestatory democracy* (Pettit, 1999, 2000). For Pettit democratic decision-making cannot merely rely on electoral systems but requires mechanisms by which citizens can contest decisions taken in between electoral rounds. Where electoral systems bind citizens to policies initiated by representative candidates, contestatory democracy offers a much more fine-grained system of (dis)approving particular decisions, options or actions. According to Pettit, broad measures of effective contestation are a prerequisite for genuine political freedom and participation. This model of contestatory democracy fits well with one crucial concern throughout the literature on disability policy, namely that disabled people are often relegated to second-class citizenship and denied full social and political participation in society (Charlton, 1998). The right to challenge in part shifts the balance back to a state where disabled people are not mere recipients of policy, as in the social welfare model, but are regarded as political partners in policy design and delivery. Being able to challenge decisions is one of the apt ways of making oneself visible, democratically speaking, and therefore rightly counted as amongst the most important political rights.

The right to challenge receives further support from its positive impact on three values that take central place in disability policy: dignity, empowerment, and publicity. As we have argued elsewhere, these values are intricately linked with the justiciability of disability rights (De Wispelaere & Walsh, 2005). Because we believe an effective right to challenge will in fact require the provision of legal remedies, the right to challenge is closely tied in with these values.

For disability rights activists, the *level* of assistance or services accessed is not all that matters; depending on how they are organised, services express a symbolic value. The core value at issue is human *dignity*. Human dignity is both inward-looking and outward-looking when considered in relation to disability services. Looking inward, dignified service provision allows the disabled person to retain his/her self-respect and pursue her life goals in an autonomous fashion when the latter offers the opportunity to actively participate in a process that highly determines the options for leading her life in a decent and satisfying manner (Engel & Munger, 2003). Dignity is tied in with participation. Looking outward, dignified service provision signals 'recognition respect' for the status of the disabled person as a moral person (Darwall, 1977).[25] By granting a disabled person a (justiciable) right to challenge, society promotes both inward looking and outward looking dignity since that person's moral status is safeguarded even in cases where service delivery itself is hampered simply because the option to *claim* one's entitlement to service delivery remains in place at all times. For legal philosopher Joel Feinberg (1980: 155), '[t]he activity of claiming, finally, as much as any other thing, makes for self-respect and respect for others, gives a sense to the notion of personal dignity'.

Next, disability rights advocates often talk in terms of the need to *empower* disabled individuals in order to counteract the various forms of oppression they suffer – wittingly or unwittingly – at the hands of the non-disabled population (Campbell & Oliver, 1996; Morris, 1997; Charlton, 1998). In addition to global, systemic forms of empowerment, the capacity to empower individuals at the micro level in their day-to-day exchange with case workers and other expert professionals is of the utmost importance to disabled persons. Where case workers typically occupy a power position vis-à-vis the disabled person, making the latter dependent on the goodwill and discretion of the case worker (Kemp, 2002), a right to challenge may balance out this inequality in favour of the disabled person. Interestingly, in many cases it is often sufficient that the case worker is aware of the proverbial stick behind the door, provided by a right to challenge the case worker's assessment or other actions/decisions where deemed fit, for her attitude to adjust.[26] But where this is not sufficient, an effective right to challenge has the power to countenance inequalities at the coalface of service delivery.

A final consideration brings us back to the politics of disability services. One of the crucial aspects of the right to challenge, especially when properly embedded in the legal system, is the fact that it 'tracks' reasons for making a decision regarding a needs assessment or service statement. The arguments informing a particular decision are in the public domain and can be traced throughout the various stages of decision-making. Such a perspective fits very well with recent work in political philosophy embracing that of Rawls and contemporary theories of deliberative democracy, which emphasises the crucial importance of publicity and public reason in the justification of social practices (Gutmann & Thompson, 1996). Under these conditions reasons for decision-making are open to public scrutiny, which in turn will positively influence the use of reasons that are acceptable to a wider constituency, as opposed to the reasoning carried out internally by bureaucratic agencies (see Richardson, 2002 for a general discussion). Publicly available reasoning then serves to mediate amongst the different perspectives and interests surrounding service delivery decisions by insisting that arguments should be brought to the fore in an attempt to reach an acceptable compromise, or else a democratic way of agreeing-to-disagree.[27] The right to challenge offers interesting opportunities for all parties to engage in an open debate about the services a disabled person is entitled to, given other legitimate claims on scarce resources. Furthermore, a decision-making process that can be publicly challenged leaves little room for political blame-shifting strategies (Hood & Lodge, 2006), such as pledging symbolic allegiance to a particular cause while leaving it up to bureaucrats to figure out the details – the sort of details that make all the difference if you are on the receiving end of the policy at hand.

Evaluating the 2005 Disability Act

In this section we examine the extent to which the Disability Act 2005 can be described as adopting a rights-based approach to the provision of services for disabled people, as interpreted through our proposed framework.

As outlined above, the Act offers one substantive right, namely the right of a disabled person to have her needs assessed. It should be noted at the outset that the definition of disability and the parameters of the needs assessment are both likely to generate problems for disabled people when the Act becomes operational. Section 7, for instance, anchors the needs assessment to health and education needs 'occasioned by the disability and the health services or education services (if any) required to meet those needs'. This leaves out crucial areas of public service provision, including notably housing provision. Other services pivotal to independent living, such as access to a personal assistant, may be included *provided they can be regarded as health-related.* Furthermore, Section 2 defines disability in a manner that excludes transient conditions and requires that a disabled person meet an impairment threshold substantially restricting their capacity to engage in occupational, social or cultural activities. These qualifications mean that, for example, a person who experiences a given mental health problem on a cyclical basis may have difficulty establishing eligibility. These problems are well-documented by the Irish disability sector and were signalled to the government in the consultation phase (Forum of People with Disabilities, 2004; Namhi, 2004; Schizophrenia Ireland, 2004).

The needs assessment will be undertaken without regard to cost or capacity to deliver the identified services. However, the resultant Assessment Report is subsequently translated into a Service Statement, which will take into account the 'practicability' of providing the services and the financial resources available. Clauses such as 'not possible or practical to provide', 'appropriate allocations', 'availability of resources', 'budget priorities' are threaded through Part 2 of the Act. It is clear from the outset that funds are not ring-fenced so that other priorities may overtake the resources demands generated by disability services (Civil Public and Services Union, 2004; IHRC, 2004, 2005: 81–82). For disability rights advocates, the lack of legally earmarked funding means the Act cannot be regarded as rights-based (Crowley, 2006).

Note that, since no minimum floor or essential guaranteed level of services is set, the Act departs from the stance adopted by the DLCG (2003) and the Irish Human Rights Commission (IHRC, 2004). Both positions had been informed by international human rights law, which obligates governments to furnish a minimum threshold or core content of socio-economic rights while also committing to progressively realising higher levels of provision (Eide *et al.*, 2001; IHRC, 2005). Further, the conditions that will render the availability of appropriate services a reality are relegated to Sectoral Plans that six government departments are obliged to prepare, demonstrating how key disability issues are to be addressed.[28] Although the Plans must be drafted following consultation with the disability sector, their content and the scope of the commitments undertaken is ultimately determined by department officials.

It should be noted that Part 3 of the Act does provide for accessibility benchmarks or standards. Sections 32–40 of the Act, for instance, supply general guidelines as to the areas that should be addressed under each plan, specify that an internal complaints system should be established by all six departments, and provide an oversight role for the Ombudsman in relation to implementation of the sectoral plans and the related general accessibility measures contained in Part 3. In turn, Sections 25–28 oblige public bodies to make public buildings, services and information accessible to disabled people within set timeframes, but again obligations are qualified by considerations as to cost, practicability and appropriateness. These benchmarks are complemented by a Code of Practice, published by the National Disability Authority, but these too leave intact a wide margin of discretion (NDA, 2006).

By and large, these guidelines are typically too general and do not provide any real opportunities for input – let alone challenge – on the part of disabled people. Although the Ombudsman may ultimately hear complaints about failure to implement general standards, there is no scope for *individual* legal redress on the part of disabled persons in the design stage, which violates a core requirement of Pettit's model of contestation.[29] In all cases, duties are tempered by conditions of practicality or resource constraints without any requirement that efforts should be directed towards improving practicality or increasing funding. It is obvious from the previous discussion that the Act fails to secure, in any robust manner, the services sought by campaigners. In addition, it performs poorly when considering how it might meet our model of disability rights by putting in place an effective right to challenge.

Commenting on the draft legislation, one of Ireland's principal disability rights groups argued that the envisaged redress process amounted to a *bureaucratic superstructure* that would waste resources and 'tie disabled people and their families into a bureaucratic battle with service providers, state agencies etc.' (Forum of People with Disabilities, 2004). There is ample reason to suggest these fears will be realised since the complexity of the administrative scheme at the heart of the Act is absolutely staggering, and any attempt at challenging a needs assessment or service delivery entails moving through several layers of *internal* review. The needs assessment is to be carried out by a Health Services Executive (HSE) official and the Service Statement drawn up by a HSE-appointed *liaison officer*.[30] Section 14 provides that a person can lodge a complaint about a determination that they do not have a disability, the standard of the assessment, the contents of the Service Statement, or a failure to provide the services outlined. But the complaint will be heard by a *complaints officer*, who is also a HSE employee, and who will either attempt to resolve the matter informally or else investigate further – although the ensuing recommendation is again contingent on the availability of resources. Adverse findings can then be further referred to an *appeals officer*. However, appeals officers are yet again civil servants, this time appointed by the Department of Health and

Children. At this point the decision is final and can be appealed only on a point of law to the High Court.[31]

Several aspects of this complicated process interfere with the right to challenge. First, the *substance* of any civil servant's decision is not open to review by an independent court or tribunal. Internal grievance processes are commonplace in the field of social provision (Cousins, 2002; Cowan & Halliday, 2003; Kenna, 2006).[32] But requiring a complainant to pass through three such tiers before a complaint is externalised, however, is not. The central point here is that a disabled individual is *effectively prohibited from* accessing an independent arbiter, such as the Ombudsman or the regular court system until the internal review procedures have been exhausted, which serves as a genuinely 'dis-abling' procedure. For these reasons alone, the Disability Act's enforcement scheme scores low on the dignity and empowerment factors we identified earlier as valuable properties of a rights-based approach.[33]

A further problem arises when we consider the value of publicity. Each stage on the path to service provision is heard in private and there is no provision under the legislation for publicising the reasons for the decisions made at various junctures. Provision is made for the publication of an annual report which addresses the 'aggregate needs identified in assessment reports prepared including an indication of the periods of time ideally required for the provision of the services, the sequence of such provision and an estimate of the cost of such provision' (Disability Act 2005, Section 13). A similar obligation is placed on each appeals officer, but no guidance is supplied as to the content of their report save that it should relate to the performance of her function under the Act (Disability Act 2005, Section 17). This level of publicity is inadequate because it only relates to 'aggregate needs', and does not offer genuine reasons for decisions but merely statements of needs identified, services provided and so on.

Avoidance of judicial oversight is a clear government imperative. As we have seen, control of the assessment, complaints and appeals procedures rests exclusively with the service providers: that is, the HSE and the Department of Health. The Taoiseach and various government Ministers have continually asserted that precluding access to the courts is designed to ensure that the costs associated with litigation do not drain the funds available for service provision. Earlier we have outlined several counter arguments. The most obvious one is that recourse to the courts only becomes an issue when rights provided for by law are violated, which hardly makes for a good argument against the use of courts. In addition, we argue that access to courts is essential to incentivise bureaucratic agents to take disability rights seriously, not treat them as a mere afterthought in a resource-limited policy context.

To revisit the question of institutionalisation briefly, the redress system for discrimination law claims operated by the Equality Tribunal serves as an interesting counterpoint. It entails the immediate externalisation of a grievance and as a quasi-judicial forum the Tribunal is completely independent of any employer, service provider or for that matter civil society interests. Although hearings are held in private, decisions are published, with provision for anonymity made in sensitive cases such as those on disability and sexual orientation grounds. Two recent cases concerning the reasonable accommodation duty imposed on service providers under the Equal Status Acts 2000–2004, underscore how an independent forum can unearth and address flawed decision-making processes in the context of needs asssessment and service delivery.[34] In both instances, adherence to fair procedures and the elaboration of reasons for service refusal and inadequate service provision were central to the Tribunal's findings.

Paradoxically, the government's litigation-avoidance rationale as expounded through the Act is likely to have the opposite effect. Failure to guarantee a minimum level of services, and in particular to 'ECHR proof' the Act, will actually increase the likelihood of resort to judicial review. The ECHR Act 2003, in force since 31 December 2003, gives the European Convention on Human Rights an interpretive status within the Irish legal system and obliges public authorities to comply with the Convention in carrying out their functions. As jurisprudence develops both within the Strasbourg system and before the UK courts (Clements & Read, 2003; Gooding, 2003; Fredman, 2006; King, 2007), litigation seeking to test these precedents on the domestic front is inevitable.[35]

Further, poor drafting means that the relationship between the various disability laws now in place will necessarily be ironed out in civil actions. For example, it is at least arguable that the Act as a whole will undercut or compromise the potential of the reasonable accommodation provisions set out under the Equal Status Acts 2000-2004 (IHRC, 2004). A Tribunal may be tempted to conclude that an accommodation sought by a given claimant has by implication been removed from the scope of the equality legislation since the Disability Act 2005 now specifies the conditions under which the service in question is to be provided.[36] As suggested by the IHRC (2004: 22), these tensions could have been managed by inclusion of a provision to the effect that the Statute did not diminish the existing legal obligations of the government.[37]

The previous analysis clearly suggests that the Disability Act 2005 fails to meet the conditions for robust rights-based legislation in relation to disability services. The failure to provide secure access to public services is exacerbated by the fact that there is no genuine right to challenge assessment, service delivery or even the wider policy context, particularly resource commitments. This failure has important consequences in relation to the political status and participation of disabled individuals in modern Irish society. As suggested before, the right to challenge is the means par excellence for disabled people to contest popular perception, including *administrative* perception, about their needs in order to participate on equal terms in society. While the government may have raised legitimate concerns about expanding costs and competing claims for scarce resources, it has responded to this concern by drafting legislation which pushes legal proceduralism to its limits. Behind the complex layers of assessment, complaints and appeals procedures, an empty formalism looms large. This is in part because the processing of disabled people's claims throughout the Act remains a matter of administrative discretion, with no recourse to independent adjudication either as a substantive means of legal redress or even as a mechanism to incentivise the administrative decision-making process.[38] The structure of multiple layers of bureaucratic executives, often part of the same (or a similar) organisation, operating as internal checks upon each other's decisions clearly favours a lock-in of initial decisions.

Furthermore, at the end of the day, no firm commitments are made throughout the legislation in terms of addressing disabled people's needs in general. In terms of resource commitments, the Act has a strong conditionality built into its main provisions. The background conditions for enabling adequate service delivery are dependent, not on the Act itself, but on the Sectoral Plans, which are drawn up with a considerable amount of discretion and local autonomy, restricted only by general guidelines and at best weak oversight to ensure these match up with concerns of the disabled population in Ireland. One clear area of concern, from a rights-based perspective, is the fact that there is no right to challenge the resource commitments themselves. These are assumed to be fixed or given, and serve as the benchmarks against which subsequent service delivery demands are being evaluated. In terms of a commitment to disability services, this is highly contingent at best, vindicating the charge of empty formalism.

In response to legitimate concerns about expanding costs and balancing disability rights with competing demands on scarce resources, the government could have taken an alternative route. Instead of empty formalism it should have adopted the perspective of fair proceduralism, as proposed by a number of disability theorists (Silvers, 1998) and developed in this paper in the form of a justiciable right to challenge. Accepting there may exist multiple legitimate perspectives on what counts as a just distribution of resources in view of varying social needs, fair proceduralism asserts that legislation provides for a process of adequately ascertaining the reasons for granting or denying certain services. Most importantly, fair proceduralism remains impartial between the perspectives of service users and providers; where the Disability Act 2005 effectively sets strict boundaries around service provision, with no right to challenge the reasons for deciding on budgets this way rather than that, fair proceduralism implies that these wider background context to be scrutinised as well. In practice, this means that a process must be available for disabled individuals seeking needs assessment and service provision to engage with those assessing their needs and deciding on service delivery. This process may result in a variety of outcomes, ranging (in theory) from all needs being met to only minimal service provision, but in all cases the reasons for the outcome are publicly stated after a fair hearing or, in ideal circumstances, a genuine mutual deliberation of both parties. A democratic state that values the participation of its disabled citizens should not settle for anything less.

Conclusion

The Disability Act 2005 will frame disability policy in relation to public services in the Republic of Ireland for decades to come. The legislation is hailed by the government as a major achievement in securing disability rights in Ireland, but the disability sector remains unconvinced. In this article we evaluate the legislation and suggest that, while it undoubtedly will improve the status quo once fully implemented, the Act nevertheless represents a missed opportunity in terms of safeguarding disability rights in Ireland.

The current legislation centres around a conception of disability rights as the right to a needs assessment, which is clearly too weak to adequately recognise the moral and political status of disabled people in Ireland. An alternative conception of disability rights grounded in a justiciable right to challenge needs assessments and subsequent decisions pertaining to service delivery in our view offers both a sound theoretical basis for understanding disability rights and a practical guideline in terms of which direction future disability policy should take. The right to challenge promotes the status of disabled persons as genuine citizens of the Republic of Ireland and would also positively affect the standards of disability service delivery. Most importantly, it would enshrine a robust rights-based approach to disability services that meets the requirements of the disability sector without causing the level of rights essentialism the government is concerned about.

Notes

A previous version of this paper was presented at an academic seminar organised by Queen's University Belfast. We are grateful to the seminar participants for comments and suggestions, and for further written comments to Keith Breen, Cillian McBride, Jonathan Seglow and Mike Timms.

1. http://www.irishstatutebook.ie/2005/en/act/pub/0014/index.html
2. The Commission was established by the government in 1993, its 1996 report contained 402 recommendations aimed at addressing the inequalities faced by disabled people.
3. *Sinnott* v *Minister for Education* [2001] 2 IR 545.
4. *Attorney General* v *X* [1992] 1 IR 1.
5. http://www.rte.ie/news/2002/0219/disability.html
6. As discussed further below, other measures in the package are an advocacy system, which initially was to be implemented via the Comhairle Amendment Bill 2004. The legislation was withdrawn and surfaced again in the form of the Citizens Information Act 2007, Section 5 of which provides for the establishment of a 'personal advocacy service'; six 'Sectoral Plans' that commit several government departments to setting out steps that will realise enhanced access to various public services; and a multi-annual Investment Programme (http://www.justice.ie/en/JELR/Pages/WP07000539).
7. www.namhi.ie/legislation/documents/TenFundamentalFlaws-DisabilityBill-DLCG.doc
8. *Dáil Debates*, Vol. 597 No. 3, 9 February 2005.
9. Government opposition to justiciable socio-economic rights is not unique to the area of disability. General objections were voiced by the then Minister for Justice, Equality and Law Reform, Michael McDowell (McDowell, 2002).
10. In April–May of 2007 every household in the Republic received a booklet which outlines the National Disability Strategy and the timetable for its implementation. The word 'rights' features once in the 16-page document and only then in the context of the Citizens' Information Service. According to the section on 'Individual Assessment' children aged under five will be entitled to have their needs assessed from June 2007 and assessments will be in place for everyone else by 2011.
11. Barnes and Mercer (2003: 116– 117) suggest this divide mirrors the division between the strategy of employing civil rights in the US and that of enhancing the welfare state across Europe, while Morris (1997) pitches the distinction in terms of care versus empowerment.
12. Health in this case also covers other forms of personal social assistance, which are all administered by the Health Service Executive (HSE).

13. A recent report suggests that 14,380 people (56.0 per cent of the disabled population) require assessment for therapeutic intervention and rehabilitation services (O'Donovan & Doyle, 2007).
14. Elsewhere we have argued in more detail that the democratic objection can be addressed in favour of justiciable disability rights (De Wispelaere & Walsh, 2005). Recent work in constitutional theory such as that concerning 'democratic experimentalism' (Dorf & Sabel, 1998; Dorf, 2003) 'constitutional dialogue' (Hutchinson, 2004; Roach, 2004; Dixon, 2007), as well as the South African experience (Davis *et al.*, 2002; Kende, 2003; Pieterse, 2004), demonstrates that courts are capable of dealing with the complex policy considerations generated by disability services, in a manner that addresses democratic and competence-based objections to their involvement.
15. Disability advocates typically take a more relaxed approach, insisting that what they require is only that the most *urgent* needs will be met as a matter of right, with higher levels of provision being secured over time (e.g. DLCG, 2003). But this strategy either implies too little or too much. On the one hand it may not tell us enough about what minimal standards to adhere to in order to safeguard the legitimate claims of disabled people in the face of competing claims. On the other hand, disabled people may insist on claims that may no longer be justified, in light of legitimate competing social priorities, as part of their claims to having their needs met. In either case, the absence of a clear indication of what is to determine the content of minimal or urgent disability rights is problematic.
16. In practice, it is expected the right to challenge will shift the balance of power considerably in favour of the service users who are typically insufficiently consulted in processes of needs assessment and service design.
17. http://ombudsman.gov.ie/en/
18. Robert Drake (1999: 184) observes that 'advocacy and representation by non-disabled people may, on occasion, achieve improvements in the circumstances of disabled people', but insists 'there are, of course, no guarantees that they will, and the views and desires of disabled people can be filtered, distorted or vitiated'. Our point is that the same problems may arise even when disabled service users are represented by other disabled people, and that only an individualised right to challenge safeguards a person's access to services.
19. See Nolan (2003) and O'Donnell (2003) for concerns about justiciable rights.
20. See the Annual Reports of the Equality Tribunal: http:www.equalitytribunal.ie.
21. Anita Silvers (1998) proposes a theory of 'formal justice' in relation to disability, based on the view that disabled people should receive those services that allow them to take up fair opportunities to contribute to society on the same basis as non-disabled people. Although we adopt a more pluralistic account in that we expand on the sort of reasons we might accept for requiring the state to provide access to services to its disabled citizens, in part to accommodate persuasive criticisms explored in Pogge (2000), we share with Silvers the perspective that such a formal/procedural approach is required to resolve competing views on what counts as appropriate needs. We also share with Silvers the expectation that this will result in fairly robust substantive entitlements.
22. See Rawls (1993: 421ff) for a statement and elucidation of the difference between justice in procedures and justice in outcomes, and Cohen (1994) and Alexander (1998) for discussion of the intricate connection between procedures and substantive justice.
23. We surmise this collective reasoning to be heavily weighted towards disabled people simply because of the urgency and comparatively strong appeal of their demands in terms of needs in a strict sense and broader forms of social and political disadvantage.
24. Estlund (forthcoming) criticises fair proceduralism on epistemic grounds, arguing it cannot generate sufficiently thick reasons to adopt a particular outcome, which are likely to generate only occasional value. However, we must keep in mind that the fair proceduralism Estlund challenges operates at the general level of collective democratic decision-making, whereas our proposal operates below that level, challenging decisions make by specific agents (typically administrators and service users) reflecting on a narrow set of reasons or goals.
25. This is precisely why the disability movement eschews certain self-referential labels and insists on employing the social model of disability which constructs the leading source of disablement as located in the external environment, as opposed to one's own body or mind.

26. Somewhat paradoxically, the presence of justiciable rights also provides a genuine opportunity for the case worker, who is often under extreme external pressure to manage her case loads in an economically sound manner, to improve their work situation. The presence of a legal threat introduces a balancing force that does not only affect the case worker but also the senior manager, who will have to take possible legal action into account and now has a genuine interest in making sure the office is not just run within budget but also in accordance with quality standards for dealing with requests for assistance. Streamlining bureaucratic incentives in accordance with disability rights is a major goal of the right to challenge.
27. Rawls (1999: 575) specifies that public reason applies in particular to three public offices: decisions of judges; discourse of government officials; and candidates running for public office. However, we would argue that major policy-making decisions in close deliberation with all relevant stakeholders should operate on similar principles.
28. The six departments are: 1) Communications Marine and Natural Resources; 2) Enterprise Trade and Employment; 3) Environment and Local Government; 4) Health and Children; 5) Social and Family Affairs; and 6) Transport. The inaugural plans were published in July 2006 and are available for consultation on the website of the National Disability Authority: http://www.nda.ie/
29. For Pettit, proper contestation requires what he terms 'editorial control', which 'cannot be exercised collectively, in the manner of electoral … control' but 'has got to be exercised by individuals or groups at a noncollective level' (Pettit, 2000: 117–118). In the context of disability rights, even single group contestation may become suspect and we recommend fully individualising the right to challenge.
30. A disabled child may either be assessed under the Disability Act or under the Education for Persons with Special Educational Needs Act 2004. If an educational need is identified following a Disability Act assessment, that aspect of the assessment must be referred to the National Council for Special Education or to the Principal of her school for the purposes of an assessment under the 2004 Act. Health needs identified in an assessment under the Educational Needs Act 2004 will be dealt with in a Service Statement under the Disability Act.
31. On this point, Section 20 of the Disability Act 2005 is explicit: 'An appeal to a court shall not lie against a determination of the appeals officer other than an appeal on a point of law to the High Court.'
32. For example, a dedicated statutory appeals system is provided for under the Social Welfare Code.
33. With respect to empowerment, it should be acknowledged that at least disabled people may be entitled to the services of an advocate, drawn from either the community and voluntary sector or the service to be instituted by the Citizens Information Board, the national support agency responsible for the provision of information, advice and advocacy to members of the public on social services (Citizens Information Act 2007).
34. *Ms D (a tenant)* v *A Local Authority* (DEC-S2007-048); *A Complainant* v *A Local Authority* (DEC-S2007-049).
35. In May 2007, the High Court awarded damages to disabled siblings, whose living conditions at a halting site operated by a public authority amounted to a breach of their rights under Article 8 of the ECHR. Cf. *O'Donnell (a minor) and Ors.* v *South Dublin County Council* [2007] IEHC 204.
36. The two main precedents to date from the Equality Tribunal are contradictory. In *Hennessy* v *Dublin Bus* (DEC-S2003-046) the Equality Officer suggested that other legislative provisions dealing with the progressive implementation of access to public services could satisfy the duty to reasonably accommodate individual disabled people under the Equal Act Status Act. A more recent decision, which is under appeal to the Circuit Court, specifies that the reasonable accommodation requirement will not be displaced by other statutory provisions: *2 Named Complainants* v *Minister for Education and Science* (DEC-S2006-007).
37. Such provision is made in the Ontarians with Disabilities Act, R.S.O. 2001, c. 32. On which see Gordon *et al.* (2002).
38. See Richardson (2002) on the complicated connections between democratic authority and administrative discretion.

References

Alexander, L. (1998) Are Procedural Rights Derivative Substantial Rights?, *Law and Philosophy,* 17, pp. 19–42.

Allen, K. (2003) Neither Boston or Berlin: Class Polarisation and Neo-Liberalism in the Irish Republic, in: C. Coulter and S. Coleman (Eds) *The End of Irish History?* (Manchester: Manchester University Press).

Baker, J., Lynch, K., Cantillon, S. & Walsh, J. (2004) *Equality: From Theory to Action* (Basingstoke: Palgrave).

Barnes, C. & Mercer, G. (2003) *Disability* (Cambridge: Polity Press).

Barnes, C. & Oliver, M. (1995) Disability Rights: Rhetoric and Reality in the UK, *Disability and Society,* 10(1), pp. 111–116.

Breslin, M. L. & Yee, S. (Eds) (2002) *Disability Rights Law and Policy: International and National Perspectives* (Ardsley, NY: Transnational Publishers).

Campbell, J. & Oliver, M. (1996) *Disability Politics: Understanding our Past, Changing our Future* (London: Routledge).

Charlton, J. I. (1998) *Nothing About Us Without Us: Disability Oppression and Empowerment* (Berkeley, CA; Los Angeles, CA: University of California Press).

Civil Public and Services Union Disability Sub-Committee (2004) *Pre-budget Submission 2005,* available online at http://www.cpsu.ie/

Clements, L. & Read, J. (2003) *Disabled People and European Human Rights* (Bristol: Policy Press).

Cohen, J. (1994) Pluralism and Proceduralism, *Chicago-Kent Law Review,* 69, pp. 589–618.

Commission on the Status of People with Disabilities (1996)A Strategy for Equality: Report of the Commission on the Status of People with Disabilities (Dublin: Stationery Office).

Cousins, M. (2002) *Social Welfare Law,* 2nd edn (Dublin, London: Thomson Round Hall).

Cowan, D. & Halliday, S. (2003) *The Appeal of Internal Review* (Oxford: Hart).

Crowley, N. (2006) Inequality – Making an Impact, paper presented at the Action for Equity conference, Institute of Public Health in Ireland, Carlingford, 17–18 October, available online at http://www.publichealth.ie/

Darwall, S. (1977) Two Kinds of Respect, *Ethics,* 88(1), pp. 36–49.

Davis, D. M., Macklem, P. & Mundlak, G. (2002) Social Rights, Social Citizenship, and Transformative Constitutionalism: A Comparative Assessment, in: J. Conaghan, R. M. Fischl & K. Klare (Eds) *Labour Law in an Era of Globalization,* pp. 511–534 (Oxford: Oxford University Press).

De Blacam, M. (2002) Children, Constitutional Rights and the Separation of Powers, *Irish Jurist,* xxxvii, pp. 113–142.

De Wispelaere, J. & Walsh, J. (2005) Rights or Policy? On the Rights-based Approach to Disability Services, paper presented at the annual meeting of the Society for Applied Philosophy, University of Oxford, 1–3 July.

Degener, T. & Quinn, G. (2002) A Survey of International, Comparative and Regional Disability Law Reform, in: M. L. Breslin & S. Yee (Eds) *Disability Rights Law and Policy: International and National Perspectives,* pp. 3–129 (Ardsley, NY: Transnational Publishers).

Disability Legislation Consultation Group (DLCG) (2003) *Equal Citizens: Proposals for Core Elements of Disability Legislation* (Dublin: DLCG).

Dixon, R. (2007) Creating Dialogue about Socioeconomic Rights: Strong-form versus Weak-form Judicial Review Revisited, *International Journal of Constitutional Law,* 5(3), pp. 391–418.

Dorf, M. (2003) Legal Indeterminacy and Institutional Design, *New York University Law Review,* 78, pp. 875–981.

Dorf, M. & Sabel, C. (1998) A Constitution of Democratic Experimentalism, *Columbia Law Review,* 98, pp. 267–291.

Doyal, L. & Gough, I. (1991) *A Theory of Human Need* (Basingstoke: Palgrave).

Doyle, A. (2003) Disability Policy in Ireland, in: S. Quin & B. Redmond (Eds) *Disability and Social Policy in Ireland,* pp. 10–27 (Dublin: University College Dublin Press).

Drake, R. F. (1999) *Understanding Disability Policies* (Basingstoke: Macmillan).

Driedger, D. (1989) *The Last Civil Rights Movement* (London, New York: St Martin's Press).

Eide, A., Krause, C. & Rosas, A. (Eds) (2001) *Economic, Social and Cultural Rights: A Textbook* 2nd edn (Dordrecht: M. Nijhoff).

Engel, D. M. & Munger, F. W. (2003) *Rights of Inclusion: Law and Identity in the Life Stories of Americans with Disabilities* (Chicago, IL: University of Chicago Press).

Estlund, D. (Forthcoming) *Democratic Authority* (Princeton, NJ: Princeton University Press).

EU Network of Independent Experts on Disability Discrimination (2004) *Baseline Study: Disability Discrimination Law in the EU Member States* (Brussels: European Commission), available online at http://ec.europa.eu/employment_social/fundamental_rights/index_en.htm

Feinberg, J. (1980) *Rights, Justice, and the Bounds of Liberty: Essays in Social Philosophy* (Princeton, NJ: Princeton University Press).

Forum of People with Disabilities (2004) *Submission to the Joint Committee on Justice, Equality, Defence and Women's Rights on the Disability Bill 2004.*

Fredman, S. (2006) Human Rights Transformed: Positive Duties and Positive Rights, *Public Law*, 2006(Autumn), pp. 498–520.

Galligan, D. & Sandler, D. (2004) Implementing Human Rights, in: S. Halliday and P. Schmidt (Eds) *Human Rights Brought Home; Socio-legal Perspectives on Human Rights in the National Context*, pp. 23–56 (Oxford: Hart).

Gooding, C. (2003) The Application of the ECHR in British Courts in Relation to Disability Issues, paper delivered at the Global Trends in Disability Law Conference, Blackhall Place, Dublin, 13 September, available online at http://www.lawsociety.ie/

Gordon, P., Beatty, H. & Holder, B. (2002) An Analysis of the Ontarians with Disabilities Act, 2001, *Journal of Law & Social Policy*, 17, pp. 15–38.

Gutmann, A. & Thompson, D. (1996) *Democracy and Disagreement* (Cambridge, MA: Harvard University Press).

Holmes, S. & Sunstein, C. (1999) *The Cost of Rights: Why Liberty Depends on Taxes* (London, New York: W. W. Norton).

Hood, C. & Lodge, M. (2006) *The Politics of Public Service Bargains: Reward, Competency, Loyalty – and Blame* (Oxford: Oxford University Press).

Hunt, A. (1990) Rights and Social Movements: Counter Hegemonic Strategies, *Journal of Law and Society*, 17(3), pp. 309–328.

Hutchinson, A. (2004) Judges and Politics: An Essay from Canada, *Legal Studies*, 24, pp. 275–294.

Irish Human Rights Commission (IHRC) (2004) *Observations on the Disability Bill 2004*, available online at http://www.ihrc.ie/

Irish Human Rights Commission (IHRC) (2005) *Making Economic, Social and Cultural Rights Effective: An IHRC Discussion Document*, available online at http://www.ihrc.ie/

Irish Times (2004a) Ahern Says Law Exceeds Global Norms, 22 September, p. 6.

Irish Times (2004b) Groups Call for Disability Bill to be Redrawn, 17 November, p. 7.

Irish Times (2005) Major Changes to Disability Legislation urged, 9 February, p. 5.

Jolls, C. (2001) Anti-discrimination and Accommodation, *Harvard Law Review*, 115, pp. 642–699.

Kemp, L. (2002) Why Are Some People's Needs Unmet?, *Disability and Society*, 17(2), pp. 205–218.

Kende, M. (2003) The South African Constitutional Court's Embrace of Socio-economic Rights: A Comparative Perspective, *Chapman Law Review*, 6, pp. 137–159.

Kenna, P. (2006) *Housing Law and Policy in Ireland* (Dublin: Clarus Press).

King, J. (2007) The Justiciability of Resource Allocation, *Modern Law Review*, 70(2), pp. 197–224.

Lawson, A. & Gooding, C. (Eds) (2005) *Disability Rights in Europe* (Oxford: Hart Publishing).

Lever, A. (2007) Is Judicial Review Undemocratic, *Public Law*, 2007(Summer), pp. 280–298.

Mabbett, D. (2005) The Development of Rights-based Social Policy in the European Union: The Example of Disability Rights, *Journal of Common Market Studies*, 43(1), pp. 97–120.

McDermot, P. A. (2000) The Separation of Powers and the Doctrine of Non-Justiciability, *Irish Jurist*, xxxv, pp. 280–304.

McDowell, M. (2002) Speech delivered at the Annual Conference of the Irish Social Policy Association, 12 September.

Morris, J. (1997) Care or Empowerment? A Disability Rights Perspective, *Social Policy and Administration*, 31(1), pp. 54–60.

Murphy, M. (2006) The emerging Irish workfare state and its implications for local development, in: D. Jacobson, P. Kirby & D. Ó Broin (Eds) *Taming the Tiger: Social Exclusion in a Globalised Ireland* pp. 85–112 (Dublin: New Island Press).

Namhi (2004)Response of Namhi to Disability Bill 2004: Submission to the Joint Committee on Justice, Equality, Defence and Women's Rights, available online at http://www.namhi.ie/

National Disability Authority (NDA) (2006) *Code of Practice on Accessibility of Public Services and Information Provided by Public Bodies* (Dublin: NDA).

National Parents and Siblings Alliance (2005) Review of the National Disability Strategy, available online at http://www.npsa.ie

Nolan, B. (2003) *On Rights-Based Services for People with Disabilities*, ESRI Policy Research Series 49 (Dublin: ESRI).

O'Donnell, R. (2003) Beyond Justiciable Rights – Standards and Quality, Paper delivered at the Global Trends in Disability Law Conference, Blackhall Place, Dublin, 13 September, available online at http://www.lawsociety.ie/

O'Donovan, M. A. & Doyle, A. (2007) *National Physical and Sensory Disability Database Committee Annual Report 2006* (Dublin: Health Research Board).

O'Mahony, C. (2002) Education, Remedies and the Separation of Powers, *Dublin University Law Journal*, 24, 57–95.

O'Mahony, C. (2006) The Right to Education and Constitutionally Appropriate Provision, *Dublin University Law Journal*, 28, pp. 422–432.

Oliver, M. (1996) *Understanding Disability: From Theory to Practice* (Basingstoke: Palgrave).

Pettit, P. (1997) *Republicanism: A Theory of Freedom and Government* (Oxford: Oxford University Press).

Pettit, P. (1999) Republican Freedom and Contestatory Democratization, in: I. Shapiro & C. Hacker-Cordón (Eds) *Democracy's Value* pp. 163–190 (Cambridge: Cambridge University Press).

Pettit, P. (2000) Democracy, Electoral and Contestatory, in: I. Shapiro & S. Macedo (Eds) *NOMOS XLII: Designing Democratic Institutions*, pp. 105–143 (New York: New York University Press).

Pieterse, M. (2004) Coming to Terms with Judicial Enforcement of Socio-Economic Rights, *South African Journal on Human Rights*, 20, pp. 383–417.

Pogge, T. (2000) Justice for People with Disabilities: The Semiconsequentialist Approach, in: L. Pickering Francis & A. Silvers (Eds) *Americans with Disabilities: Exploring Implications of the Law for Individuals and Institutions*, pp. 34–53 (New York/London: Routledge).

Quinn, G. (2000) Rethinking the Nature of Economic, Social and Cultural Rights in the Irish Legal Order, in: C. Costello (Ed.) *Fundamental Social Rights: Current European Legal Protection and the Challenge of the EU Charter on Fundamental Rights*, pp. 35–54 (Dublin: European Movement).

Quinn, G. (2003) Policy Responsibility 'For' or Legal Responsibilities 'To' Persons with Disabilities?, Paper delivered at the Conference Global Trends in Disability Law –Setting a Context for Irish Law Reform, Law Society of Ireland, Blackhall Place, Dublin 13 September.

Quinn, G. (2007) The New UN Convention on the Rights of Persons with Disabilities – Drafting Process and Contents, Paper presented at the Irish Human Rights Commission Briefing on the International Convention on the Protection of the Rights and Dignity of Persons with Disabilities, 19 April 2007, available online at http://www.ihrc.ie

Quinn, G. & Bruce, A. (2003) Towards free and inclusive societies for people with disabilities, in: S. Quin and B. Redmond (Eds) *Disability and Social Policy in Ireland*, pp. 182–199 (Dublin: University College Dublin Press).

Rawls, J. (1993) *Political Liberalism* (New York: Columbia University Press).

Rawls, J. (1999) The Idea of Public Reason Revisited, in: J. Rawls (Ed.) *Collected Papers* (Cambridge, MA: Harvard University Press).

Richardson, G. & Genn, H. (2007) Tribunals in Transition: Resolution or Adjudication, *Public Law*, 2007 (Spring), pp. 116–141.

Richardson, H. (2002) *Democratic Autonomy* (Oxford: Oxford University Press).

Roach, K. (2004) Dialogic Judicial Review and its Critics, *Supreme Court Law Review*, 23, pp. 49–104.

Roulstone, A. (2003) The Legal Road to Rights? Disabling Premises, *Obiter Dicta*, and the Disability Discrimination Act 1995, *Disability and Society*, 18(2), pp. 117–131.

Runswick-Cole, K. (2007) 'The Tribunal was the Most Stressful Thing: More Stressful than my Son's Diagnosis or Behaviour': The Experiences of Families Who Go to the Special Educational Needs and Disability Tribunal (SENDisT), *Disability and Society*, 22(3), pp. 315–328.

Schizophrenia Ireland (2004) *Briefing Document for Disability Bill 2004*, available online at http://www.recover.ie/

Silvers, A. (1998) Formal Justice, in: A. Silvers, D. Wasserman & M. B. Malhowand (Eds) *Disability, Difference, Discrimination* (New York: Rowman and Littlefield).

Toolan, D. (2003a) An Emerging Rights Perspective for Disabled People in Ireland: An Activist's View, in: S. Quin & B. Redmond (Eds) *Disability and Social Policy in Ireland*, pp. 171–181 (Dublin: University College Dublin Press).

Toolan, D. (2003b) Will Government Share the Feeling or Wait …, Paper presented at the Irish Social Policy Association Seminar Disability Legislation: Policy and Practice, 5 June, available online at http://www.ispa.ie/newsevents/

Waddington, L. and Diller, M. (2002) Tensions and Coherence in Disability Policy: The Uneasy Relationship Between Social Welfare and Civil Rights Models of Disability in American, European and International Employment Law, in: M. L. Breslin & S. Yee (Eds) *Disability Rights Law and Policy: International and National Perspectives*, pp. 241–282 (Ardsley, NY: Transnational Publishers).

Waldron, J. (1999) *Law and Disagreement* (Oxford: Oxford University Press).

Walsh, J. (2006) Unfamiliar Inequalities, *Northern Ireland Legal Quarterly*, 57(1), pp. 155–184.

Whyte, G. (2002) *Social Inclusion and the Legal System: Public Interest Law in Ireland* (Dublin: Institute of Public Administration).

Whyte, G. (2004) Rights and Judicial Activism, in: B. Fanning, P. Kennedy, G. Kiely & S. Quin (Eds) *Theorising Irish Social Policy*, pp. 165–191 (Dublin: University College Dublin Press).

Whyte, G. (2006) The Role of the Supreme Court in our Democracy: A Response to Mr Justice Hardiman, *Dublin University Law Journal*, 28, pp. 1–26.

How to Think About Marriage: Autonomy, Equality, Recognition

PETER MORRISS

Introduction

The question of how we should think about marriage is currently firmly on the political agenda in Ireland. In 2006 alone, four Reports were issued, by various official bodies, investigating family law.[1] Part of the reason for this uncharacteristic flurry of official interest is the realisation that the Irish Constitution in this area no longer accords with reality. There is a near-consensus that legal changes are required to deal with the rapid growth in non-marital cohabitation. Further, there is considerable pressure to allow some official status to gay couples. In February 2007, the Dáil debated a Bill to create a status of Civil Union for gay couples, carrying all the rights and responsibilities of marriage, although without the name.[2] The government majority voted down the Bill, but only – it claimed – because it wanted to bring in its own, better, Bill at a later date. In the parliamentary debate, not one TD spoke against the principle of state recognition of homosexual couples.

So, change is in the air. In the words of the Law Society: 'There is little doubt that the Irish family law system now requires nothing less than a major overhaul if it is to meet the increasing demands placed on it. The law must now root itself in reality and not emotive or traditional rhetoric.'[3] However, I want to suggest that the very fact that *four*, different, bodies presented proposals on marriage is part of the problem. Each Report looks at a sub-set of the possible issues, without any apparent coordination between them. As one might expect from politicians and lawyers,[4] there has been little attempt to think about what *general* principles should apply here. I suggest that we should return to first principles to think again about marital law. Among the principles I think we should investigate are the three in my subtitle: autonomy, equality and recognition.

Autonomy

Autonomy is widely recognised as an important value in modern Ireland. It is, perhaps, a *default* value, such that anyone who proposes infringing autonomy is required to give a *reason* for doing so, whilst those who wish to enhance autonomy need give no reason other than that they *are* enhancing autonomy. It is no surprise that one of the values explicitly mentioned in these documents is autonomy, which both the Law Reform Commission and the Working Group on Domestic Partnership think should be one of the objectives of legal reform.[5]

Yet Western states currently refuse to allow people the autonomy to choose the marital arrangements they might want. Each state imposes its own understanding of what marriage is; if you'd rather live in a different sort of marriage – well, you can't. What is more, the state can (and does) unilaterally alter the terms of the understanding it imposes. Thus in Ireland before 1997, anyone who wanted to marry had no choice but to agree to be legally married for life. In 1997 that option was removed, and replaced by one requiring marriages to be subject to (a certain sort of) no-fault divorce. To anyone who is concerned with autonomy, this limitation should seem astonishing.

There is no reason why this should be the case. There is no reason why those who want no-fault divorce should not have it; but, at the same time, those who would like their marriage to allow for no divorce – or for limited fault-based divorce – should be allowed to have the marriage of *their* choice.[6] If autonomy really *is* the default value, then the current Procrustean[7] approach is unacceptable; any understanding of marriage should be allowed, provided there are not good reasons for *not* allowing it. The onus of proof is on those who would limit autonomy.[8]

It might be claimed that we do have more autonomy than I am here allowing; for we are now far more tolerant than we used to be of sexual practices that differ from the perceived norm. People who wish to enter into non-marital or adulterous or homosexual or polygamous sexual relationships can do so; they now suffer relatively little social opprobrium,[9] and break no laws – providing, that is, they don't claim that their relationships are *marriages*.[10] Does this not fully respect our autonomy?

I would like to argue that it does not. For, at present, any such relationships are, literally, outside the law: that is, any agreements that the parties might make are not legally enforceable. The leading case here is *Ennis* v *Butterly* ([1996] 1 IR 426). Bernadette Ennis and Colm Butterly were in a relationship with each other; both were married, but separated from their respective spouses. They entered into a cohabitation agreement to live as man and wife; Ennis gave up her business in order to be a full-time home-maker; in return, Butterly promised to make her a partner in his business. When Butterly failed to carry out his part of the bargain, she sued under the contract – and lost, as all cohabitation contracts are 'illegal and unenforceable' (*Ennis* v *Butterly* [1996] 1 IR 427).

This is a weakness. Such a relationship is intended to be enduring, and maybe life-long; it is one in which the parties undertake to make considerable sacrifices – sacrifices which they may be willing to make only on the understanding that the other party will carry out their part of the agreement. It is understandable that some people might be reluctant to make these sacrifices if there is no legal framework to prevent the other person walking away from their commitments. Part of what marriage law does is to provide such a legal framework.

So our autonomy can be enhanced if we are able to enter into legally enforceable, long-term agreements.[11] Intimate and personal agreements are no different from any others. Concern for autonomy should certainly not impose legal enforcement on those who do not want it – who think, perhaps, that their love is sufficient, or that their relationship would be demeaned by being brought under the jurisdiction of the law. But equally, it should allow those who *do* want such legal backing to have it. Currently, this applies only to those who marry.

So I am arguing that marriage law fulfills a useful function in providing a legal framework for our relationships. But it is too rigid: it offers only *one* such framework. Rather, it should respect people's different views and understanding of their relationships. So a respect for autonomy requires us to treat those agreements that people enter into with each other as legally enforceable if the parties *want* them to be treated as legally enforceable.[12] The implications for this are far reaching. It would allow people to enter, should they wish, into legally enforceable marriages that do not allow divorce, or allow only fault-based divorce. It would allow homosexuals to enter into such agreements just as readily as heterosexuals. Indeed, it would include relationships not involving sexual intercourse or sexual attraction. It would not restrict the number of the parties to two. Whether these agreements should be called *marriages* is, at this stage of the argument, irrelevant. All I am suggesting is that if you (plural) want to create some unorthodox domestic arrangement, and want that arrangement to be legally enforceable, then it should be enforceable. The principle of autonomy requires no less.

In the rest of this article I will explore some of the implications of this position. I will do so by employing a distinction, made in an important article by Tamara Metz, between the *instrumental* status of marriage, and its *constitutive* status (Metz, 2007). The *instrumental* status involves the 'concrete, delineable goods' (Metz, 2007: 200) that follow from marriage; the *constitutive* status sees marriage as an expressive good, 'a highly public celebration of the ideals of mutuality, companionship, intimacy, fidelity, and family' (Metz, 2007: 201, quoting the Massachusetts court in *Goodridge* (2003) 27). The instrumental aspect requires equality; the constitutive status involves recognition.

Equality

The instrumental benefits of marriage have always been considerable. If your spouse dies, you will be allowed to claim on their pension (if they have one), to avoid inheritance tax, and, if living in a rented property, to inherit the tenancy. If your spouse leaves no will, you nevertheless have a claim on their property; even if there is a will, it is overridden if it does not make suitable provision for you. If your spouse was wrongfully killed, you can recover damages; if he or she is ill, and needs looking after, you are entitled to take time off work to do so. If your spouse is taken into hospital you have the right to visit, and the right to be consulted on their treatment if they are not able to give their own informed consent. If your spouse abandons you, you may have a claim against them for maintenance payments. To turn to happier considerations, you are considered the parent of any child you or your spouse has. You are entitled to adopt, jointly becoming parents. If you emigrate or become a refugee, your spouse is entitled to enter the country to join you. And the full list of instrumental benefits is much longer than this.

In recent years, all these rights[13] have been made gender neutral; more recently still, many, but not all, of them have been extended to cohabiting heterosexual (but usually not homosexual) couples; some have been extended to other family members.[14] The equality agenda in Ireland has been to treat husband and wife the same (whilst extending appropriately more favourable treatment to the weaker party, usually taken as the wife); to extend to cohabiting couples as many as possible of the rights held by married couples; and to not discriminate on the basis of sexual orientation.[15]

I want to argue that this, whilst laudable, does not go far enough; indeed, the whole approach adopted by human rights law (as expressed, for instance, in the European Court of Justice) is inadequate. The mistake is to give too narrow a scope to equality, and put too much weight on the notion of discrimination.

The European Court equates equality with opposition to discrimination.[16] The notion of equality that is employed is that 'similar situations shall not be treated differently unless differentiation is objectively justified' (HRC, 2006: 17).[17] Thus any attempt to invoke equality in domestic relationships has to proceed in three stages: first, one has to establish that people in some relationship are treated less favourably than similarly placed married people; second, that the relationship is similar enough to marriage to warrant the comparison; third, that there are not 'objective justifications' for the different treatment.[18] Any such claim can, then, be rebutted by showing that the relationship is not sufficiently like marriage to count as 'similar'.

To illustrate how this jurisprudence goes astray, I want to consider some recent cases on the issue of whether a cohabitee of someone who has died can continue to live in the home they shared with the deceased. First is an English case (although the relevant Irish law is similar); second, an English case interpreting the European Convention on Human Rights; third, the European Court interpreting the same Convention.[19]

The facts in the first case were as follows. John Thompson had lived in a rent-controlled flat in London from 1972 until his death in 1994. Since 1976, he had lived there with his gay lover, Martin Fitzpatrick. When Thompson died, Fitzpatrick applied to the landlord to take over the tenancy of the flat; the landlord refused. Fitzpatrick then claimed that he had the right to the tenancy under the Rent Act. This Act gives the right to take over a tenancy to a surviving spouse, if living with the tenant, or a cohabiting partner 'living as his or her wife or husband'; family members, who have lived there for the last two years, also have the same right, under less favourable terms. Fitzpatrick claimed that he was a cohabiting partner; or, failing that, that he was a member of Thompson's family. The House of Lords found that he did not qualify as a cohabiting partner, as husbands and wives had to be of opposite sex; he did, however, qualify as a member of Thompson's family.

The next case had similar facts; but now the UK Parliament had enshrined the European Convention on Human Rights into English law, and so the House of Lords had to take account of it. They concluded that a long-term cohabiting gay couple was indeed similar to a cohabiting heterosexual one; that there was no acceptable policy reason for treating the gay couple worse than the heterosexual one; and that therefore the surviving partner had the right to inherit the tenancy on the same terms as a heterosexual partner.

The third case was somewhat different. It concerned two sisters, in their eighties, who had lived together all their lives. They had built a house together 30 years previously, which they owned in their joint names; in their wills, each had left her share to the other. However, when one of them died, the other would be liable to pay inheritance tax on her sister's bequest; the amount of tax was more than the surviving sister would be able to afford, and she would therefore have to sell the house. They wanted the European Court to declare that it was contrary to the European Convention to levy tax in such circumstances – particularly as they would not be liable for inheritance tax if they were married, or were a gay couple who had registered under the (recently introduced) Civil Partnership Act. The European Court, by a majority of 4–3, found against the sisters, in part on the ground that they had not made out that they were in an analogous position to a married couple, and in part because, even if they had, a state 'cannot be criticised for pursuing, through its taxation system, policies designed to promote marriage' (*Burden*: Judgment: 17). These two considerations hang together, as it is only in so far as sisterly cohabitation is *not* similar to marriage (or sexual cohabitation) that it makes sense to use taxation policy to promote the latter and not the former. I agree with the minority of the European Court that this decision was unjust.

Let us return again to the partnership of Martin Fitzpatrick and John Thompson. The agreed facts indicate that this was (as it were) more than just a long-term sexual relationship. The two are described throughout the judgment as 'in a longstanding, close, loving and faithful, monogamous, homosexual relationship'.[20] But, beyond this, Thompson became severely disabled in 1986, and required constant care; in response, Fitzpatrick gave up his job, and for over eight years cared for him 24 hours a day.[20] There is little doubt that this self-sacrifice increases his moral claim to remain in the flat that he had made his home (subject to paying the rent). But, legally, more seems to depend on the sexual nature of their relationship. All the judges in *Fitzpatrick* v *Sterling*, like the European Court in *Burden*, were adamant that sexually cohabiting couples were legally different from those in non-sexual relationships. They thus distinguished *Fitzpatrick* from a previous case, in which a similar amount of care was shown but in a relationship that was not sexual. In that case (*Joram Developments Ltd* v *Sharratt)*, Lady Salter, a widow aged 75, formed a platonic relationship with Frank Sharratt, a young man of 24. She invited him to live in her flat, which he did for nearly 20 years until she died, aged 94; although they were unrelated, they called each other aunt and nephew. The county court judge described the quality of the relationship in very similar terms to the judge in *Fitzpatrick*:

> He stuck by her to the end. Nobody else in her family did so. Had it not been for the presence of [Sharratt], in the last five years she would have been obliged to enter a nursing home ... She was able to remain in her home, to be looked after by a much younger person ... Their relationship was sensitive, loving, intellectual and platonic. (Judge Solomon, in *Joram*, [1979] 1 WLR 5)

Yet Sharratt was refused the right to take over the tenancy. The Law Lords decided that he could not be a member of Lady Salter's family, for adult strangers can not form a familial relationship unless it is sexual.[22]

I submit that this approach is flawed. Instead of picking over the concept of 'the family' or that of a married couple, to establish what is sufficiently similar to it, we should look to the purpose of the legislation and then extend it to all those for whom the purpose fits.[23] Lord Clyde suggested in *Fitzpatrick* that '[t]he purpose of the statutory provisions on succession ... [is] to ensure that the [tenant's] security of tenure is not weakened by the inability of those closely bound to him to remain in residence by right after his death' (*Fitzpatrick*, [2001] 1 AC 52). If this, or something like it, *is* the justified reason for the existence of the right to inherit a tenancy, then it should go to *all* relevant people: certainly a person who has shared the home for 20 years should be entitled to its benefits, whether or not their relationship with the registered tenant was sexual.

The daft result of the existing jurisprudence is that it privileges sexual (even adulterous) relationships. If (under the present law) Lady Salter and Frank Sharratt had chosen to have a sexual relationship, he could have stayed on in the flat after her death; because neither of them was so interested, he could not. It is difficult to think of a sensible rationale for such an outcome. Yet such absurd conclusions are inevitable if we adopt the European Court's approach of extending the benefits of marriage to relationships judged to be 'similar', and denying them to relationships that are not similar.[24] It is, after all, a necessary requirement of marriage that there is a sexual relationship between the parties,[25] so it is inevitable that sexual relationships will be privileged over non-sexual ones, whether or not that is appropriate.

The Canadian case of *Brunette* c. *Québec* provides a further example of the lack of flexibility of the anti-discrimination approach.[26] Patricia Brunette was a severely disabled woman, who was unable to live alone without assistance. She was looked after by her elderly mother; but when her mother had to go into a home, Brunette invited Guy Émard, who was also unable to live alone because of mental problems, to share her house. Their relationship was not amorous or sexual; but it was characterised by a high degree of intimate inter-reliance. After they had lived like this for ten years, the Ministry of Social Security withdrew Brunette's welfare payments (her sole source of income), as she was deemed to be living in a 'marriage-like' relationship. On appeal, this was reversed, the Court ruling that, because of Brunette and Émard's lack of reciprocal sexual interest, their relationship was *not* like a marriage, and so her benefit was restored. But in order to produce this clearly sensible outcome, the Court had to go through some nifty – and dubious – footwork to find that their relationship was not marriage-like.

This seems a crazy way to proceed. There would seem to be excellent policy grounds for encouraging disabled people to support each other by living together: their autonomy would be greatly enhanced, and the cost to the state would be less.[27] Yet our law is based on our Procrustean obsession with fitting people into the categories 'married' or 'not married', however inappropriate these categories might be. It is time to rid ourselves of this obsession.

That such a radical rethink is indeed possible is shown in the Law Commission of Canada's Report, *Beyond Conjugality*. It, too, thought that autonomy and equality were important values that should inform public policy, and it examined these values more closely than any of the Irish Reports (or, indeed, all of them together). One form of equality that it thought was important was *relational equality*, which is concerned with equalising 'the legal status among different types of relationships' including 'conjugal and non-conjugal relationships which may share the functional characteristics of emotional and financial interdependence' (LCC, 2001: xi).[28]

What this points to is that there are *reasons* for the large number of instrumental benefits of marriage. The reasons have to do with the high degree of emotional and/or financial interdependence (and dependence) that we expect in a marriage, and a feeling that the law should acknowledge this, thus treating married couples in a different way from strangers. The way to decide who should qualify for these instrumental benefits is to consider the reasons that justify the benefits, and then grant the benefits to all those covered by the reasons.

To this end, the Law Commission of Canada proposed a four-step methodology to be used in investigating how widely instrumental benefits should be extended.

1. Are the objectives of the law legitimate? [If not, then the benefits should be withdrawn from married couples.]
2. Do relationships matter [as a basis for determining the benefits]?
3. If relationships matter, can individuals be permitted to designate the relevant relationships themselves?

4. If relationships matter, and self-designation is not feasible or appropriate, is there a better way to include relationships?
   (LCC, 2001: xii–xiii and 29–30)

The greater part of *Beyond Conjugality* is an application of this methodology to a large range of Canadian laws.[29]

I want to apply this approach to some examples discussed by the (Irish) Law Reform Commission but not by the Law Commission of Canada; this will bring out the difference in the approaches employed.

The first concerns reform of the Domestic Violence Act (see LRC, 2006: ch. 4, section D). This Act was initially intended to protect spouses and children from domestic violence, by allowing them to obtain barring orders, and similar protections, against a violent spouse. It was extended in 1996 to include some cohabitants. The Commission recommends that the protections be extended to all cohabiting couples, whether different- or same-sex. It further recommends that someone should be able to apply for a Safety Order against a person with whom they are *not* cohabiting, if (but only if) they have a child in common (LRC, 2006: section 4.23).[30]

But why is there any need to specify a relationship here? Why cannot the defences against domestic violence be available as a protection against *anyone* who threatens domestic violence? Doubtless *most* perpetrators of domestic violence fall into these (now expanding) categories; but surely domestic violence is wrong whoever does it, and if protections are justified against certain categories of people, they are justified against all people. This shows the need to ask the Canadian Law Commission's second question: do relationships matter here at all?

Next, here are two of the Law Reform Commission's proposals in the area of health care.

(1) Visitation Rights

> If a cohabiting partner goes into hospital for treatment, there is no automatic right of visitation for the other partner. … [A]n automatic right of visitation should exist for both opposite-sex and same sex cohabitants. (LRC, 2006: section 4.33)

I should say at once that my own (happily, limited) experience of visiting (and being visited) in Irish hospitals is that everybody who wishes to visit is allowed to do so; nevertheless, presumably there are circumstances when some system of limitation would need to be imposed. But why limit by the nature of the relationship? Why not accord to each patient an appropriate number of visitors, and allow them to choose who they wish to visit them? Some people might prefer to be visited by their children or parents, rather than their partner; others might prefer a close friend. We should not limit patients' autonomy in this regard. Further, these proposals would leave anybody who happens *not* to be cohabiting without any visitors at all; that seems unjustly discriminatory. So here we should simply allow each individual to designate his or her own significant other(s).

(2) Consent and Treatment

> The Irish Medical Council has recommended that a doctor treating a seriously ill person who is unable to communicate or understand should confer with the patient's family before reaching a decision on 'the use or non use of treatments which will not contribute to recovery from primary illness'. While Medical Council guidelines recommend consultation with the next of kin and/or the spouse of a person, no provision is made for consultation with a cohabiting partner.
>
> *The Commission recommends consideration to be given to include cohabitants within the category of persons with whom a doctor should confer when treating* [such] *a seriously ill patient...* (LRC, 2006: sections 4.36 and 4.37; footnotes omitted)

Here, again, there seems no reason why the patient cannot specify who they wish to be consulted on such matters.[31] Many people might prefer, for instance, that the doctor consult with a trusted GP or solicitor, rather than with a possibly distraught loved-one (who may well themselves be old or unwell); relieving one's partner of such traumatic choices might be a kindness to them. Autonomy and equality should surely allow freedom of choice in such a matter. Even if the person becomes incapacitated suddenly and unexpectedly, there is no reason why he or she should not have expressed views on the matter in advance; this could be kept on their medical database.

I am therefore suggesting that we should look at what a relationship *does*, rather than see whether it is sufficiently 'similar' to a marriage to warrant extending to it the instrumental benefits of marriage. The key features are emotional and financial interdependence. Marriages necessarily involve sex; emotional and financial interdependence may, but need not, involve sex. If it is interdependence that we are interested in, then there is no need to enquire into people's sexual habits. This point sounds too obvious to be worth stating, yet the structure of discourse has overlooked it. Of the four Irish Reports I have been discussing, three are concerned exclusively with sexual relationships (rather coyly called 'intimate relationships' by the Law Reform Commission).[32] The fourth – the Paper on Domestic Partnership – does at least acknowledge the existence of non-sexual relationships: it divides domestic partnerships into three distinct cohabiting groups:

- Opposite-sex couples
- Same-sex couples
- Non-conjugal relationships, (Domestic Partnership, 2006: section 1.07).[33]

But it is not helpful to distinguish relationships in this way; we should leave *sex* to one side and concentrate on *interdependence*. A close personal relationship should be considered as a category in its own right. That is the approach of *Beyond Conjugality*, reflected in its title, and it is the one advocated here.

Recognition

The ceremony of marriage is presumably important as a way of publicly recognising the commitment of the parties to each other. Therefore, the recent interest in recognition would seem to be relevant to a consideration of marriage. Yet the Irish Reports that I have been discussing concentrate almost exclusively on the instrumental aspects of marriage; reading them, one might think that all that marriage is about is getting one's hands on a range of benefits. Only one mentions any non-instrumental rationale for having an institution of marriage: the Domestic Partnership *Report* lists recognition as one of its guiding principles, describing it as 'about acknowledging the existence, legality or validity, of particular relationships through a formal approval or through giving legal status whereby the relationship is treated as worthy of consideration and protection. Recognition is about the status and standing of a group [*sic*] in society and how society values and affirms any particular group' (Domestic Partnership, 2006: section 1.13).

The invocation here of the status of a *group* points to the communitarian perspective often adopted in the 'recognition' literature. This suggests that we should think of ourselves primarily as members of social groups, through which we become aware of who we are. If the culture of the group to which we belong is belittled – or the group itself is – then we will grow up as damaged individuals. To avoid this, such groups should be treated with respect.

At present, the group that feels itself denied recognition in the most significant way is that of gays and lesbians, who often claim to be subordinated because their relationships cannot be accorded the status of marriage.[34] It is for this reason that the Domestic Partnership *Report* considered that recognition is about the status of *groups*, rather than about the status of the individuals who are (or are not) married.[35] Yet the difference of recognition can be met in two ways: marital status can be made available to homosexual couples on an equal footing with heterosexual ones, or heterosexual unions can be accorded no legal status, just like gay unions at present.[36] Thus the claim of equal treatment for homosexuals does not provide an independent reason why the state should recognise marriage at all. It is *that* question that we must consider.

The best treatment of this is by Metz, who starts with Hegel. Hegel saw marriage as a contract, in which individuals transcend their individuality, to form themselves into a unit 'deeply intertwined with each other and with the community that confers marital status' (Metz, 2007: 203). But, for Hegel, the state is more important than the community: the state is the ethical authority through which individuals transform themselves into a transcending union.

Metz rejects the Hegelian notion of the state: for her, the state does *not* function as an ethical authority (Metz, 2007: 205–206). The state should therefore not be concerned with marriage's constitutive status. But that does not mean that we have to do without marriage: marriage can be disestablished and passed to civil society,[37] to communities. That would have the advantage that those who have different understandings of what marriage is, can have the marriage that they want (or they can, at least, if there is a suitable community with the same understanding) (Metz, 2007: 206–207).

What Metz does, then, is to see marriage as a rite of passage; like other rites of passage, it serves both to mark and to create a change in status for the participant(s). We do not usually expect the state to be involved in rites of passage. Metz therefore proposes that the state should play no part in the constitutive aspects of marriage; it should neither create marriages, nor should it recognise any distinction between the married and unmarried.

This has the advantage of allowing autonomy, and increasing the separation between church(es) and state. Indeed, it would *enhance* the significance of churches (and also non-religious communities), as the state could no longer impose on them its own understanding of marriage.

There is a further, more immediate, advantage. The Irish Reports discussed here fear that a constitutional referendum, extending state recognition of marriage to gay partnerships, would be too divisive. Yet they are also worried that equality would be violated by the introduction of a *separate* category of civil union for homosexual, and not heterosexual, partnerships. Metz's suggestion removes this difficulty: the state can simply ignore the matter altogether.[38]

Metz's approach is thus very appealing, and deserves serious consideration. But I am worried about the central role given here to community. It is easy to talk vaguely and loosely about community,[39] and it is often difficult to discuss this idea dispassionately. Sometimes 'community' seems to work as a secular equivalent to God, and perform equally implausible miracles. Some of that seems to be going on here. The account of marriage as a transformative rite of passage produced by a community is unclear: I'm not sure how community involvement is supposed to produce this transformation. Presumably the claim here is not the instrumental one that the transformation is more likely to succeed if the community is involved. Instead the community is somehow seen as intrinsically necessary for the transformation. But why this should be the case is rather a mystery.[40] And, for what it is worth, it seems to be an uninteresting mystery for an increasing number of Irish people who, far from wishing to get married before their community, choose to get married abroad – to such an extent that the diocese of Dubrovnik recently wrote a strongly worded letter to the Irish Bishops' Conference asking them to discourage 'wedding tourists' to Croatia (*Irish Times*, 2007).

It is also not clear to me whether Metz's pluralist vision, appealing though it is, would suffice. She removes Hegel's fixation on the state, and replaces it with a more diverse picture of an individual (or couple) in 'their community'. But this is oversimplistic. A person is usually a member of many overlapping communities: they may, for instance, be gay *and* Catholic. Insofar as recognition of their status is important to them, it may well be from *many* of their communities: it may be important to them that the gay community recognise their partnership, but important also that their neighbours and co-religious do. Thus 'lesbian/gay weddings symbolically claim that lesbian and gay couples are not estranged from the values of the wider communities to which they consider themselves affiliated … [E]ach of these weddings makes the claim that the marrying couple are members of the wider community …' (Lewin, 1998: 86).

This raises the question of whether the state might not, after all, be the best body for recognising such relationships. For one thing that the state can do, that communities cannot, is speak for the *whole* of society. And that may be a valuable task.

Doubtless, bringing in the state in this way can give rise to worries: Alasdair Macintyre has suggested that seeking state recognition is a 'disastrous' invocation of the ideal of the *Volk* (Macintyre, 1999: 132); Metz also has this worry (Metz, 2007: 207–208). We should certainly always be aware of this danger. But we must also not forget the dangers of handing recognition over to communities. Communities are not always the most tolerant of social entities, and usually not the most inclusive. By definition, the state's remit runs wider: it is to be concerned about *all* citizens.[41]

An example of the dangers that can occur when communities are in control of rites of passage is the funeral of the first Irish President, Douglas Hyde, in 1949. As Hyde was a Protestant, his funeral took place in the Protestant cathedral in Dublin. The members of the cabinet, who were all Catholics, accompanied the funeral cortege to the cathedral; but they could not enter for the funeral itself, as the Catholic Church at that time forbade its members from attending Protestant religious services; so they had to hang around outside, and rejoin the procession when it left the church.[42] If the *state* had been in control of the funeral, that exclusion could never have happened.

The Catholic Church was, if anything, even more intolerant of cross-community marriages. As late as 1963, the very powerful Archbishop McQuaid of Dublin was insisting that 'The [Catholic] Church … forbids everywhere and most severely the marriage of a Catholic with a non-Catholic' (quoted in Fuller, 2002: 17). When, in exceptional circumstances, the Church gave a dispensation to allow such a 'mixed marriage', it insisted on stringent conditions that stressed the superiority of the Catholic faith, and did not allow a proper ceremony; the wedding 'was treated as a second-class affair' (Fuller, 2002: 17). Allowing marriages to be conducted solely by communities may, then, leave little room for marriages between people from *different* communities. The autonomy allowed here is to *communities*, not to individuals. This is a worry for those who do not embrace the stronger versions of communitarianism.

So I am suggesting that there is a case to be made for a somewhat paradoxical position. This is that the state should not grant any legal significance to marital status itself, but *should* be prepared to *create* marriages. Ideally, the state *alone* should perform the required ceremonies; for if rival groups are allowed to perform them, then some will inevitably be seen as more valuable – more status-enhancing – than others. But doubtless that smacks too much of Robespierre. The more tolerant (if wishy-washy) solution is for the state to allow anyone who wishes to perform marriages to do so, whilst also performing them itself – all the while recognising that such a ceremony has constitutive, but not instrumental, significance.

But seeking recognition from either state or community has the big drawback that our self-respect then depends on the approval of others, with all the dangers that entails.[43] Perhaps more emphasis should be put on the desirability of striving ourselves to be happy with our relationships, whatever form they might take. This could lead to a debunking of the significance of such ceremonial rites of passage. Or, rather, to say that those who are unable or unwilling to engage in them have no cause for complaint – or as little cause as Muslims and atheists have for not being able to take First Communions. Rather than create a state equivalent (or parody) of such a ceremony, those who don't qualify should perhaps just shrug and get on with their lives. Symbolic recognition is only important for those who choose to recognize the symbols. We could, instead, deny to both state and communities the power, by imposing *their* symbols on *our* lives, to control our sense of self-worth.

So perhaps the Irish Reports discussed here are wise in concentrating on the *instrumental* benefits of marriage: if the practical disadvantages that the unmarried currently suffer were all removed, would there be any further case for worrying about the inequalities of differential constitutive recognition?

Interdependence and Care

There is another important element in Metz's article. She proposes that '[l]egitimate public welfare goals traditionally treated through marriage … would be addressed through an intimate caregiving union (ICGU) status' (Metz, 2007: 197).[44]

As I have already indicated, care-giving is an important component of marital and non-marital relationships alike, and many unmarried people commit themselves (either full-time or part-time) to caring for specific others who are dependent on them. Such care-giving is socially crucial, and morally invaluable. Hence the centrality, to political philosophy, of Metz's intimate care-giving unions.

However, I would want to stretch Metz's conception, perhaps beyond breaking point. I would first want to stress, again, that 'intimate' should not mean 'sexual'; ICGUs should encompass the Burden sisters, Lady Salter and Frank Sharratt, and Patricia Brunette and Guy Émard, just as much as Martin Fitzpatrick and John Thompson. What counts here is any union in which people care for each other.

If we want to put sex to one side, and look at dependence, interdependence and caring, then we should not model our approach exactly on marriage. One example of the difference that adopting this approach might bring is that there is no reason to be fixated on *couples*. We generally regard marriage as something that should take place between two, and only two, people, and hold polygamy in abhorrence. But interdependence can well occur, quite legitimately, between any number of people: we are all familiar with the interdependence that can exist in a household of up to a dozen people. Disabled people, just like children and the elderly, often have several adult carers. In so far as such dependence requires instrumental benefits and recognition, they should be provided. This should not raise any qualms about 'undermining marriage', for what is provided has nothing to do with marriage; even if married couples do qualify, they do so because they also exemplify the relevant interdependences.

One poignant example of an emotionally interdependent relationship is the following (taken from Stacey, 2003: 335–336). Lisa and Kat, a long-standing lesbian couple, have two children. The children's father is Michael, a gay man and good friend, who acted as sperm donor. Michael is in a relationship with Joaquin; both take an active part in the child rearing. The children are loved and well cared for by all four 'parents' and their extended kin. But because of the 'couple model' we are used to, Lisa (the biological mother) is either treated as a single parent (which she is definitely not), or has to choose to register either Kat or Michael as the child's 'other' parent; Joaquin can have no standing at all, even if, as a matter of fact, he spends more time with the children than any of the others. The existing Procrustean approach to relationships insists that this comprehensible and functional multi-party relationship must be treated as if it contained only two core adults. If we start by looking at varieties of interdependence, rather than starting with our expectations of the conjugal model, we will not make that mistake.

But a focus on ICGUs is too narrow. ICGUs are *one* form of care-giving, and a very important one. But insofar as it is *care* that we are concerned with, we should consider *all* desirable ways of providing care; we should not privilege one form. Thus we should consider both marriages and ICGUs as subsets of the wider category of care provision. I want to suggest, further, that that is not done at present in Ireland; that that is a serious failing; and that this failing has unrecognised implications for recognition.

Most care-giving does take place in the setting of ICGUs. But many people in Ireland are not in ICGUs: they live alone. In that they are not part of an ICGU, they are necessarily amongst the most vulnerable and defenceless sector of the population. Yet they are ignored in these discussions. Take the All-Party Committee on the Family. Its Report points out very early on that 21.6 per cent of the households in Ireland contain just one person; this is the second most common form of household.[45] Of these, 41 per cent are elderly persons; looked at another way, 26 per cent of people over 65 live alone (Committee on the Constitution, 2006: 22–23). This is clearly a significant proportion of the most vulnerable members of society. The Committee next defines a 'family' as consisting of a cohabiting couple, or adult(s) and child(ren), thus reducing the number of households by nearly 30 per cent, and eliminating all one-person households.[46] People in one-person households do not get another mention in the Report.

But there is considerable insult added to this injury. One important way that the Irish state accords recognition is by doing so in the Constitution: many of the most contentious parts of the Constitution are about symbolic recognition.[47] The section on the family opens: 'The state *recognises* the Family as the natural and primary unit group of Society …' (Article 41.1.1 [emphasis added]).[48] The All-Party Committee does not propose to change that wording.[49] That excludes all those in single-person households. Marginalised here are the bachelor farmer, the spinster teacher, the widow or widower whose children (if any) have grown up and left home – even the priest. All these do not have the solace of an intimate partner to share their life and give them bodily and emotional care; on top of that they are demeaned as unimportant by the Constitution. Meanwhile, everybody seems obsessed about a possible slur given to those who already have all the emotional benefits of cohabitation. Equality seems to have been completely lost sight of. I would therefore suggest that it is unacceptable for the Constitution to privilege people in one sort of domestic arrangement over those who (whether through choice or circumstance) are in another sort – particularly when these unprivileged are also amongst the most vulnerable members of society.

There is an alternative approach. First, all reference to the family should be removed from the Constitution, or the family redefined so as to include single-person households and unrelated couples who look after each other, like Lady Salter and Frank Sharratt.[50] But, second, there should be a recognition of the vulnerability, and need for care, of those who are *not* in intimate care-giving unions. There should certainly be recognition of the noble and self-sacrificing work done by carers within the home. But there should also be recognition that many do not have this, and that important intimate care is given *outside* unions – by, for instance, nurses. That care is no less important. I have been arguing that the State has a duty of recognising *all* its citizens, not just those in intimate unions. One way that this can be done is by the inclusion in the Constitution of an undertaking that the State cares *about* all citizens, and will therefore undertake to care *for* those who are unable to care for themselves (temporarily or permanently), and who do not have anybody on hand to care for them. That would probably require a commitment to a welfare state; for a welfare state provides, along with its instrumental benefits, an important symbolic statement of the state's recognition of our equality, vulnerability and need for care.[51] That would provide some recognition of the worth of all.

Conclusion

In summary, I have argued: (1) that contracts dealing with domestic relationships should be capable of being legally enforced; (2) that the state should not privilege any form of domestic relationship, nor should it impose one understanding of marriage on those who have other understandings; (3) that the 'equality' approach to instrumental benefits is misguided; instead we should ask the *reasons* for the benefits and then use these reasons to determine who should qualify for these benefits; (4) that there are arguments for the state leaving recognition of marital unions to communities; but there are also arguments that the state is precisely the sort of body that should be creating such unions; there are also arguments that people should not be seeking recognition for their unions from either state or community; (5) in any case, any such recognition should have no impact on the availability of instrumental benefits; and (6) the state should recognise the need of everybody for care, and undertake to provide that care when necessary.

Notes

1. Committee on the Constitution (2006); HRC (2006); Domestic Partnership (2006); LRC (2006). A further Report (*Report of the Study Group on Pre-nuptial Agreements*, 2007) appeared when this article was nearing completion.
2. Civil Unions Bill 2006. This was debated in Dáil Éireann on 20 and 21 February 2007.
3. The Law Society's submission to the Committee on the Constitution, reproduced in Committee on the Constitution (2006: A161). The Society's proposals for change disappointingly fail to meet its own requirements.
4. With the exception of the Committee on the Constitution, whose members were drawn from the Oireachtas, the bodies producing the Reports mentioned in footnote 1 consist almost entirely of lawyers – which is both surprising and regrettable.
5. Unfortunately, the Law Reform Commission did not express this ideal too well: 'The Commission is of the view that the State should respect the choice [*sic*] people make in relation to their own private lives. The objective of reform in this area does not necessitate far-reaching rights on [*sic*] cohabitants' (LRC, 2006, section 1.14, n. 45). The Working Group on Domestic Partnership expressed itself rather more clearly, if scarcely more grammatically: 'autonomy encompasses the rights and the capacity of an individual to freely choose the form that one's personal relationships will take rather than have decisions made for them' (Domestic Partnership, 2006: section 1.14).
6. In 1967 it was proposed that, for those who married in a religious ceremony, the rules of that religion regarding dissolution of the marriage should be followed by the state (Committee on the Constitution, 1967: 44). This proposal received a hostile reaction from the Catholic Church: see Whyte (1980: 347-9). I am proposing a variant of this: that marriages not allowing divorce (or allowing only fault-based divorce) should be allowed to anyone who might want one. This proposal should surely be acceptable to the Catholic Church. For similar suggestions (made by an erstwhile anti-divorce campaigner) see Binchy (1995: 71–74), and *Irish Times* (2005). Of course, if this tolerance is to be accorded to those with a Catholic understanding of marriage, then it has also to be accorded to those with other beliefs.
7. Some critics have described this as a 'one size fits all' approach (e.g. Stark, 2001), but that metaphor is not apt: garments warranting this description fit the wearer comfortably, whatever his or her shape or size. This flexibility is precisely *not* what current marriage laws offer.
8. I expand on the arguments of this section in Morriss, Liberalism and Marriage: An Underexplored Tension, (unpublished paper), which is a companion piece to this one.
9. However, schoolteachers may still lose their job if their private sexual behaviour is deemed incompatible with their school's religious ethos: see *Flynn* v *Power* (1985). This legal privilege of religious organisations to flout equality requirements, which are binding on everybody else, was explicitly recognised in the (misnamed) Employment Equality Act, 1998: section 37(1).
10. It is possibly acceptable to have sexual *relationships* with two people at once; it is a criminal offence to have *marriages* with two people at once.
11. For fascinating discussions of these issues, see Elster (1979) and Elster (2000).
12. Subject to a range of familiar restrictions. I enumerate and explore these restrictions in Morriss, Liberalism and Marriage: An Underexplored Tension, (unpublished paper).
13. There are, of course, also obligations incurred by marriage; but I will focus on the rights, as do these Reports.
14. For summaries of the current state of the law, see the Reports in footnote 1.
15. A good example of this approach is HRC (2006). More generally, see Baker *et al.* (2004).
16. 'The terms 'equality' and 'non-discrimination' are sometimes used synonymously by the ECJ.' (HRC, 2006: 17 n. 69). I draw on this Report here, as it expresses European jurisprudence clearly and – so far as my other reading allows me to assess – accurately.
17. Here, as elsewhere, I have omitted footnotes referring to cases.
18. 'An objective justification will be established if the differential treatment pursues a legitimate aim, and if there is a reasonable relationship of proportionality between the means employed and the aim sought to be realized' (HRC, 2006: 52).

19. The cases are *Fitzpatrick* v *Sterling Housing Association Ltd* (2001), *Ghaidan* v *Godin-Mendoza* (2004), and *Burden and Burden v The United Kingdom* (2006–2007). For helpful commentary on the first of these, see Glennon (2000). Note: after this article was completed, *Burden and Burden* was referred to the Grand Chamber of the ECHR, which heard the case on 12 September 2007. No judgment has been delivered by 23 October, the deadline for completing this article's proofs. References to this case are therefore to the judgment of the Chamber.
20. Lord Slynn, in *Fitzpatrick* [2001] 1 AC 32. It is not clear to me whether the faithfulness and monogamy of the relationship is relevant to Fitzpatrick's claim. For a critical comment on this phraseology, see Lord Millet's dissenting judgment in *Ghaidan*; he thought that its use misunderstood the rationale of the legislation, which is that qualification for the tenancy should depend on status and not merit (*Ghaidan* [2004] 2 AC 557, para. 100).
21. The disability, which was caused by a blood clot on the brain after a fall, resulted in Thompson being tetraplegic and unable to speak.
22. If an adult adopts a child – legally or *de facto* – then the child becomes a member of the adult's family. But, strangely, there is no concept of adopting an adult in modern European law.
23. Some gay activists have also advocated this approach: e.g. Gay and Lesbian Rights Lobby of NSW (1994).
24. For some support for my claim that a legal 'equality-regime' is inadequate, see Graycar and Millbank (2000).
25. The inability to have a sexual relationship is, and always has been, a ground for annulling a marriage.
26. For a discussion, see Cossman & Ryder (2001: 304–6).
27. These points are made frequently in the judgment: *Brunette* paras 15, 19, 25, 60, 62, 67.
28. The other sort of equality advocated is equality *within* relationships (covering gender neutrality).
29. LCC (2001) Chapter 3, Part 2 (which is more than half of the whole Report).
30. The rationale is that some violent fathers have used their right of access to their child to harass the mother.
31. When Lady Salter went into hospital, she designated Frank Sharratt as her next of kin: see *Joram*, [1979] 1 WLR 6.
32. HRC (2006) does briefly mention non-conjugal relations (pp. 137–138), but has little to say about them.
33. The chapter on non-conjugal relationships (HRC, 2006: ch. 9) is the shortest and thinnest in the report, and makes no proposals. But this thinking seemed to influence the Minister of Justice, Equality and Law Reform, who gave, as one reason for opposing the Civil Unions Bill, its failure to include non-conjugal relations (McDowell, 2007a: cols 1806, 1807; McDowell, 2007b).
34. The preferred form of self-referral at present is LGBT, denoting lesbians, gays, bisexuals and transsexuals. The presence of bisexuals here is intriguing. Presumably, in this context, recognition of bisexuality should require the possibility of the marriage of at least three people: how *else* can bisexuality be recognised? But nowhere in the mainstream literature have I seen even a hint at such a possibility; the B in LGBT seems to be put in just for show. For such unwillingness to think through the implications of what they are saying, see the submissions to the Oireachtas Committee from Gay and Lesbian Equality Network, Gay and Lesbian Unions Eire, Irish Council for Civil Liberties, Johnny Gay Peer Action Charity Group, Labour LGBT, LGBT Campaign – TCD and USI, Lesbians in Cork, and The Workers' Party of Ireland, all included in Committee on the Constitution (2006) Appendix 3.
35. This emphasis is probably helped by the presence in the Working Group of the Director of Policy Change at the Gay and Lesbian Equality Network.
36. Nancy Fraser is one of the few writers to notice this (Fraser, 2000: 115).
37. One should say, passed *back*: marriage was controlled by church and community, not the state, until late in the nineteenth century. There is no comprehensive history of marriage in Ireland; but see Cosgrave (1985).
38. This would probably require the removal from the Constitution of Article 42.3.1°, under which 'the State pledges itself to guard with special care the institution of Marriage'. Attempting to repeal this clause might itself be divisive, but only if not properly handled. After all, Article 44.1.2°, which

pledged the State to recognise the special position of the Catholic Church, was removed in 1972, without controversy (Whyte, 1980: 53–56, 163–165, 349–350, 388–389).

39. This is perhaps particularly prevalent in Ireland. I was amazed to discover, on moving here some ten years ago, that I was automatically a member of 'the settled community'. This is Irish-speak for all those who are not 'members of the Travelling community' (that is, Irish gypsies). As I had just emigrated from my own country to a place in which I knew nobody and nobody knew me, I felt neither settled nor part of any (Irish) community.
40. There is perhaps a parallel here with a church's role in conducting such a transformation. But it is at least clearer how a god could perform (or assist) such a transformation.
41. I cannot explore here the extent to which the state should *also* be concerned about non-citizens who reside within its territorial boundaries (or, indeed, about its impact on non-citizens abroad). Note that whilst communities that cross state boundaries (for instance, religious ones) may contain more members than states do, that does not make them more *inclusive*.
42. See Fuller (2002: 16–17). For original reports see *Irish Times*, 5 July 1949, p. 4, 6 July 1949, p. 7, and letters on subsequent days.
43. This is pointed out by Jones (2006: 40).
44. See Metz (2007: 208–211) for discussion of ICGU status.
45. Committee on the Constitution (2006: 22) (which is the fourth page of the Report proper). The figures are from the 2002 census.
46. Committee on the Constitution (2006: 23–24). To be exact, 28.2 per cent of households are discarded: in addition to the 21.6 per cent of single-person households, 7.1 per cent of households are (unspecified) 'non-family households', whilst 0.4 per cent of households consist of more than one family unit.
47. The importance of this symbolism is shown in the interminable, and very heated, debates over the exact form of words by which abortion should be completely prevented in the Constitution – whilst granting a constitutional right to have an abortion abroad, so that the actual abortion rate of Irish women is around the European average.
48. Other passages bestowing recognition include the contentious Article 41.2.1° ('In particular, the State recognises that by her life within the home, woman [*sic*] gives to the State a support without which the common good cannot be achieved'); the now deleted article recognising the Catholic Church (see n. 38); and the *not* deleted recognition of religion in Article 44.1.1° and the Preamble.
49. A minority of the Committee proposed inserting a sentence into the Constitution stating that the family is not necessarily based on marriage, and then: 'All persons, irrespective of their marital status, have a right to family life' (Committee on the Constitution, 2006: 129). I am at a loss as to what that could mean when applied to a single adult – unless the suggestion is that a single adult has ceased to be a person.
50. These two proposals are equivalent, as if the latter were adopted any statement to the effect that 'the State recognises the Family' would become empty, as it would 'recognise' everything.
51. For powerful statements of this view, see Titmuss (1970) and Ignatieff (1984).

References

(a) Official Reports

(1) Irish

Committee on the Constitution (1967) *Report* (Dublin: Stationery Office).

Committee on the Constitution (2006) The All-Party Oireachtas Committee on the Constitution, *Tenth Progress Report: The Family* (Dublin, January 2006).

Domestic Partnership (2006) The Working Group on Domestic Partnership [chaired by Anne Colley], *Options Paper, Presented by the Working Group on Domestic Partnership to the Tánaiste and Minister for Justice, Equality and Law Reform, Mr Michael McDowell T.D.* (Dublin, November 2006).

HRC (2006) J. Walsh & F. Ryan, *The Rights of* De Facto *Couples* (Dublin: Irish Human Rights Commission, March 2006).

LRC (2006) The Law Reform Commission, *Report: Rights and Duties of Cohabitants* (LRC 82 2006) (Dublin, December 2006).

Report of the Study Group on Pre-nuptial Agreements, 2007, [chaired by Inge Clissmann] (Dublin, April 2007).

(2) Other

LCC, 2001: Law Commission of Canada, *Beyond Conjugality: recognizing and supporting close personal adult relationships* (Ottawa).

(b) Cases

(1) Irish

Ennis v *Butterly* [1996] 1 IR 426.

Flynn v *Power* [1985] ILRM 336.

(2) Other

Brunette c. *Québec* [2000] R.J.Q. 2664.

Burden and Burden v The United Kingdom (European Court of Human Rights, December 2006, as revised March 2007; available on ECHR website).

Fitzpatrick v *Sterling Housing Association Ltd* [2001] 1 AC 27.

Ghaidan v *Godin-Mendoza* [2004] 2 AC 557.

Goodridge v *Dept of Public Health* (2003) 440 Mass. 309.

Joram Developments Ltd v *Sharratt* [1979] 1 WLR 3 and 928.

(c) Secondary Sources

Baker, J., Lynch, K., Cantillon, S. & Walsh, J. (2004) *Equality: From Theory to Action* (Basingstoke: Palgrave).

Binchy, W. (1995) Pluralism, Religious Freedom, and Marriage Law, *Doctrine & Life*, 45 (January), pp. 71–74.

Cosgrave, A. (Ed.) (1985) *Marriage in Ireland* (Dublin: College Press).

Cossman, B. & Ryder, B. (2001) What is Marriage-Like Like? The Irrelevance of Conjugality, *Canadian Journal of Family Law*, 18, pp. 269–326.

Elster, J. (1979) *Ulysses and the Sirens* (Cambridge: Cambridge University Press).

Elster, J. (2000) *Ulysses Unbound: Studies in Rationality, Precommitment, and Constraints* (Cambridge: Cambridge University Press).

Fraser, N. (2000) Rethinking Recognition, *New Left Review* (n.s.) 3 (May/June), pp. 107–120.

Fuller, L. (2002) *Irish Catholicism since 1950: The Undoing of a Culture* (Dublin: Gill & Macmillan).

Gay and Lesbian Rights Lobby of NSW (1994) *The Bride Wore Pink: Legal Recognition of our Relationships, A Discussion Paper* (2nd edn, Sydney: Lesbian and Gay Legal Rights Service).

Glennon, L. (2000) *Fitzpatrick* v *Sterling Housing Association Ltd* – An Endorsement of the Functional Family?, *International Journal of Law, Policy and the Family*, 14, pp. 226–255.

Graycar, R. & Millbank, J. (2000) The Bride Wore Pink … To the *Property (Relationships) Legislation Amendment Act 1999*: Relationships Law Reform in New South Wales, *Canadian Journal of Family Law*, 17, pp. 227–282.

Ignatieff, M. (1984) *The Needs of Strangers* (London: Chatto & Windus).

Irish Times (2005) Binchy Argues for Legal Right to Lifelong Marriage, 26 August.

Irish Times (2007) Croatian Church to Discourage Irish Weddings, 15 February.

Jones, P. (2006)Equality, Recognition and Difference, *CRISPP*, 9, pp. 23–46.

Lewin, E. (1998) *Recognizing Ourselves: Ceremonies of Lesbian and Gay Commitment* (New York: Columbia University Press).

Macintyre, A. (1999) *Dependent Rational Animals: Why Human Beings Need the Virtues* (London: Duckworth).

McDowell, M. (2007a) *Parliamentary Debates (Official Report), Dáil Éireann*, 20 February.

McDowell, M. (2007b) Labour's Civil Union Bill Would Not Stand Up, *Irish Times*, 2 March.

Metz, T. (2007) The Liberal Case for Disestablishing Marriage, *Contemporary Political Theory*, 6, pp. 196–217.

Morriss, P. Marriage & Liberalism: an Underexplored Tension, (unpublished paper).

Stacey, J. (2003) Toward Equal Regard for Marriages and Other Imperfect Intimate Affiliations, *Hofstra Law Review*, 32, pp. 331–348.

Stark, B. (2001) Marriage Proposals: From One-Size-Fits-All to Postmodern Marriage Law, *California Law Review*, 89, pp. 1479–1548.

Titmuss, R. M. (1970) *The Gift Relationship: From Human Blood to Social Policy* (London: George Allen & Unwin).

Whyte, J. H. (1980) *Church and State in Modern Ireland 1923–1979* 2nd edn (Dublin: Gill and Macmillan).

The Regulation of Public Space in Northern Ireland

CIARÁN O'KELLY & DOMINIC BRYAN

Context

On 10 September 2005, an Orange Order march was rerouted away from part of the Whiterock area of west Belfast. The marchers had intended to pass along the Springfield Road but an alternative route was imposed by the Northern Ireland Parades Commission in order to avoid their passing houses with nationalist occupants. The rerouted parade had been due to take place at the beginning of June 2005 but had been postponed in the hope that the Orange Order could either find or force a more advantageous resolution at the end of the summer. Having observed no meaningful engagement between the Orange Order and nationalist residents in the intervening months, however, the Parades Commission ruled for the rerouting a second time in September (PCNI, 2005a).

The 2005 marching season in Northern Ireland had been tense. A general sense of frustration in loyalist communities, in part at other decisions made by the Parades Commission, combined with the internal politics of loyalist paramilitary groups, had produced perfect conditions for violent confrontations between marchers and their supporters on the one side and the police and security services on the other (Davenport, 2005). These conditions came to fruition in the wake of the march's rerouting with three days of rioting that resulted in millions of pounds worth of damage, live rounds exchanged, 30 police officers injured, and a total cost in terms of policing of £3 million. The Chief Constable of the Police Service of

Northern Ireland described the original Orange Order parade as having 'become illegal' (BBC Online, 2005) with marchers determined to breach the Parades Commission's determination, thus producing the confrontation that sparked the riot.

The events of September 2005 seemed all the more unfortunate to some people because they appeared to be a 'throwback to the early days of the Troubles or, more recently, the worst days of the Drumcree crises in the mid nineties' (Davenport, 2005). No doubt levels of violence surrounding marches have, at least as measured in terms of policing costs, fallen significantly since the late 1990s (Hamilton & Bryan, 2006: 184f). The September 2005 riots, therefore, looked like an anomalous blip in a general downward trend. That said, the riots served to remind observers of ongoing tensions over parades. Resentment continued to brew in the unionist and loyalist part of the community over ground they saw as ceded to republicanism since the beginning of the peace process.

Given these tensions, how are we to explain the reduction in violence around parades since the late 1990s? Jarman has addressed a wide range of reasons why this might be the case (Jarman, 2003). We will focus on a single narrower factor, however: the impact of the Parades Commission as a regulator of public space.[1] We will examine the effect that the organisational form the Northern Ireland Parades Commission has taken has had on the marching controversy. We argue that the cause of conciliation – one of the Commission's formal aims – is not helped by the Commission's structure.[2] While violence might not return to the levels of a decade ago if the Parades Commission were to be abolished overnight, any reduction in violence would not be a consequence of the Commission's existence. This will always be the case so long as law is regarded in Northern Ireland as imposed from without, not authored from within.

Our argument is set out in three sections. In the first section we discuss the Commission as a public body and what this might mean for its effect on Northern Ireland's political and social landscape. We give an account of precisely what sort of public body the Parades Commission is, in terms of the formal architecture of the state. This gives us a significant insight into the division between the stated purpose of the Commission and its actual effects. Drawing on aspects of Iain Ayer's and John Braithwaite's 'responsive regulation' model, we set out the range of options for action available to the Commission and the manner in which those options are used. We question why it is that, regarding the 7 per cent of marches that are deemed controversial, mediated solutions have proven somewhat elusive? Informed by the discussions in the first and second sections, in the third section we discuss the Commission in terms of its accountability and legitimacy and suggest some means by which it might be reformed with conciliation in mind. We argue that it is difficult to envisage a deliberative resolution of the parades dispute. Given the factors we set out in the second section, the Parades Commission is simply not designed for developing a sustainable long-term solution to the use of public space. This is especially so given the distance between law-making and the subjects of law in Northern Ireland.

The Parades Commission as Public Body

The origins of the Parades Commission and of Northern Ireland's marching disputes have been addressed in great detail elsewhere (Bryan, 2000; Hamilton & Bryan, 2006). It suffices here to say that the Parades Commission was set up in response to the political, public order, and policing crisis caused by parades in the mid-1990s. This crisis had been boiled over at Drumcree in 1995 and again in 1996, where the police's blocking of an Orange parade from the mainly nationalist Garvaghy Road area in Portadown, County Armagh had served as a rallying point for loyalists and others. A compromise was reached in 1995, but led to seriously bad feeling on the nationalist side when the Orange Order fêted the compromise as an historic victory for them (Bryan, 2000: 3).

When Orangemen were blocked from marching down the road on 9 July 1996, a wave of pre-meditated protest and widespread public disorder swept across Northern Ireland. In the midst of this mayhem, a Catholic taxi driver was murdered on the evening of 9 July. As the 12th approached, and fearing outright chaos, the police changed their decision and forced the march down the Garvaghy Road, producing three days of serious rioting in nationalist areas in which another man died (Bryan, 2000: 5–6). In a sense, however, although the Orange Order had won the 1996 battle, they lost their struggle to march freely along the Garvaghy Road because the confrontation led to government moves that would lead to a shift in the balance of power around parades.

A significant outcome of the Drumcree confrontation was the initiation of the 'Independent Review of Parades and Marches', chaired by Peter North. The terms of reference for the 'North Review' were to examine 'the adequacy of the legal provisions covering parades, the power of the police and Secretary of State, the possible introduction of new machinery such as a tribunal for deciding on parade disputes and the possible introduction of a code of practice for public demonstrations' (Bryan, 2000: 171). The Review, published in 1997, proposed that parading be regulated by an independent commission. The commission was to facilitate mediation between conflicting groups and, should no compromise be forthcoming, would adjudicate on how parades and marches ought to proceed.

In 1997 the police were better prepared to counter violence in Drumcree but actually decided that the parade should proceed along the route. Despite impressions at the time, this was something of a pyrrhic victory for the marchers. The police had avoided confrontation in the knowledge that the following year, in 1998, the new legal body would be making the decisions however. In 1998 the Parades Commission made its determination that the Drumcree parade would be rerouted. No Orange march has gone down the Garvaghy Road since.

The Drumcree debacle and other crises (notably on the Ormeau Road in Belfast and also in Derry) exposed some serious problems with the regulation of public spaces in Northern Ireland. Most importantly, the police's enforcement of public order put them in the unenviable position of having to adjudicate on parade routes, very often within hours of the parades starting. Their adjudications were made on public order grounds, on whether re-routing a parade or allowing it to proceed would produce the most disorder. Unfortunately, police adjudication produced perverse incentives towards violence on the part of antagonistic groups. If a group's members could threaten more violence than their opponents, then they would get their way.

The Parades Commission was established on a non-statutory basis in 1997. When the Labour party came into power, the Commission was given a formal role under the 1998 Public Processions (Northern Ireland) Act (TSO, 1998). It was not met with universal acclaim and remains somewhat unpopular among members of the Unionist community. The Orange Order have consistently rejected the Commission's rulings and have called for its abolition or, more recently, for a review of its functioning.[3]

In 2006, 7 per cent of Parades came to the attention of the Commission in some shape or form, although not all were ruled on (PCNI, 2006: 3). As the North Review envisaged, and the Act prescribed, the Commission must have regard to five criteria in adjudicating on marches: potential for public disorder; disruption to the life of the community; impact on community relations; failures regarding the guidelines in the Commission's code of conduct; and the desirability of allowing a procession along a particular route (TSO, 1998, section 8(6)). In practice these criteria have been interpreted rather widely by the Commission. Factors such as the prevailing political atmosphere, the cumulative effect of marches and the sensitivity of march-organisers, as manifested in their actions, to local concerns have been cited in Commission adjudications (Hamilton, 2007: 97).

The Commission places a significant emphasis on its mediation functions, by which it nominates Authorised Officers, effectively local fieldworkers to assist local communities in resolving parading disputes (Hamilton & Bryan, 2006). Recently, it has placed a greater emphasis on furthering its mediation function, regarding local compromise as a far more acceptable outcome than adjudication (PCNI, 2006: 2). In essence, however, while the Commission has the *discretion* to accept compromises between groups its *power* lies in its adjudicatory capacities.

We will return to this in more detail in the second section. For the moment, however, let us examine the Commission itself as an *agency*. The formal character of the Commission is fundamental to our understanding of its role, or lack of a role in producing a genuine resolution to the parades dispute, something we will return to in the third section.

UK governments have long regarded quasi independent agencies as having particular benefits in the governance of the state. Even the Blair administration, which advocated a significant reduction in the number of agencies before rising to power, has actually vastly increased the number and range of agencies through its terms in office (Flinders, 2004b: 886ff). The agencification of governance provides states with a very powerful tool. Governments have stated that the establishment of agencies provides us with an efficient and effective means for engagement at a more local level than can be managed from the monolith of central government. It provides opportunities for the local softening of what would otherwise be hard law. How this is articulated has changed somewhat over the years. The Cabinet Office's 1998 Public Bodies report, which lists all quasi-autonomous public bodies active in the UK, emphasised appropriateness and cost effectiveness as the key motivations behind the establishment of agencies (Cabinet Office, 1998: vii). By 2002, the stated motivation had been reduced to talk of effectiveness, with agencies being the 'best means of delivering the function required' (Cabinet Office, 2002: v).

This might certainly be the case, but agencification also has the advantage of insulating politicians from areas of policy that they would prefer not to address directly. Agencies, as such, can act as 'buffer zones' (Flinders, 2004b: 898) or 'teflon coats' (Hood, 2002: 17) between policies and politicians. Indeed, this may have been an important reason for establishing the Parades Commission. The Commission could insulate politicians from blame for specific events. At the same time, politicians could be simultaneously be seen to act by allowing for regular reviews of the Commission's functioning as demanded under public bodies protocols.

Given this it appears that the primary motivations behind establishing the Commission had less to with conciliation – its stated aim – and more to with avoiding, through the exercise of administrative power, the sort of crises that arose in the mid-1990s. The Commission as constructed has something of the 'mongrel' about it (Hamilton & Bryan, 2006: 156), with an attachment to the idea of conciliation sitting uneasily with its wielding of significant regulatory power over public spaces in Northern Ireland. This ambiguity is borne out in Cabinet Office and Northern Ireland Office categorisations of the Commission. From the point of view of the Cabinet Office, it is a wielder of hard law. The NIO, on the other hand, may yearn for a somewhat softer governance of the situation.

From its inception in 1998 until 2005, the Parades Commission was regarded as an independent regulator by the Cabinet Office's agencies and public bodies team. Regulation is defined by the Cabinet Office as 'exerting powers over, or imposing burdens on, other organisations or individuals; by means of inspection, licensing, referral to another decision-maker (particularly with binding advice), accreditation or enforcement' (Cabinet Office, 2005b: v). In 2003, however, a Better Regulation Task Force report recommended that independent regulators be brought within the public bodies database, where each non-departmental public body (NDPB) is listed, categorised and described (BRTF, 2003). As a result, the Parades Commission and other independent regulators were designated as public bodies in 2005.

When it was included in the database, the Commission was regarded as a 'tribunal' NDPB, a definition repeated in 2006 (Cabinet Office, 2005b: vi; Cabinet Office, 2006: 325). Some months earlier, however, prior to the publication of the Public Bodies report, the Northern Ireland Office had, in passing, defined the Parades Commission as an *executive* NDPB (NIO, 2005: 21). The process of categorisation may seem somewhat arcane, but it indicates a significant ambiguity between departments as to the Commission's role. After all, tribunal NDPBs are supposed to 'operate with jurisdiction in a specialised field of the law, independently of Government'.

Executive NDPBs, on the other hand ought to function 'deliberately at a remove from ministers,' so as 'to permit a service or function to be carried out independently, at arm's length from the Government.' (Cabinet Office, 2005a: 4–7). That the Parades Commission was, in the end, categorised as a tribunal NDPB may be quite telling.

Specifically, from the perspective of central government, it is the adjudication theme and not the mediation theme that drives the Parades Commission. As a regulator and as a tribunal NDPB the emphasis is on law enforcement rather than on engagement with local communities. This is entirely consistent with the urgent needs presented by the Drumcree crisis and other events related to marching. In short, the enforced regulation of public spaces remains at the heart of government approaches to the Commission's role.

As far as the Parades Commission is concerned, moreover, its value lies in precisely the manner in which it does and *does not* perform one of the normal functions of public bodies. While, on the mediation side, the Parades Commission is sufficiently local to facilitate dialogue between groups, when it comes to adjudication, the Commission's power lies precisely in its distance from the local environment and from events on the ground. It is ultimately an agency wielding coercive power that has the discretion not to wield that power.

Handing the adjudicatory power over to an independent body has some obvious benefits for the police, for government, and for other members of the political sphere. When adjudication powers were shifted to the Commission, the police could avoid formulating policies on the hoof, and can now stick with enforcing the Commission's rulings. Second, the shift in powers benefited political actors who could sidestep involvement in parades disputes by ceding sovereignty over the matter to an external agency and distancing themselves from its decisions. This was particularly important in 1997 and 1998 when crucial political talks were underway which led to the Good Friday Agreement.

While, in the wake of the establishment of the Parades Commission, the police have retained their public order powers to make decisions on the day, they have not used them. They have benefited from being 'one stage removed' from adjudications over marches and thus are insulated from anything but the duty to implement Commission decisions (Jarman, 2003: 98). Once decisions were removed from actors on the ground, moreover, and once it was realised that the police would implement decisions no matter what threat of force was wielded against them, violence was reduced.

This is because the Commission is simply not amenable to persuasion through violence or protests on the day (Jarman, 2003: 98). Violence and protests are not good forms of communication from the ground to the agency. In fact, on the day itself, there is little if any means by which communication can happen. The Commission's formal, rules-based character means that the only possible communications can be admitted through applications, objections and appeals. In this situation, the bureaucratic character of the agency, not its capacity to maintain a local presence, is the key to its power.

Benefits for political actors have been less direct. Nevertheless, they are very real. While judgements over the potential for public disorder were made by the police, in an environment where public disorder could either disrupt a parade or force one through a neighbourhood, blame could easily spill over onto the doors of governments and politicians. After all, as Hamilton has pointed out (Hamilton, 2007), every party to the dispute could claim that their rights were being trampled by the agents of the state, especially where parading adjudications appeared to be entirely *ad hoc*. The Parades Commission solved the problem of blame by implication for politicians because adjudications are now distant from political control.

This form of power arising from an administrative structure is not entirely unproblematic, however. The incentives produced by the Parades Commission only go so far as to encourage people to follow the rules it has instituted. If they follow those rules strategically, then the violence and discord surrounding parades can be damped down without at all solving the problems that are at the root of the disagreement. The *modus vivendi* reached will only exist so long as the Parades Commission exists to enforce it. The Parades Commission encourages nothing more than the following of its rules. While that might produce valuable outcomes, it ought not to be mistaken for the production of a consensus that would involve actual conciliation between opposing factions.

Moreover, while the north report may have envisaged that the Parades Commission would eventually render itself redundant, the Commission is designed so that this is most unlikely to happen. It is a coercive device rather than an instrument for promoting conciliation. This is why the Commission's character as a public body is fundamental to an understanding of possibilities for conciliation in Northern Ireland.

The Parades Commission as Regulator

As we said above, while the Commission has the discretion to accept compromises between groups its power lies in its power to adjudicate. In this section we outline some limitations on the Commission's adjudicative power as it is manifested in Northern Ireland's political and social landscape. Whereas in the previous section we argued that it is the Commission's status as a distant and rule-bound public body that is the key to its power, in this section we argue that that power, while leading to a reduction in violence, has hitherto not been sufficient to bring about much in the way of mediation between conflicting parties. The fact that this is changing slowly in the face of the Commission's regulatory strategy, we argue, has more to do with calculations of opposing groups as to how to gain advantage in the face of the Commission's coercive force than it has to do with genuine conciliation.

The Parades Commission's regulatory strategy can be seen as a variant on Ayers and Braithwaite's 'responsive regulation' model (Ayers & Braithwaite, 1992). Drawing on and adjusting 'tit-for-tat' strategies in game theory, Ayres and Braithwaite hypothesise that regulatory enforcement ought not to be seen as a binary process, with enforcement either happening or not happening. Where regulation is a binary process, the only enforcement power available to the regulator is often the power to suspend or withdraw a licence or otherwise shut a regulatee down. As Ayres and Braithwaite note this sanction 'is such a drastic one that it is politically impossible and morally unacceptable to use it with any but the most extraordinary offences.' In these situations, punitive legal architectures can actually result in under-enforcement of regulatory rules (Ayers & Braithwaite: 1992: 36).

It is better, Ayers and Braithwaite argue, for regulation to be backed up by a series of measures, ranging from the mild to the catastrophic (both for the regulator and often for the regulatee). In these circumstances, the regulator can either ratchet enforcement measures up until they get a response from the regulatee. 'Every escalation of noncompliance by the firm,' they write, 'can be matched with a corresponding escalation in punitiveness by the state' (Ayers & Braithwaite, 1992: 37). So, the base of the pyramid, representing the bulk of regulatory arrangements, might involve self-regulation. Then, moving up the pyramid, regulator intervention becomes ever-more punitive. Even if the regulator-regulatee relationship settles into an equilibrium where they both work to a menu of punishments matched to various actions, punishments ought to settle at the level just above that where they become disincentives to bad behaviour.

A related aspect of the enforcement pyramid as described by Ayers and Braithwaite is that each ratcheting up of enforcement is both a punitive action in itself and is a form of communication to the regulatee that 'socially suboptimal compliance with regulatory goals' are not sufficient to satisfy the regulator (Ayers & Braithwaite, 1992: 38). As the regulator climbs higher up the pyramid, the incentives for compliance increase. That said, these incentives are produced 'at the cost of increasingly inflexible and adversarial regulation.' Given this, 'clear communication in advance of willingness by the state to escalate up the pyramid gives incentives to both the industry and regulatory agents to make regulation work at lower levels of interventionism' (Ayers & Braithwaite, 1992: 38-–39). The pinnacle of the pyramid, in this model, involves punishment sufficiently onerous as to be akin to mutually assured destruction in theories of warfare. There are few incentives if any for anyone to allow things to get to this point but it is imperative that the regulator communicate a willingness to enforce even to such a costly point. 'Lop the tops off the enforcement pyramids,' Ayers and Braithwaite write, 'and there is less prospect of self-regulation, less prospect of persuasion as an alternative to punishment' (Ayers & Braithwaite, 1992: 39).

In short, the Ayers and Braithwaite enforcement pyramid is a 'benign big gun', designed to instil an adequate culture of self-regulation in the regulated industry. The more punitive the big gun, so the logic goes, the more likely it is that self-regulation will happen. The lessons to be drawn from this are that the 'big gun' at the top of the pyramid drives behaviour towards compliance and that the manner in which the scale of sanctions is wielded acts as a communicative device between regulator and regulatee.

Although Ayers and Braithwaite focus their attention on the public regulation of firms, others see the enforcement pyramid as a tool for realising social justice in a wider range of ways. According to Christine Parker, for instance, the pyramid might be used by 'mothers, lovers, bosses, creditors, unions, and generals struggling for justice in child-rearing, relationships, employee management, finance, industrial relations, international trade and warfare' (Parker, 1999: 71). For Parker, the base of the pyramid is composed of the achievement of justice according to endogenous ordering, where people resolve their differences in ways that they themselves formulate. The further up the pyramid they go, the more formal the legal measures they people deploy. Just as with Ayers and Braithwaite, however, Parker argues that 'people would settle matters lower down when they found that matters could be settled in a way that protected their rights at that level' (Parker, 1999: 76).

In some, if not in most circumstances, it is possible to imagine that the higher, formally legal, echelons of the pyramid would not be required for endogenous ordering to occur in people's social lives. The Braithwaitian assumption that action at the lower level is a function of possible action at a higher level does not mean that action at a lower level can *only* happen in the light of possible punitive actions (Scott, 2004: 160). Nevertheless, an enforcement pyramid is an effective mechanism where trust between parties is absent, either because of their formal characteristics (as is sometimes the case regarding the regulation of corporations) or because trust is more or less entirely missing, as is the case in Northern Ireland (O'Kelly, 2006). Where mistrust is prevalent, Ayers and Braithwaite's adjusted tit-for-tat game may act as an effective substitute.

So, how are we to see the Parades Commission's regulatory behaviour through the enforcement pyramid frame? It is not the Commission's compatibility with the model that is interesting, although it does in practice employ a scale of sanctions against various groups. Rather, it is precisely the Commission's divergence from the model that is revealing. This divergence falls into two related areas.[4]

First, whereas the conventional enforcement pyramid model has regulator–regulatee behaviour driven down towards the pyramid's base, the Parades Commission's behaviour very often sees enforcement ratcheted up towards the pyramid's peak. Second, whereas the Ayers and Braithwaite model predicts that the enforcement pyramid will involve communication and learning about acceptable regulatee behaviour, evidence of enforcement being regarded as communication is lacking.

Before examining these divergences, however, let us examine the components of the Commission's enforcement pyramid. While, as we saw above, the Commission's powers are often seen as a simple division between its meditative and its adjudicative roles, the adjudicative role is, strictly speaking, itself spread across a range of possible determinations (as required in section 2(2)b that includes placing on restrictions on the use of flags and emblems on parades and ordering major changes to parading routes (section 8(1)). In accordance with section 7 of the Act, those intending to protest must give notice of their intentions and the Commission may place restrictions on the number and manner of protests (Jarman, 1999: 1429).

Given this range of sanctions, we can sketch a rough taxonomy for a Parades Commission enforcement pyramid (Figure 1). At the base of the pyramid, we have the most desirable situation where disputes are successfully resolved through Parades Commission-sponsored mediation. Akin to a form of self-regulation in the style of Ayers and Braithwaite, mediated resolutions represent the outcome that the Parades Commission advocates for the regulation of disputes over parades. Legislatively speaking, the Parades Commission has the same powers of the police to impose a resolution to a dispute if mediation fails. In practice, the imposed resolution is subject to judgements as to the degree to which the parade (or attendant protest) goes beyond acceptable bounds of behaviour as set out in the Commission's Code of Conduct (PCNI, 2005b). These range from the imposition of various conditions, such as on the behaviour of those involved, numbers of participants or the like through a Code of Conduct, adherence to which is, in theory, to be monitored by the Parades Commission. Lack of adherence should bring consequences for future applications. Beyond this, a parade may be re-routed away from potential trouble-spots. Finally, it is possible for a parade to be banned outright by the Secretary of State for Northern Ireland (Jarman, 1999: 1422).[5]

Returning to the divergences with the Ayers and Braithwaite model, the purpose of the enforcement pyramid is to highlight the manner in which the regulatory regime at the base of the pyramid is achieved because transgressors risk encountering a more punitive regime further up towards the peak. The pyramid as a regulatory and communication device assumes that all players are good calculators of the costs

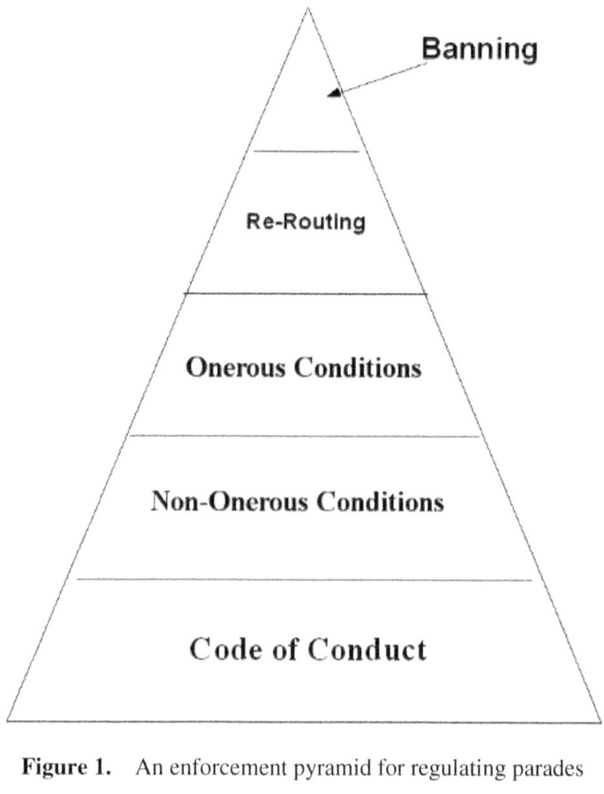

Figure 1. An enforcement pyramid for regulating parades

and benefits of any set of behaviours and learn from the shape of the pyramid. What, however, are we to conclude from the fact that, so far at least, there has been no discernible trend towards mediated settlements in Northern Ireland?

Certainly, we do not conclude that the various parties to disagreements in Northern Ireland are either irrational or are poor readers of their own interests. Rather, we draw four conclusions, especially in the light of the fact that, although the Parades Commission frequently reaches the higher echelons of the pyramid, the actual banning of parades by the Secretary of State has not happened since the Parades Commission has been in operation. First, the enforcement regime vis-à-vis contentious parades is not so punitive as to force groups into mediation. Indeed, certain levels of confrontation may actually be *desirable* to groups in conflict. Second, the Code of Conduct is not adequately enforced, there is only very limited monitoring of compliance, and there is insufficient, indeed next to no, connection made between the principles enshrined in the Code of Conduct and the development of a broad understanding of human rights. Without these elements in the Commission's behaviour, its capacity to communicate expectations to those who are subject to its rulings is severely curtailed. As such, the lower level of the regulatory pyramid is ineffective. Third, the Ayers and Braithwaite model envisages regulation being directed against relatively unified agents or groups. The Northern Ireland parading conflict is far more diffuse than this with intra-group conflicts almost doing as much to shape the environment as inter-group conflict. Fourth, pyramid-as-communication in the manner Ayers and Braithwaite intended may require a certain fundamental understanding of law as legitimately enforced in order to work smoothly. Where law is contested or is regarded as an exercise in pure power, it simply becomes one more component in the conflict environment, to be exploited and manipulated in accordance to a group's current interests. We shall examine these issues in turn.

The Regime is not Sufficiently Punitive

At one level the observation that the regime is not sufficiently punitive as to produce the desired (on the part of the regulator) results is entirely trivial. After all, we can assume that wherever mediation is successfully resisted, the regime is by definition not sufficiently punitive. The more interesting question, however, is over the grounds for resisting a level of enforcement that is acknowledged to have rather high costs associated with it, namely the regulation of public processions culminating in the enforcement of route-changes on marches. One reason why the Orange Order might prefer to pay these costs than to engage in mediated discussions is that entering into mediation is itself highly burdensome.

There are two primary problems with the pursuit of mediated agreements. First, the very engagement in dialogue itself involves parties at least implicitly acknowledging the legitimacy of their opponents' claims and stepping back from the absoluteness of their claims. As Parker said above, people would settle their differences voluntarily if they felt that their rights could be protected in doing so (Parker, 1999:

76). As regards parades, there is a significant loss of strategic face involved in entering into negotiations. From the perspective of the Orange Order, acknowledging the idea that the objections of local residents are sufficient to trigger examination of their processions is anathema to their sense of their own legitimacy. The thinking seems to be: 'why engage with people who seek to deny rights that are obviously yours?' The standpoint of nationalist residents, on the other hand, is rooted in the idea that the marches are deliberate provocations and, rather than seeking to march in public spaces as neutrally conceived, the loyal orders specifically choose to march where they can provoke. All this stands apart from the fact that thirty years of violent conflict have fuelled resentment and mistrust between both sides of the community (and often between specific individuals).

It is difficult to engage in mediation if these perspectives are maintained. In a sense, if an acknowledgement of the legitimacy of the other's claim was possible the conflict would automatically be defused. As things stand, and as we have said above, engagement can only happen at a strategic level where legitimacy is not acknowledged but the opponent's power to block progress towards one's aims is.

A second problem with mediation is that even getting to the strategic interaction stage may prove difficult because the maintenance of some level of conflict, whether violent or non-violent, may actually be of value to participants, or a particular section of the participants, especially within the ritualistic constraints of many public disturbances in Northern Ireland. It may, at least, be more valuable than the achievement of a settlement. Various political actors have long regarded movements like the Orange Order as useful in achieving their aims, even though they were by no means entirely biddable. Social and political authorities could not decide whether clashes involving Orangemen were signs of the loyal enforcement of good order or of illegitimate vigilantism. Perceptions tended to teeter between the two. For instance, as Bryan points out regarding confrontations at Portadown during the mid-1980s, they produced in politicians 'a sense in which they were unable to control some of what was taking place, but also a concern that other groups were trying to gain political legitimacy from the confrontations. As senior Orangemen and UUP politicians called for restraint, others could be seen as greater 'defenders of Protestantism' (Bryan, 2000: 159). At the same time, the politicians and senior Orangemen could not entirely disassociate themselves from Orangeism, for fear of ceding support to hardliners, but instead had to continue in their attempts to shape it towards their own ends (Bryan, 2000: 178).

The Lower Level of the Regulatory Pyramid is Ineffective

A Code of Conduct, that has been revised on a number of occasions by the Parades Commission, was designed to provide a common basis on which behaviour in public space could be understood and regulated as regards parades and protests. The idea is that, at a lower level than requires police enforcement, organisers and participants become aware of and act on the responsibilities that are associated with their right to freedom of assembly. Ideally, for instance, displays of flags representing paramilitary organisations would be recognised as being unacceptable, or behaviour would be restrained when a parade passes a place of worship.

On the one hand, poor adherence to the Code of Conduct should, in theory, induce sanctions for parade or protest organisers in the years that follow their breaching the code. On the other hand, consistent adherence could ensure that the rights and obligations involved in freedom of assembly are widely understood. The outcomes of the Code of Conduct, in theory, could be evidence based and transparent. A system of monitors was set up to provide the Parades Commission with information on adherence to the code. This information would go beyond that provided by the police, who are concerned with clear breaches of the law. This, in theory, provides the lowest level of the regulatory model and offers the possibility that across Northern Ireland event organisers gain an understanding of the common responsibilities that flow from the rights they are claiming. Such a common understanding, shared by all those involved, would reduce the likelihood of confrontation.

In practice this has only had a limited effect. The system of monitoring and feedback introduced by the Parades Commission has been poorly run and inadequately resourced. The recruitment of trained volunteer monitors has been limited and peripheral to the tasks undertaken by the Parades Commission with monitors, who are effectively on the front line of adherence to a Code of Conduct, being undervalued.

In addition, monitoring has been limited to relatively few contentious parades so that the Parades Commission has very limited information on the level of adherence to the Code of Conduct in the more than 3,000 events held annually in Northern Ireland.

This means that there are often inconsistencies on what is allowed and not allowed in different parts of Northern Ireland, inconsistencies which organisers, such as the members of the Orange Order, are well aware of. This inconsistency is made worse since, in the processes of negotiation that have taken place over parades and protests, outcomes can be arrived at that seem to fly in the face of the Code of Conduct. As such, the authors, as well as participants in events, are aware of incidents when flagrant breaches of the Code of Conduct were ignored in the following years so that ongoing negotiations would not be undermined.

As a result, the transparency of the Code of Conduct is lost in the smoke and mirrors of private negotiations. The lowest level of the regulatory pyramid is almost totally ineffective and any common understanding of the responsibilities that derive from the right to freedom of assembly that in turn might provide a basis for longer term settlement and reduction in conflict, is completely lost.

A Lack of Unified Groups

It is safe to say, furthermore, that, as fissures have appeared in communities, whether in terms of paramilitary control over communities or in terms of divisions over political questions, public processions have become far more hardline (Hayden, 2005). So, parading organisations have become more entrenched precisely at the moment that pressure has grown for compromises over parades.

Given this, therefore, a second reason why the enforcement regime may be above the mediation baseline is that Ayers and Braithwaite tend to assume that the target industry can act as a relatively homogeneous interlocutor with the regulator. This may indeed be an accurate assessment of regulation in the industries at the heart of their study. It is certainly not true of the various groups involved in the parades dispute in Northern Ireland, though. In a sense, there is not one parading problem in Northern Ireland. There are countless distinct local problems.

Whatever the number, local mediation is not buttressed by a sense of common agency on the parts of various interlocutors. A solution to a problem in Portadown cannot be expected to automatically inform attempts to diffuse disputes on the Ormeau Road, for instance. Neither, for that matter, would Orangemen or protesters in Portadown necessarily give way on matters of importance to them in exchange for reciprocal compromises in Ormeau. Local disputes are resolutely local, even if they resonate across Northern Ireland. This is primarily because disputes are driven by the sensitivities, histories and personalities belonging to whatever locale the proposed march is to take place in. Second, it is undoubtedly because the issue of parading and attendant protests is resolutely visceral: a compromise thirty miles away has little bearing on the progress of *my* parade, or does little to ease the tension created by a parade passing *my* front door. On top of all this, it is difficult, even within the Orange Order, to discover people whose authority stretches beyond the local. It is interesting to note that in recent years, in a number of areas, there has been attempts to set up fora that comprise the range of Unionist and loyalist interests including the loyal orders, political parties, and loyalist paramilitary groups. Correspondingly, although the same cannot be said for the Catholic community, where Sinn Féin holds much greater hegemonic power in working class communities, we ought not to overestimate the power republicans have to agreements where distant compromises trump local concerns.

Legitimate Law and State Power

A third reason why equilibrium enforcement is not placed at the base of the pyramid is because the very concept of a regulator–regulatee relationship assumes a certain attachment to legitimate law. This point is crucial to the discussion of legitimacy and power in the next section of this paper. A sense of law as a manifestation of general democratic consensus is entirely missing *vis-à-vis* parading in Northern Ireland. The attachment is required if calculations as to the best form of engagement with a regulator are to include an assumption that the regulator's powers are rooted in legitimate law. While both sides of the parading disputes in Northern Ireland make reference to law, it is safe to say that many actors regard law as one more contested component in their political environment.

Part of the reason for this must be that the regulation of parades by the police in Northern Ireland prior to the establishment of the Parades Commission gave the distinct impression that law was to be regarded as a matter of power politics, entirely open to contestation. The character of public order legislation meant that the resolution of parades disputes were, at base, determined by shows of force designed to persuade the police that one community or other could create the most disruption if they did not get their way. The Drumcree dispute reinforced that impression as the police, quite understandably wishing to minimise public disorder and violence, reversed decisions over parades. The Parades Commission, on the other hand, has by no means provided a solution to the legitimacy-of-law problem. Indeed, the frequency with which senior politicians and Orangemen call for the Commission's abolition suggests that they regard it as a strategic innovation designed to undermine their position.

In short, the Parades Commission does provide an enforcement pyramid through which public spaces in Northern Ireland are to be regulated. Given the region's social and political environment, however, the enforcement pyramid does not work as Ayers and Braithwaite envisage. At least as regards controversial parades, enforcement tends towards the top of the pyramid, not the bottom. For the variety of reasons set out above, this suggests that the enforcement scale provided by the Commission does not provide the incentives for, or a necessary basis upon which to produce, negotiations. Or rather, that those incentives provided do not outweigh the incentives to behave contrary to its regulatory strictures.

The Parades Commission and Legitimacy

All that said, the Parades Commission has clarified the regulatory landscape as far as parades are concerned. It has also removed police and politicians from the dispute, at least by distancing decision making from the political sphere and by separating adjudications from events on the ground. In that sense, it has performed an important function. Where to now, however? Is the Commission a permanent feature in Northern Ireland, or, as it itself envisages, will it eventually render itself redundant?

Indeed, this is how the Commission envisages things. It looks forward to its own dissolution, 'when there is no need for a statutory body to place restrictions on the rights of others and where parades have ceased to be a focus of community tensions' (PCNI, 2006: 2). Moreover, 'the Commission making decisions is not going to make things better in the long term. The Commission maintains that the only way to achieve long-term solutions to these disputes is for all parties to work to make a genuine attempt to 'listen to' and 'address' the concerns of those with whom they differ' (PCNI, 2006: 3). Again, however, it is unrealistic to expect that the Commission, as conceived, works as anything more than a force for preventing violence around the parades dispute.

Despite its work we suspect that conciliation, where it happens, will probably not arise from the Parades Commission's existence. As we set out in the previous sections, the Commission's design as a public body distances decision-making from events on the ground and insulates both police and politicians from the ramifications of the parades dispute. Moreover, while strategies have shifted in response to the Commission's creation, thus leading to a reduction in violence, a shift towards negotiation aimed at resolving parades disputes has been slow in coming.

While agencies, as Flinders puts it, are 'an integral layer of any modern democracy, contributing expertise, providing arenas for civic participation and reducing the need for ministers to get ensnared in the minutiae of government' (Flinders, 2004a: 783), the manner in which they function may well expose the contradictions between accountability and independence in the governance of society. Moreover, it becomes increasingly obvious that legitimacy is not a given for quasi-autonomous agencies; and finally that divisions of responsibility between agencies and their ministerial masters may not at all be clear-cut (Christensen & Lægreid, 2006).[6] In short, their distance from parliamentary and other oversight bodies may be the key to the effectiveness of agencies. Whether this distance is a price worth paying is an open question. At the very least, however, some thought has to be given to how any specific agency fits into the overall governance of a state (Flinders, 2004a: 783).

As far as the Parades Commission is concerned, it could not be better designed as a tool of relatively raw administrative power in responding to the marching dispute. It leaves a lot to be desired, however, in terms of any effect we might want it to have in terms of developing a consensus on how public spaces ought to be shared in Northern Ireland. For Hamilton, a shared ethical vocabulary of rights is essential if public spaces are going to be used without conflict:

> If the vocabulary of rights is used merely to legitimate liberty-limiting interventions with little effort being devoted to generating consensus about the content and scope of the rights engaged (and their role in discriminating between valid and invalid harms and benefits), the contribution of a rights paradigm to resolving conflicts over freedom of assembly will be irrevocably diminished. (…) In the absence of ethical grounding, a rights discourse is likely to seem irrelevant and can gloss over the fundamental questions raised by the reconstruction project. (Hamilton, 2007: 100)

In other words, the Commission does very little to diminish the idea that rights can only be traded and never shared.

Shane O'Neill makes a similar point from a discursive perspective. He objects to the Commission's being 'insufficiently accountable in its determinations on contentious marches that have not been resolved through local dialogue. It has also been accused of engaging in trade-offs, of making judgements that are insufficiently clear or consistent, and of caving in to the greater threat of violence' (O'Neill, 2000: 42). The criteria by which the Commission makes its adjudications, O'Neill argues, 'are too vague to allow for transparently impartial and consistently principled judgements.' Second, he continues, 'by allowing considerations that are responsive to the greater threat of violence to impinge on their deliberations, the criteria lack a critically normative edge, since they will reflect and reproduce the balance of illegitimate power' in the society (O'Neill, 2000: 42).

While it is certainly the case that the criteria and processes for judgement that the Commission follows allow threats of violence to be taken into account in an indirect manner, our analysis suggests that the Commission, in practice, has been less responsive to direct threats of violence than the police had been in pre-Commission times. On the criteria by which the Commission's adjudications are made, however, it may well be the case that they are one element in producing obscure or opaque judgements, with little clear direction as to any consistent principles which ought to underlie the regulation of public spaces in Northern Ireland.

While the Commission's adjudications do tend to set out their thinking at great length (PCNI, 2005a), they tend to provide forms of 'supply-sided' legitimacy and accountability. That is, adjudications tend to be steeped in the procedures and in the legislative powers under which the Commission has formulated its rulings. The rulings, explaining their precise fit with the Public Processions (Northern Ireland) Act, seem primarily calculated with possible judicial review of decisions in mind. Communication with parties to specific disputes on the ground does not come across as a particularly significant priority for the Commission. In this environment, questions of legitimacy and accountability are only understood in a narrow sense: the Commission is only accountable to the body of law within which it functions. Its outputs are designed as formal inputs for other legal processes, not as communications with the subjects of regulation. So, as O'Neill and Hamilton point out from their distinctive perspectives, the accountability and legitimacy gaps lie in the lack of engagement between the Commission and the people who are the subjects of its adjudications.

As the previous sections suggest, however, the problem lies with the entire environment in which adjudications are made. Where law is made at a distance, the impression may be that enforced regulation of public space may simply be one more issue where decisions are imposed rather than, say, arising from the democratic will of the people to whom the laws are directed. Without a sense on the part of the subjects of law that they are also the authors of the law to which they are subject (Habermas, 1999: 260), there is little prospect for institutions to communicate with the citizenry as much more than coercive devices of external powers.

The question of legitimacy is difficult when it comes to specific institutions. While citizens may be willing to adhere to laws that are applicable to all in some general sense, the regulation of rituals and the use of public spaces in a divided society throws up some profound difficulties. The precise specificity of rituals that makes them worthwhile to participants also means that regulations are often targeted disproportionately at one section of a divided community more than another. This makes arguing from more abstract principle much more difficult.

That said, it is possible to envisage a situation where institutions are legitimated to a greater extent, at least in terms of their functioning and in terms of their relationship to formal democratic institutions. Following the full restoration of the Northern Ireland Assembly in May 2007, there is a possibility of devolving justice and policing matters to Northern Ireland. A report on the devolution of justice and policing is due to be laid before the Assembly in early 2008. It may be that devolution will include the bringing of the Parades Commission's administration within the Assembly's formal remit. Moreover, the ongoing Review of Public Administration is likely to produce new arrangements for local government in Northern

Ireland. Such a move will go some small way towards addressing the distance between the Parades Commission and the people over whom it rules. That is not to say that a strict legal and institutional legitimacy, where a body clearly and transparently fits the state's overall architecture, equals political legitimacy, where the body's power is willingly accepted by those who are subject to its power. It does restore a relationship between agencies and representative democracy, however. At the very least, in other words, devolution might give the Commission a polity to speak to.

Conclusion

We believe that it is in this light that the current trend towards mediation ought to be regarded. The failures of the Commission are not symptomatic of an agency whose remit is too narrow or is even mis-directed. Rather, the Commission's problems are symptomatic of a wholesale body of law that is constructed at a distance from the people of Northern Ireland.

In this paper we contend that the reduction in violence around parades is not a symptom of reduced inter-communal tensions. It is, rather, in no small part a result of the specific institutional character and regulatory function of the Parades Commission. The character and function of the Parades Commission as established, it ought to be noted, derives not simply from its formal role in the statute books, although that is very important, but in the expectations its establishment creates on the parts of participants on all sides of the parades issue *vis-à-vis* how they interact with the state over the uses of public space.

The Commission has been very successful in communicating that strategies of violence were not going to lead to results when it came to groups either forcing parades along contested routes or preventing parades using those routes. This success has been rooted in the fact that the coercive power that backs up its adjudications is far more substantial than anything that can be summoned by supporters and opponents of parades.

Where the Commission has been less successful, *vis-à-vis* its stated aims, has been in communicating any coherent sense of the principles by which public space might be shared. Neither has it been particularly successful in promoting the idea that public space ought to be shared at all. In part this is because the institutional architecture of the Commission is not in fact disposed towards these aims. It is also partly because the aims of violence-reduction or of wider political agendas have prevented the Commission from building a consistent stance. Finally, the position of the Commission in Northern Ireland's political culture reflects a wider problem of legitimacy, where there is little sense of state force being anything more than force in itself (as opposed to a force willingly accepted as part of legitimate rule).

For the Commission to do more than counter force with greater force, we would not need to see a consensus on parading alone. We would need to see a sense of the law as a shared, perhaps local, project, belonging to the people over whom it rules, where the authority of law is less a matter of force and more a matter of authorship.

Until then the Parades Commission remains just one more actor in Northern Ireland's social environment using force to get its way.

Notes

The authors would like to thank Cillian McBride, Jurgen de Wispelaere, John Garry, Shane O'Neill and Michael Hamilton for comments and discussion on this work.

1. Regulation might be understood as a 'sustained and focused attempt to alter the behaviour of others according to defined standards or purposes with the intention of producing a broadly identified outcome or outcomes, and which may involve mechanisms of standard-setting, information-gathering and behaviour-modification' (Black, 2003: 65).
2. By conciliation, we mean something similar to that described in John Rawls's *Political Liberalism* (Rawls, 1993). In the instance of the Parades Commission, an overlapping consensus on how rights to public space ought to be shared might develop. This consensus need not have the emotive tone of *reconciliation* but it ought to involve a range of settlements and compromises that reveal a commitment to sharing public space that goes beyond mere strategic motives. Thus, conciliation involves a deeper disposition than a *modus vivendi*, where behaviour might change but dispositions do not.
3. The UUP is committed to abolishing the Parades Commission (UUP, 2007). The DUP's manifesto for the 2005 parliamentary and local elections pledged to work for the Commission to be 'replaced' (DUP, 2005). In its manifesto for the 2007 Assembly elections (DUP, 2007), the party still described the Commission as 'part of the problem' but had settled for a review of the Commission's functioning.
4. It is important to note that we do not intend our discussion as a test of the Ayers and Braithwaite model. Rather, we are using the model as a vehicle for clarifying some of the problems we identify with the Parades Commission as a regulator.
5. This power, available under the 1987 Public Order (Northern Ireland) Order, has only been used once since its inception. In the wake of violence at Drumcree, Secretary of State Patrick Mayhew banned a 1996 Apprentice Boys march in Derry when talks between the Apprentice Boys and residents broke down (Jarman, 2003: 96; Hamilton, 2003: 159).
6. A longer list could undoubtedly be derived from Christensen and Lægreid's discussion.

References

Ayers, I. & Braithwaite, J. (1992) *Responsive Regulation: Transcending The Deregulation Debate* (Oxford: Oxford University Press).

BBC Online (2005) *Rioters 'Intended To Kill Police'*, 11 September (Belfast: BBC Northern Ireland), available online at: http://news.bbc.co.uk/2/hi/uk_news/northern_ireland/4235278.stm

Black, J. (2003) Enrolling Actors in Regulatory Systems: Examples from UK Financial Services Regulation, *Public Law*, Spring, pp. 63–91.

BRTF (2003) *Independent Regulators* (London: Better Regulation Commission).

Bryan, D. (2000) *Orange Parades: The Politics of Ritual, Tradition and Control* (London: Pluto Press).

Cabinet Office (1998) *Public Bodies* (London: Cabinet Office).

Cabinet Office (2002) *Public Bodies* (London: Cabinet Office).

Cabinet Office (2005a) *Classification of Public Bodies: Guidance for Departments* (London: Cabinet Office).

Cabinet Office (2005b) *Public Bodies* (London: Cabinet Office).

Cabinet Office (2006) *Public Bodies* (London: Cabinet Office).

Christensen, T. & Lægreid, P. (2006) Agencification and Regulatory Reforms, in: T. Christensen & P. Lægreid, *Autonomy and Regulation* (Cheltenham: Edward Elgar).

Davenport, M. (2005) *Parade Riots Point To Deeper Unrest*, 11 September (Belfast: BBC Northern Ireland), available online at: http://news.bbc.co.uk/2/hi/uk_news/northern_ireland/4236282.stm

DUP (2005) *Parliamentary and Local Government Elections 2005 Manifesto* (Belfast: Democratic Unionist Party).

DUP (2007) *Assembly Elections 2007 Manifesto* (Belfast: Democratic Unionist Party).

Flinders, M. (2004a) MPs and Icebergs: Parliament and Delegated Governance, *Parliamentary Affairs*, 57(4), pp. 767–784.

Flinders, M. (2004b) Distributed Public Governance in Britain, *Public Administration*, 82(4), pp. 883–909.

Habermas, J. (1999) *The Inclusion of the Other: Studies in Political Theory* (Cambridge MA: MIT Press).

Hamilton, M. (2003) *Rights, Relationships and the Struggle for Recognition: Parade Disputes and Public Order Law in Northern Ireland*, PhD Dissertation, School of Law, University of Ulster.

Hamilton, M. (2007) Freedom of Assembly, Consequential Harms and the Rule of Law: Liberty-Limiting Principles in the Context of Transition, *Oxford Journal of Legal Studies*, 27(1), pp. 75–100.

Hamilton, M. & Bryan, D. (2006) Deepening Democracy? Dispute System Design and the Mediation of Contested Parades in Northern Ireland, *Ohio State Journal on Dispute Resolution*, 22(1), pp. 133–187.

Hayden, L. (2005) Gangland Glamour, 16 November (London: The Guardian), available online at: http://society.guardian.co.uk/societyguardian/story/0,,1643087,00.html

Hood, C. (2002) The Risk Game and the Blame Game, *Government and Opposition*, 37(1), pp. 15–37.

Jarman, N. (1999) Regulating Rights and Managing Public Order: Parades Disputes and the Peace Process, 1995–1998, *Fordham International Law Journal*, 22(4), pp. 1415–1439.

Jarman, N. (2003) From Outrage to Apathy? The Disputes over Parades, 1995–2003, *Global Review of Ethnopolitics*, 3(1), pp. 92–105.

NIO (2005) *Devolving Policing and Justice in Northern Ireland: A Discussion Paper* (Belfast: Northern Ireland Office).

O'Kelly, C. (2006) Public Institutions, Overlapping Consensus and Trust, *Critical Review of International Social and Political Philosophy*, 9(4), pp. 559–572.

O'Neill, S. (2000) Liberty, Equality and the Rights of Cultures: The Marching Controversy at Drumcree, *The British Journal of Politics and International Relations*, 2(1), pp. 26–45.

Parker, C. (1999) *Just Lawyers: Regulation and Access to Justice* (Oxford: Oxford University Press).

PCNI (2005a) *Determination Made in Relation to the Whiterock Temperance Lol 971 Parade Notified to Take Place in Belfast On Saturday 10 September 2005.* (Belfast: Parades Commission for Northern Ireland), available online at: http://www.paradescommission.org/Uploads/docs/ACF697F.doc

PCNI (2005b) *Parades and Related Conduct: A Code of Conduct.* (Belfast: Parades Commission for Northern Ireland), available online at: http://www.paradescommission.org/publications/PDF/ACF440B.pdf

PCNI (2006) *Parading in a Peaceful Northern Ireland: Forward View and Review of Procedures 2006–2007* (Belfast: Parades Commission for Northern Ireland). available online at: http://www.paradescommission.org/publications/PDF/PC_wayforward.pdf

Rawls, J. (1993) *Political Liberalism* (New York: Columbia University Press).

Scott, C. (2004) Regulation in the Age of Governance: The Rise of the Post-Regulatory State, in: J. Jordana & D. Levi-Faur (Eds) *The Politics of Regulation: Institutions and Regulatory Reforms in the Age of Governance*, pp. 145–174 (Cheltenham: Edward Elgar).

TSO (1998) *Public Processions (Northern Ireland) Act 1998* (London: The Stationary Office), available online at: http://www.opsi.gov.uk/acts/acts1998/1998002.ht

UUP (2007) *A Fair and Inclusive Society* (Belfast: The Ulster Unionist Party), available online at: http://www.uup.org/policy_society.htm

Identity, Unity, and the Limits of Democracy

CILLIAN MCBRIDE

Introduction

What is it, if not ethnicity, that makes a collection of individuals into a people, a collective political agent? In particular, can a divided society find a distinctly democratic way to resolve its difficulties and forge a common citizenship without implicitly relying on some unacknowledged link between citizenship and ethnicity? Nationalists, of course, will welcome any such link, arguing that it is indeed an implicit and necessary assumption of citizenship and nationalists of a liberal bent will argue that, provided the national identity involved is suitably inclusive, this link plays an essential role in motivating social cooperation (Miller, 1995). Others, however, more sensitive to internal diversity, are rightly critical of the cultural assimilationism which even an inclusive nationalism requires. An alternative solution then is that offered by multiculturalists, who believe, such as nationalists, that cultural membership cannot be divorced from citizenship, but conclude that, as the nation-state is a utopian ideal rather than a fact on the ground, we must opt for a formally group-differentiated citizenship which will licence the institutional recognition of cultural pluralism (Kymlicka, 1995; Tully, 1995). With the right institutional arrangements, groups may exercise political autonomy *as groups*, within the same state. Both nationalists and multiculturalists, however, join in rejecting what they see as an implausible liberal ‘neutralism’ which seeks to decouple thicker group memberships from citizenship, as the only way in which to render it properly inclusive (Tamir, 1993: 106).[1]

My aim in what follows is to set out an interpretation of democratic citizenship which is consistent with this ‘decoupling’ strategy but which is not liable to the standard critiques of ‘neutralism’: that it is too thin, and that it is implicitly biased in favour of the dominant cultural group and the political status quo. What I need, first of all, is some account of the unity of the demos which is consistent with a broadly impartialist, liberal-egalitarian outlook. Second, if we are to avoid the charge that liberal egalitarians are compelled to simply take the boundaries of the state and citizenship for granted, and, therefore, *implicitly* favour national majorities, then I need some account of how this view might allow for critical reflection on the boundaries of the state. Here the task will be to steer a course between the Scylla of nationalism and the Charybdis of a cosmopolitanism that has nothing to say about borders other than that they must all ultimately be abolished. I take it that a liberal egalitarian account of the unity of a democratic people cannot remain silent on this question, but rather must offer some account of how state-borders might become the subject, rather than simply the presupposition of democratic politics.

My strategy involves two components: one, institutional, and the other attitudinal, specifically, ‘recognitional’, both answering to different aspects of public reasoning. The institutional component, which centres on the conditions of forming a determinate collective will, serves as an alternative to nationalist accounts of popular sovereignty (Habermas, 1998; Pettit, 1999). The recognitional component, which turns out to be central to the practice of public reasoning, provides the basis for a non-culturalist account of the unity of a people. Taken together, I argue that these elements allow us to conceive of a democratic politics *about* state-boundaries that centres on the idea of a public as something to be constructed, rather than on the unity of a pre-political people.

I shall be taking a hard case as the focus of my discussion, first, because the liberal-egalitarian case will be strengthened if we can show that it can cope with such cases (and cope better than its rivals), and second, because one promising way to approach the question of what constitutes the unity of a democratic people should be to start with an examination of a society that conspicuously lacks this unity in the hope that we can identify the missing element. The hard case I have in mind is, of course, Northern Ireland, and it is a hard case for two reasons: because a divided society like this seems to provide the best possible example of the strength of nationalist identifications and the weakness of any thin commitment to constitutional essentials; and because the nature of the conflict concerns the boundaries of the demos itself, and here nationalist and cultural accounts more generally seem to have a crucial logical advantage: they can provide a clear account of *who* the people are and, consequently, *where* the boundaries of the demos *ought* to lie. The liberal egalitarian alternative, however, seems entirely ill-equipped to provide any guidance whatsoever on this score, being concerned with how things ought to be arranged *within* a state whose boundaries are treated as given, but essentially silent on the question of where those boundaries should lie.

In response, I suggest first, that the apparent strength of nationalist accounts turns out to be their greatest weakness. Nationalism's much vaunted motivational force is the very thing that renders it so extremely divisive and a force for political instability in the real world, in contrast to the imagined world of already achieved nation-states. In a divided society, nationality will not serve as the basis for common citizenship, but rather as the basis for ongoing conflict. With respect to the question of borders, as I have indicated above, it is clear that a liberal egalitarian view cannot simply confine itself to the justice of institutions within state boundaries, but must also have something to say about those boundaries themselves. The thrust of the argument here, however, is that contrary to appearances, democratic theory has a wealth of theoretical resources for providing practical guidance on *handling* the 'boundary problem', and not that such theories can ultimately resolve the logical conundrum itself (Whelan, 1983). Democrats can live with the circularity identified by the boundary problem, provided, of course, that this does not place boundaries entirely beyond the reach of democratic politics. Accordingly, I shall not aim to offer a conclusive answer to the Northern Ireland's 'constitutional question'. This would be to ask too much of an egalitarian political theory. What I do hope to offer, however, is an indication of how the respective political projects of both Irish Nationalism and British Unionism may be rationally, and legitimately pursued, and how a democratic politics about borders ought to be conducted.

Demos and Ethnos: The Limits of Democratic Politics?

Why is it that the nationalist account seems to offer the most coherent solution to the problem of identifying the demos? Clearly it is because nationalists have at their disposal an independent criterion for identifying the demos, i.e. it is treated as identical with the ethnos. Ostensibly pre-political criteria such as language use and shared cultural practices, etc. serve to pick out who 'the people' are, independently of any reference to the boundaries of actual states and legal criteria of citizenship (Gellner, 1983).

One important objection to this account is that, in the real world, states are almost never clear-cut nation-states, and to treat the majority ethnos as the political demos means that members of the minority will be consigned to second-class citizenship, which is clearly repugnant. For this reason, egalitarians will be attracted to purely territorial accounts of the limits of citizenship. If the criterion of civic membership is given by a territorial limit rather than by ideas about descent or cultural membership, then, in circumstances of ethnic diversity, it will be possible to avoid institutionalising hierarchical, ethnically exclusive, relations between different groups within the populace. If, by contrast, we identify the citizenry with a particular ethnic group or a dominant narrative about cultural identity and political agency, then those who fall outside this group, while still subject to the same burdens entailed by citizenship, will be demoted to a second-class status. Lying within the borders of the state but outside the borders of the people, their interests will count for less, and their voices will be discounted in 'public' deliberation. The attraction of a simply territorial criterion, i.e. residence within the territory, is obvious: to the extent that one is subject to the laws, and must bear the burdens of citizenship, then one is entitled to participate in public affairs on an equal footing, with entitlement to the same rights as any other resident.

Clearly, no state operates, as yet, with such a purely territorial account, although few remain committed to a thoroughgoing *jus-sanguinis* model of civic membership. Most States, while they permit naturalisation, will still operate a distinction between citizens and resident aliens, the latter having a more narrowly circumscribed set of rights than that former, despite being subject to the burdens of citizenship: i.e. they are regarded as bound by collective decisions, but are denied the right to participate in decision-making, i.e. political citizenship (over and above limited access to welfare and some civil rights). This produces the curious irony, that ex-pat citizens may often have voting rights, but resident aliens (who are subject to the decisions in question while ex-pats are not) typically do not (Benhabib, 2004). Be that as it may, it is clear that the moral argument favours the territorial criterion: what matters is participation in a particular set of cooperative relations, and to the extent that one is resident in a state and accepts the burdens of citizenship then one is morally entitled to the same rights as everyone else participating in this scheme. Increasingly, too, there are moves in the direction of legal recognition of this case: EU citizens may participate in local elections of the member state in which they reside, regardless of nationality, while some states permit certain categories of resident alien to vote in national elections too.[2] It may be utopian to suppose that any state will ever be wholly free from attempts to exploit exclusive interpretations of the demos in domestic politics, but the notion of a purely territorial criterion for civic membership is evidently conceptually coherent, morally attractive to egalitarians, and also, to some extent, already embodied in existing institutions.

It would not seem to be of much use, however, in offering guidance as to how to respond to the problems posed by divided societies such as Northern Ireland. The problem which the territorial criterion responds to is that of hierarchical relations *within* a given territory: it has nothing to say about where the borders of any territory ought to be. While it is premised on the idea that everyone within the territory should have the right to participate on an equal footing in deliberations about public affairs, the attempt to make the borders of the public itself the subject of democratic deliberation runs into the familiar problem that there can be no democratic decision about the borders of a democratic state because democracy *presupposes* the existence of a clearly delimited people entitled to participate in such decisions. When questions about where to draw the line delimiting the territory and therefore the demos arise, an appeal to purely civic, democratic, values and principles is powerless simply because this question must be settled first as a precondition of democratic politics. While the territorial criterion can weaken the grip of an exclusivist politics about the nature of the demos, here it seems to reach its limit. The boundaries of the demos are contestable in the strong sense that what might count as a democratic decision concerning those boundaries will be determined by prior choices about who is to count as the demos in the first place, which is, of course, the very point at issue (Gallie, 1955–1956).

This can be clearly illustrated with reference to Northern Ireland. If this were primarily a sectarian conflict, centred on religious communities, then it would, in a sense, be less intractable. Instead, it is primarily a *national* conflict in which national divisions have been reinforced by an overlapping religious division (Ruane & Todd, 1996: 22–30; McGarry & O'Leary, 1995).[3] The conflict, then, is precisely about the boundaries of the territory and, by implication, the nature of the demos, i.e. the political people. Who has a right to participate in such a decision is what is directly at issue. Unionists will want to say that the appropriate demos is the UK, although, given the apparent indifference to their fate exhibited by most of their fellow Britons, confining the right to vote in any border poll to Northern Ireland itself has clear attractions for UK governments. Nationalists naturally believe that this loads the decision against them and would prefer the decision to be taken by Ireland as a whole, excluding GB. Dublin and London for their part, are happy to confine the decision to Northern Ireland itself for, although any change in Northern Ireland's status would have considerable implications for the citizens of each jurisdiction, neither is keen to move Northern Ireland to centre-stage in the domestic politics of either polity. At any rate, it would seem that there is no clear answer to the question as to 'who votes?'; whatever answer is adopted appears to presuppose the very answer that such a vote is to decide. Evidently, this is not just a logical problem but a serious political problem too: this is the very source of Northern Ireland's inability to establish stable political institutions enjoying robust legitimacy.

One way to develop the sort of democratic position that we are concerned with here would be to simply insist on the idea that a commitment to democracy simply *is* a particular view of the internal organisation of states and that, as democrats, we should properly have nothing whatsoever to say about boundaries. Certainly, the view adopted here is that our primary focus should always be on ensuring that the internal institutional configuration of any state should be such as to permit equal participation in collective decision making. To the extent that this is the case, then secessionist pressures must be correspondingly weak – the primary solution to boundary problems will always be an internal solution. However, while it is clearly an implication of the view adopted here that we should not care too much about state boundaries, there are obviously good reasons to avoid simply endorsing existing state boundaries. Liberal egalitarians do indeed, as liberal nationalists affirm, take the existence of boundaries for granted (Tamir, 1993: 117), but this does not mean that liberal egalitarians are committed to endorsing whatever *configuration* of boundaries we find ourselves confronted with. Nationalists will, of course, insist that we cannot take existing boundaries at face value: to do so would simply be to endorse the current set of hierarchical relations between national groups. Liberal nationalists are right to argue that liberal egalitarians cannot simply ignore the issue of boundaries: at the very least it would be irresponsible to avoid addressing an issue that is after all a key source of political conflict. Having said that, it is worth noting that liberal nationalism is itself particularly studious in avoiding discussion about the external boundaries of the state, and is altogether more comfortable with discussions about integrating individual immigrants into the nation's public culture. The liberal nationalist prefers to build nations around existing states, rather than to build states around existing nations, as orthodox nationalism demands. Some cosmopolitans will respond that far from ducking the issue of state boundaries, they actually have a substantive position on it: a world of states is morally untenable, and boundaries must be eliminated. While this cosmopolitanism (which may exist more in the minds of non-cosmopolitans than anywhere else) offers substantive moral reasons for thinking that boundary disputes ought not to play a role in our politics, the avoidance of this issue on the part of liberal nationalists is rather more puzzling, suggesting a distinctly utopian view of the politics of nationalism in which the difficult questions about the political coexistence of nations have simply been swept under the carpet. The liberal-egalitarian view adopted here, however, takes its lead from mainstream cosmopolitanism in that it rejects the idea of a world-state as undesirable (for Kant on tyranny (Kant, 1970: 113)), and affirms the value of maintaining a range of multi-level democratic institutions as the best way to discharge cosmopolitan obligations (Pogge, 1992). If plural jurisdictions are to be part of this world, then liberal-egalitarians will, however, need to develop some account of how we might have a democratic politics which takes the configuration of these boundaries as its subject, and not simply as its founding presupposition.

Given that we cannot plausibly duck the question of redrawing boundaries, is there anything that we can say about it between the polar opposites presented by the nationalist commitment to national self-determination on the one hand, and the cosmopolitan vision of a world without borders on the other? The first point to make is that there do appear to be good, non-nationalist, reasons for recognising a right to secession on the part of minorities, of the sort sketched by Buchanan (1995). (I dissent from his endorsement of the cultural survival rationale, however, taking any right to secession to be contingent on violations of the traditional civil, political and welfare rights). What does the work in Buchanan's account is the idea of the violation of individual rights: where this occurs, individuals may act in concert to reorganise the state in such a way to eliminate such abuses. Where this is impossible to effect within a particular state's institutions, then secession is a legitimate goal. The steps that may be permissible to successfully secede are themselves subject to the usual caveats about the permissible use of force. National identity clearly plays a role here in serving as a *marker* for the purposes of discrimination, on the one hand, and, presumably, in identifying candidate states for the purposes of secession on the other hand, but the argument does not rely upon any putative right to *national*-self-determination per se. Rather it is simply the case that for rights-violations of a certain sort, i.e. those directed as individuals identified as members of a minority national group, secession, quite contingently, becomes a *possible* remedy in a way that it is not for members of other groups subject to similar discrimination. For these groups, it is simply the case that emigration will be the only practical option where internal reform cannot be effected.

The Limits of Nationalism: Division and Misrecognition

The sort of pure egalitarian, democratic, view canvassed above, which seeks to decouple national and civic identity faces one apparently insuperable obstacle: it sets out a vision of the internal organisation of states, but *logically* must remain silent on the question of their proper boundaries. I want to suggest now, that the apparent advantage enjoyed by nationalism in this respect is illusory. The multicultural theory of ethnic accommodation has some clear advantages over the nationalist model, and has rightly focused our attention on a range of potentially useful institutional devices, but I shall indicate why it too is theoretically ill-suited to address the difficulties of constituting democratic citizenship in a divided society.

The nationalist account purports to offer a determinate answer to the question of where state boundaries should lie, i.e. that they should be coterminous with nations. However, faced with a divided society like Northern Ireland, it runs into the difficulty that where two nationalities are in contention over the same piece of territory, it cannot decisively resolve the question in favour of one side or the other (Miller, 1995). Affirming that *both* nations have a right to self-determination simply fails to offer a determinate answer as to which group should control the territory in question.[4] Partition/repartition is not an attractive solution for the simple reason that in the real world, populations are typically intermingled in such a way as to defeat tidy territorial carve ups: each act of partition creates new national minorities, which is of course, unacceptable from a nationalist perspective. The only practical solution to this problem consistent with nationalist presuppositions will be to supplement territorial partition with forced population movement (or worse): imposing new borders is never enough to solve the problem of national minorities.

In the context of Northern Ireland, this dilemma of indeterminacy has led Nationalists and Unionists to adopt interpretive strategies which try to present the conflict in terms which make it easier to resolve in theory, if not in practice. Nationalism's traditional strategy for getting around this dilemma involves a simple denial that Unionists are truly British in the first place. If they can be interpreted simply as Irish people who are, however, in deep denial about their true identity then the coherence of the nationalist project is not threatened. Of course, Irish nationalism officially aspires to reconstitute Ireland in impeccably civic terms (Whelan, 1996), and this encourages the interpretation of Unionists in primarily religious terms: insofar as they are not British but Protestant there is no obvious difficulty, logical or practical, in integrating Irish Protestants into an Irish republic – a move which has already been successful with respect to the Protestant minority in the South. To the extent that there is a *national* conflict, on this view, it has been conducted between Nationalists and 'the Brits' – where the 'Brits' are understood to be the English, not the British, Unionist, population. The requirements of nationalist political theory, then, have forced Irish nationalism to 'misrecognise' the Unionist community to the extent that nationalism refuses to recognise that Unionists see themselves as British.

Unionists, it is fair to say, do not have such a unified interpretation of the conflict, possibly because their position as defenders of the constitutional status quo seems not to have encouraged the elaboration of a Unionist *project* as such, over and above the minimal aspiration to avoid inclusion in an Irish republic(Coulter 1994).[5] As Irish Nationalists are committed to changing the status quo, they clearly have an incentive to develop a more elaborate case for constitutional change. The most promising strand of unionism, from a liberal-egalitarian perspective, is a civic, largely integrationist, politics which presents unionism as driven by an attachment to a civic interpretation of Britishness (Aughey, 1990). On this view, unionism is itself a form of constitutional patriotism to a set of political institutions which are shared between several different constituent nations (Habermas, 2001).[6] This model has a symmetrical relationship to the civic version of Irish nationalism: it holds out the prospect of integrating the other side as equal citizens, primarily, however, under a religious description, i.e. Protestants can become Irish citizens on the nationalist view, while Catholics can become British citizens on the Unionist view. This repeats the mistake of misrecognising the nationality of the other side, but also reflects a significant failure on the Unionist side, to recognise the ethnic and religious baggage with which the favoured civic identity has been laden. Unionism, even in its civic variants, has typically failed to appreciate that institutional ties between political unionism and Protestant organisations such as the Orange Order, and cultural attachments to a particular, increasingly outdated view of Britishness, which harks back to a monocultural, Protestant, imperial past seriously undermine their attempts to present Britishness not as a national but as a civic identity (Robbins, 1990; Colley, 1992).[7] To be sure, Irish nationalism is also guilty of similar self-deception to the extent that even its self-consciously republican variant is still wedded to a thick cultural model of Irishness as Gaelic, if not, officially at least, to Irishness as Catholic. This exclusive tendency is arguably stronger in the loyalist, Northern Ireland-nationalist, strands of unionism, which has hitherto shown little interest in integrating, or assimilating the Irish nationalist population.

Not only does the logic of nationalism produce inevitable blind-spots on both sides here – blind spots affecting both their interpretation of their opponents and of themselves, the conflict itself has arguably accentuated exclusivist tendencies within both camps which serve to undermine moves in the direction of inclusive civic nationalisms, whether Irish or British. It's not hard to see why this might be so: to the extent that each community sees itself as under threat, whether from the British State, or from republican terrorism, the incentive to strengthen group solidarity and morale by reinforcing those features of collective identity which underline the differences and distinctiveness will be strong as these provide a bulwark against assimilation, and against backsliding by more moderate tendencies within one's own community (Ruane & Todd, 1996: 60). To the extent that Nationalists, for example, resist assimilation into a historically hostile British state, through emphasising their distinctive Gaelic identity and culture, then this will undermine attempts to present the nationalist project in terms of a secular, inclusive, continental republicanism, which can provide the underpinnings for an Ireland in which 'Catholic, Protestant and Dissenter' can share as equals. Not only are these tendencies evident as distinct currents within nationalism and unionism more widely but they are evident in the case of Sinn Féin especially, within the same political organisation.[8]

At this point the liberal nationalist can, of course, insist that this sort of social and political division is precisely what the emphasis on a strong, inclusive, national identity is designed to remedy. With deeper roots than a purely institutional focused constitutional patriotism, this sort of national identity can prevent the emergence of this sort of division, something which multicultural models of 'plural monoculturalism' will only encourage (Sen, 2006: 157). However, it is not clear, first of all, that the attempt to strengthen national identity will not actually accentuate divisions, a dynamic evident in the Northern Ireland case, nor is it clear just what work the distinctively *national* components of this shared identity are actually doing. While it is certainly desirable to live in a state characterised by a shared public culture (Miller, 1995), and the absence of social division centred on ethnicity, it is not clear that the liberal nationalist can provide us with any useful guidance on the practical matter of how we might achieve such as state if we don't already inhabit one, for in a society like Northern Ireland it is clear that a shared civic people won't be built on the foundations of either British or Irish nationalities as things currently stand (Todd, 1995).

This is one reason why multicultural solutions appear to be more practicable than liberal nationalism's unhelpful strictures on maintaining a shared public culture and national identity: in the real world, we may be able to assimilate immigrants when they turn up on our shores, but the attempt to assimilate indigenous national minorities will only accentuate conflict, over and above concerns about the moral permissibility of attempts to do so. It is hard to imagine that any of the measures employed to build nation-states, the coercion entailed in forging political, linguistic, and religious, unity in particular, could be endorsed today.

The Limits of Multiculturalism: Plural Monoculturalism?

The multiculturalist solution, or at least its general orientation towards internal solutions, whether in terms of federal arrangements, group-representation, or consociationalism, is clearly more attractive (Kymlicka, 1995; Tully, 1995). To the extent that multicultural citizenship is an umbrella, under which a range of cultural memberships may flourish, it must be more attractive to pluralists than the nationalist alternative which operates with the crude tools of assimilation, partition, domination, and/or expulsion. The problem here is that multiculturalism has never shaken off the communitarianism from which it was born (Taylor, 1994; Benhabib, 2002). It is concerned above all with accommodating groups' concerns with preserving their cultural identity and practices. This makes it ill-suited to coping with the problems of a divided society, to the extent that the task of overcoming these divisions requires the *transformation* of relations between groups, and by implication, relations *within* groups: the relations groups have to their own history, traditions, and projects (Ruane & Todd, 1996). Divided societies, one might say, have already got a well-embedded de-facto group-differentiated citizenship and need rather to overcome, rather than reinforce this. The founding move of multicultural political theory was to recognise that some marginalised groups wish to resist assimilation/ integration, while the central problem for a divided society like Northern Ireland is to work out how to integrate already separate communities under a common citizenship(Kymlicka, 1989).

This basic orientation renders multicultural political theory deaf to complaints about 'tribalism', a phenomenon universally acknowledged to be central to Northern Ireland's problems and regularly manifested in a depressing inability by members of each community to acknowledge the legitimate complaints of the other and to rise above the sterile assertion of an exclusive victim status. By making cultural survival its central concern (Spinner-Halev, 2000), multicultural political theory lacks the resources to offer guidance on how best to strengthen those forces within communities which may prompt the sort of critical self-examination which is required to undermine sectarianism. While the suggestion that a looser, less comprehensively assimilationist model of civic integration is desirable is certainly sound, the multicultural model of celebrating a plurality of internally undifferentiated cultural blocs is decidedly less attractive. This model relies, despite loud protestations to the contrary, on a fundamentally privatised, apolitical conception of culture, which is inimical to internal diversity and public contestation – phenomena which may be better sustained by a more traditional liberal concern with individual freedom and toleration (Barry, 2001). Furthermore, a misplaced focus on securing esteem recognition for particular cultural practices may in fact fuel a competitive and destructive cultural politics which will undermine integration in the name of securing 'respect' for one's particular 'tradition (MacGinty and duToit, 2007).

That said, the multicultural predilection for difference-sensitive institutional solutions is sound, even if the culturalist rationale offered for them is not. While some in Northern Ireland believe that building a common citizenship requires us to resist 'sectarian' measures such as 50/50 police recruitment, or the formal power-sharing arrangements entailed by the GFA, it is clear that a non-culturalist, liberal egalitarian rationale can be offered for these innovations. Indeed, the hope that we could build equal citizenship without monitoring the 'perceived community background of job applicants' or without taking positive steps to increase Catholic recruitment to the PSNI may look suspiciously like a case of well-intentioned people simply wishing the world away. Fortunately, liberal egalitarian political theory can licence justifications for departures from strict equal treatment which serve to bolster equal opportunities and in doing so, build confidence in the fairness of shared institutions. The goal of breaking down the sectarian monoliths does not commit us to an impotent 'difference-blindness' which is unable to respond to the facts of social division.[9] Having indicated why both nationalist and multiculturalist models of citizenship fail to address our central concerns, I want to proceed now to the construction of my two-stage account of an alternative model of liberal-egalitarian citizenship. This requires me to outline, first, the sort of deliberative/republican model of political autonomy which will justify the adoption of some of the counter-majoritarian devices favoured by multiculturalists to protect minorities, while ditching the idea that we must have our political autonomy mediated by group membership in any but the weakest sense.

Political Autonomy: the Institutional Basis of Collective Decision-Making

Both nationalist and multiculturalist accounts regard political autonomy as group mediated, albeit with differing views regarding the institutions required to allow groups to exercise political autonomy qua groups. I reject this group-mediated account of political autonomy in favour of an account which is normatively individualist, although not ontologically atomist (Pettit, 1993). What this amounts to is a rejection of populist accounts of democratic rule, which treat institutions as the medium whereby the will of the group is translated into action. Multiculturalism, while pluralist with respect to 'peoples', and counter-majoritarian in outlook, endorses a view which has the same basic structure: democratic institutions are simply instruments for translating the will of the peoples concerned into actions.

The alternative view, endorsed here, is that democratic institutions are constitutive of an authoritative *democratic* will, such that without these institutions there may be social groups but no collective *will* as such (Habermas, 1998). This is not an atomist view which would deny that there are ever *any* collective intentions, but only those of individual agents (Searle, 1995). Rather, the point is that while we can assign collective intentions with a relatively high degree of determinacy to relatively small collectives, in tightly circumscribed contexts, concerning relatively simple decisions, the larger the group, and the more complex the intentions the more difficult it will be to identify a unique candidate amongst the range of possible *interpretations* of the collective's will. To that extent, the will must be indeterminate without the sort of formal mechanisms that make a collective will possible. We needn't hesitate to ascribe a collective intention to a group of students in a seminar room to end early and break for lunch, without going to the trouble of taking a vote, but when a state's budget priorities are at stake, involving all manner of complex trade-offs, then talk of collective intention is essentially empty in the absence of formal decision-making procedures.

In addition to the issue of indeterminacy there is also the legitimacy question: not only must a group have formal institutional mechanisms for turning the intentions of members into a genuinely *collective* will, it must have mechanisms of a particular sort if we are to attach moral weight to the expression of this will. This is to say, that if these mechanisms do not afford each group member a substantively equal opportunity to influence the outcome of the group decision-making process, but rather have a hierarchical character which does not permit equal opportunities to all to influence the outcome of collective deliberation, then we are entitled to discount group claims on the grounds that they are the product of internal inequality, rather than of a freely formed collective will (Cohen, 1997).

Groups may resist internal democratisation, of course, and citizens may legitimately opt out of politics, but to the extent that they seek to be political actors; expressions of collective intentions should be weighted according to the character of their internal deliberations. By this I mean that they will carry less authority in public deliberations in the judgements of those participating. We should be entitled, as deliberators, to discount those expressions of group interest by community figures where we have reason to suppose that the views expressed, are the product of inequality. Without institutions, collective agency is indeterminate and, without the right sort of institutions, i.e. those that give members an equal say in forming that will, we ought not to take the pronouncements of spokesmen as authoritative.[10]

It is, then, the *institutions* of democratic government which make it possible for collections of individuals and/or collections of groups, to have a determinate, collective will that is binding on all. There is no collective will prior to these institutions; rather these are constitutive of the collective political will. This is only binding to the extent that the institutions treat all as equals. We should be clear here that rejecting group mediated political agency does not entail a rejection of groups per se, whatever that might mean, but only of the view that their status as political agents can be taken at face value, or that they must serve as the building blocks of a political theory. Nor does it suppose that political autonomy can be enjoyed by individuals without collective action: Political autonomy is a public good in the sense that it must be jointly produced. This normatively individualist account of democratic politics neither denies that groups exist, nor that there is such a thing as cultural membership, or situatedness, and it does not treat democratic decision-making simply as a matter of aggregating individual preferences. Political autonomy is a public good produced by individuals acting in concert, who participate in forming a collective will through a process of public reasoning (Pettit, 1999).

The normative individualism that stresses the need to guarantee each citizen an equal share of political autonomy also justifies the adoption of measures to promote a more inclusive politics, gender quotas for parliamentary candidates for example (Phillips, 1995), but also devices such as the formal power-sharing arrangements set out in the GFA. On the view set out here, these are justified not because people have a fundamental right to govern themselves through their ethnic blocs, but simply in order to protect individual members of minorities from the risk of majority domination. These counter-majoritarian measures are justified not in the name of the value of preserving cultural identity, but rather as devices to guarantee each citizen an equal share of political autonomy. The particular justificatory route adopted is important, however, for the individualist rationale, unlike the culturalist, dictates that institutional designs must also guard against the risk of supporting 'internal' hierarchies which will stifle cultural contestation and inclusive deliberation (Pettit, 1997; Sunstein, 2003).

This model of collective decision-making belongs to a family of deliberative conceptions of democracy inasmuch as the interpretation of political autonomy involved includes a conception of public reason, and what Rawls terms, the 'duty of civility', i.e. the obligation on all citizens to refrain from seeking to employ the shared coercive power of the state for private ends (Rawls, 1993). To this extent it is at odds with purely aggregative models of political decision-making, which are open to the problem of majority domination (Elster, 1997). Legitimate collective decisions follow a process of public reasoning in which unreasonable personal preferences will be exposed as lacking the requisite public justification. On its own however, this account appears to be incomplete for by tying the possibility of forming a legitimate collective will to a determinate set of political institutions, it appears to have no way out of the paradox of democratic foundation outlined above: taking democratic institutions themselves to be constitutive of the demos still leaves us without an account of where those boundaries should lie, or rather without an account of how we might have a democratic politics about the limits of the demos. In what follows, I shall argue that this problem can be resolved, in theory at least, with reference to a particular conception of recognition, and of the public sphere.

Recognition and Reason: Imagining and Constructing the Public Sphere

A plausible model of deliberative democracy has two components: institutional and recognitional. On the one hand, the ideal of public reasoning needs to be embodied in a set of institutions which make it possible for citizens to form a determinate collective will, while, on the other hand, the same ideal of public reason indicates that these institutions should be configured in such a way as to promote the practice of public reasoning. This practice, I suggest, must be thought of as one in which the notion of respect recognition plays a central role (Honneth, 1992, 1995; Fraser & Honneth, 2003). To see why this is so, we must reflect on what is involved in public reasoning.

Goodin suggests that we think of public reasoning as having two aspects, an external reflective aspect and an internal reflective component (Goodin, 2000). The former refers to the business of reasoning in public as it were, when we engage our fellow citizens in actual dialogue about our common affairs. The latter refers, by contrast, to the internal dialogue that we all, as deliberating agents, carry on in our minds. Much of the literature on deliberative democracy stresses the external collective aspects of deliberation, seeing it as the kernel of a potentially radical direct democratic challenge to representative institutions, and there is a corresponding suspicion of any stress on the internal reflective aspect of deliberation. This is presumably because internal reflective deliberation can be carried on without any actual collective dialogue taking place at all, so to insist upon its importance may also be to weaken the case for greater direct participation in decision-making. These misgivings are misplaced, however, for while it is true that internal reflective deliberation is independent of external collective deliberation, it is also the case that in the right circumstances, external collective deliberation can serve a useful role in correcting flaws in our individual internal deliberations, whether by exposing flaws in our reasoning, correcting errors of fact or by enlarging our moral imaginations. Here, however, it is the link between the imagination and internal reflective public reasoning that is significant.

It is clear that there are considerable limitations on the scope of external collective deliberation: the number of people with whom we can realistically hope to engage in dialogue of this sort can only ever be extremely limited, even allowing for the opportunities afforded us by the internet and the emergence of the blog, welcome as these are. What matters, Goodin suggests, is that we try to expand citizen's imaginations, such that they can imagine the lives and arguments of others whom they could never hope to meet in their day to day life (Goodin, 2000). Of course, this is not just an optional add-on to the business of public reasoning, a theoretical fix to make up for the difficulties posed by mass-society: the imagination *necessarily* plays a central role in public reasoning. When we accept the burdens of public reasoning we undertake to provide reasons for our preferred policies which are in principle acceptable to our fellow citizens, allowing for the fact of reasonable ethical pluralism, and this means that we must imagine ourselves presenting our reasoning before an imagined public that exceeds the range of persons with whom we actually have an opportunity to voice our arguments (McBride, 2003). We must consider the interests of those who we may never meet – those not only geographically distant from us, but also who are *socially* distant, occupy very different social locations and live very different lives. Further, we must, of course, not only consider their interests but also seek to engage with the best arguments we can imagine them making against our preferred policy – and not confine ourselves to those arguments which are in fact voiced, which may be flawed in various ways. To do otherwise would be to fail in our obligation to extend equal consideration to the interests of those affected and would allow us to exploit inequalities in the distribution of argumentative skills (which are presumably the product of other social inequalities) (Young, 2000).

Our reasoning, it is often said, is essentially public, in that for anything to count as a reason, it must be capable of being adopted by another. We can press this point, as O'Neill suggests, to the conclusion that reasoning cannot be limited to particular groups, whether of churches or bodies of citizens but must always be in some sense open to inspection by others – to engage in reasoning then is always to place oneself before the tribunal of reason itself, where it's composition cannot ultimately be limited to an audience of our own choosing (O'Neill, 1997). Public reasoning, then, is not simply the reasoning of a particular group of citizens about their common affairs, but is reasoning which can always be overheard so to speak – it becomes available for others to assess, and those who engage in it are obliged to open themselves to the criticism not just of a particular bounded 'public' but to an imagined public, which is in principle unlimited.[11] To try to circumscribe the audience of public reasoning is to betray the essentially limitless character of reason, and one's obligations as deliberating agent.

How, then, does this account of the imagined public of public reasoning serve to clarify the problems at hand: the unity of the demos and the possibility of a democratic politics of state-boundaries? With respect to the unity of the demos, it suggests, first, that to engage in public reasoning we must extend a certain sort of recognition to those potentially affected by our preferred policies. The duty of civility requires us to take their interests into account and, in so doing, to consider their stated views of these interests. They must, quite simply, *count* as equals in our deliberations. This is clearly an example of respect recognition, the universal recognition we extend to others simply by recognising them as equal members of the moral community (Honneth, 1992). The centrality of this mode of recognition to deliberative democratic politics is often obscured by the assumption that recognition is first and foremost a matter of endorsing the self-image of particular cultural groups and/or adopting group-differentiated institutions of various sorts.[12] It is clear, however, that public reasoning does not require us to extend this thicker, esteem-based, mode of recognition to others. Rather we are required to respect their right to define themselves as they please, and to *consider their own view of their interests*, even if ultimately we choose to withhold esteem recognition from their particular identity (or aspects thereof) and to discount their stated interpretation of their interests (McBride, 2005).

What this means for a divided society such as Northern Ireland should now be clear: an egalitarian view of citizenship requires citizens to extend this fundamental form of recognition to those who belong to the alternative community – where this means that those others are to count as genuine equals in deliberation. This is not a matter of endorsing or valuing their *particular* identities but of recognising their right to be counted as part of the projected 'we' of public deliberation, the 'we' to whom one seeks to justify one's arguments. While democratic institutions make a collective *will* possible, it is this act of mutual recognition on the part of deliberating agents which brings a demos, a democratic *people*, into being.[13] A demos is simply the 'we' created by the act of recognition required by public reasoning, and it acquires a will where there are the institutional mechanisms that permit a determinate will to be formed. While citizens may remain highly critical of aspects of each others traditions and culture, and choose to reject arguments made in their name, this is very different from the sort of disregard detailed above in which Irish Nationalists, for example, simply refuse to recognise, i.e. respect, the right of Unionists to define themselves as British. This disregard is aimed at simply excluding difficult problems from one's deliberations, a misrecognition of the other which constrains deliberation, while a critical engagement with the cultural identity of the other can be premised on recognition of the other's right to view themselves through the particular lens in question, even where this lens is judged to be flawed in some ways – these interpretations are, modified, reconstructed and sometimes rejected in the process of deliberation, but cannot, consistent with public reasoning, be excluded from deliberation from the outset.

The first key implication of this argument is, firstly, that a functioning deliberative democracy requires a significant recognitional component. Against the culturalist view that the politics of recognition is fundamentally concerned with according esteem to particular cultural identities (Thompson, 2003), the view set out here centres on the moment of universalist respect recognition required by the practice of genuinely public, i.e. unrestricted, reasoning. It is this moment of recognition that constitutes the unity of a people, and not some allegedly pre-political ethnic identity.

Liberal nationalists advance some way in this direction by seeking to locate nationality in a shared 'public culture' rather than in a pre-political ethnicity. However, the liberal nationalist account of public culture fudges the issue of publicity; if it is to be a genuinely nationalist public culture then one must endorse patently absurd nationalist readings of universal values, e.g. that toleration is a *uniquely* British value, while, on the other hand, to admit that these values are indeed universal, robs them of their distinctively national flavour (Miller, 1995). Liberal nationalists are right, however, to think that a body of citizens should be bound to one another by a sense of solidarity and not merely by sharing a formal legal status. The argument from recognition through public reasoning indicates that this solidarity takes the form of a civic trust which is sustained through practices of public reasoning, i.e. it is through the conduct of democratic politics that civic trust is built, rather than relying on pre-political aspects of culture or identity (Habermas, 1998).[14]

Second, it is a clear implication of the view set out here that the demos must inevitably have fuzzy boundaries to the extent that it is an imagined phenomenon, constituted by the sort of recognition required by unrestricted public reasoning. This must appear, at first blush, to be a fatal weakness – it seems to rob the demos of clearly defined boundaries for simply to recognise another as a member of my imagined public seems to include them in the demos. This degree of inclusiveness, however, threatens to rob the notion of the demos of its content and commit us to an implausibly stateless cosmopolitanism.

This should not be surprising – this is an egalitarian view at heart, and as such it must have cosmopolitan implications: we cannot, as egalitarians impose artificial constraints upon the equal consideration of interests. It is inevitable then that our imagined publics must spill over the bounds imposed by actual state borders, and include many who are not, strictly speaking, our fellow citizens at all. Equally, the same public-expanding recognition seems to work at the sub-state level, extending beyond formal politics to many day-to-day interactions in which we may find ourselves called upon to consider the interests of others. I take it that these are indeed the implications of the sort of egalitarian view set out here, which requires us to deliberate about the interests of others and in so doing extend respect recognition to them. It points both to cosmopolitanism on the one hand, and towards the democratisation of social relations (Pateman, 1970) on the other, and it cannot plausibly be confined to particular states, or to the world of formal politics within given states (Pogge, 1992).

Taken together with the institutional component of democratic autonomy, however, these potentially disturbing implications may appear less utopian in aspect. We need institutions to make a collective political will possible, to enable us to act in the world. To this extent state-boundaries continue to serve a purpose, and their boundaries will be relatively clear, at least, they will be clear enough to prevent disputes about the jurisdiction of particular collective acts. Our imagined public will always spill over these boundaries, which is as it should be given that the impact of our actions, private and public, will often do so as well. The idea of an unbounded imagined public is, however, compatible with that of a bounded state to the extent insofar as our public reasoning has two aspects. On the one hand, it is directed towards forming a will, i.e. taking a decision. As such we are obliged in the first instance to confine our deliberations to considering the interests of those potentially affected by the decision in question. This may not only be confined to our particular state, but even to subsets of the citizenry within that state (Goodin, 2007). However, even where our deliberations are restricted in this way by the nature of the decision before us, they remain open in the sense that our reasoning is always open to inspection by others not involved in our own particular political process, and must be so if it is to count as reasoning at all. Even where we are not directly affected by decisions taken in other states, we may follow their citizens' deliberations, and adopt views for and against particular positions adopted therein. While, as citizens they may not be obliged to justify themselves to us, as reasoning agents they should not be indifferent to counterarguments and reconstructions, no matter what their source. As deliberating citizens, we form a collective will for a particular state, but our reasoning is always open to all.

Of course, where our actions affect others then we are obliged to take them into consideration in our deliberations, even if they lie beyond our borders. Indeed, we may find that this obligation may be best discharged by establishing transnational deliberative fora of various sorts to support our deliberations and to make collective problem solving possible with those lying outside the borders of our state. What emerges, on this view, is not a picture of a world-state, but rather of a world of imagined publics which is never wholly coterminous with state boundaries and in which these boundaries themselves may be placed in question *within* a democratic politics which is concerned with determining the appropriate configuration of institutions for coping with the problem at hand. Our guiding principle here is the idea that we need to avoid exclusions which involve those affected by decision-making both within and without existing state borders.

Sometimes this will be a matter of establishing transnational institutions, while, in other circumstances, it may be a matter of shifting those borders themselves, to avoid inclusion in arrangements where are our interests are not given due consideration. This latter situation involves secession on the one hand, but also (and this is where the difference with traditional nationalist models of secession becomes clearer) of finding or, better still, building a home, i.e. of constructing a public in which one can participate as an equal. While the traditional nationalist model takes the identity of a people for granted, on this public-reason-centred view, this is too simple, for not only must one ensure that one extends genuine recognition to everyone within one's current political institutions, but also seek the same recognition beyond one's current borders, from those within one's preferred political destination. This is best understood, not as a matter of simply reuniting a pre-existing people, but of constructing a new public, inclusive of all its potential citizens. The liberal-egalitarian secessionist must engage with the interests both of those who would become a minority under any new arrangements, but also seek to engage the interests of those in the proposed destination state – for there could be no justification for joining a polity in which one's interests would not receive equal consideration. Because public reasoning has a dual aspect, a limited decision-oriented aspect and an unrestricted reason-oriented aspect, one can now make sense of the idea of a democratic politics of borders as one which proceeds by enlarging the public through engaging the deliberative imagination of all those concerned, regardless of where they stand with respect to current state boundaries. The goal of such a politics is not to align borders with ethnicities, but to align borders such that those already participating in the informal public deliberations of a given state can participate fully in its collective *decision*-making. Whether constructing transnational deliberative fora, or opting to secede from and/or unite with existing states, the guiding principle is given by the idea of political autonomy – the right to participate as an equal in deliberations about the decisions which affect one's life. The logical conundrum of the boundary problem is not solved – decisions cannot but be taken within existing democratic institutions, but it can be handled, and it should be clear now that democratic theory has at its disposal, non-nationalist, public reason centred resources to guide how we might handle a democratic politics about state boundaries.

Conclusion

How might we think of such a politics proceeding in a Northern Ireland context? First, to the extent that Nationalist and Unionists seek to pursue their political projects consistent, broadly speaking, with a liberal egalitarian outlook, then each must take, as its first priority, the development of the 'internal' recognitional component of democracy. While the GFA has provided a set of formal power-sharing institutions apparently capable of ensuring equal political autonomy, what clearly remains is to strengthen the informal, attitudinal component of public reasoning, which is necessary if democratic politics is to be conducted within Northern Ireland. This will not be a matter of forging a national identity as a precondition of democratic politics, but of engaging in genuine public reasoning in which participants expand their democratic imaginations in order to genuinely include others as equals in their deliberations rather than excluding them from the outset through misrecognition and caricature. Through the practice of unrestricted public reasoning a demos may be forged. While such a demos may not share a national *identity* – the common citizenship to be constructed here is built on the inclusiveness of public reasoning, and not by pre-political identities – it would, however, possess the *unity* proper to a democratic people.

Of course, both Nationalists and Unionists have ambitions that extend beyond Northern Ireland, albeit in different directions. Clearly, the liberal egalitarian cannot offer a determinate answer to whether Northern Ireland ought, as a matter of justice, to be British or Irish. In this respect, however, the liberal egalitarian is, of course, no worse off than the nationalist. The position sketched here can, though, offer some guidance on how each project may legitimately proceed. First, it is clear that the disastrous politics of anglo or of hiberno-phobia have no place in this picture. To insist that Britain or Ireland are foreign countries whose affairs are of absolutely no concern to one or other community within Northern Ireland is an absurd position which ignores the complexity of interactions between these states. Regardless, then of the ultimate constitutional outcome of Northern Irish politics, the sort of trans-national/cross-regional institutions established under the GFA are likely to be permanent features of the political landscape, as would be required by the all-affected principle (these institutions are nested, of course, within a larger European context of similarly overlapping jurisdictions).

On the view adopted here, we must be sceptical too of attempts to represent solutions such as joint British–Irish sovereignty over Northern Ireland as required by *justice*. On a culturalist view, whether nationalist or multiculturalist, we might, for example, suppose that, if cultural groups possess a basic right to self-determination as groups, then a fair solution would be one which simply awards joint-sovereignty over Northern Ireland to British and Irish governments, rendering it both British and Irish territory. This rationale for joint-sovereignty can remain silent, of course, on the question of internal democracy within Northern Ireland, being compatible, for example with allowing citizens to exercise their rights to political autonomy through participation in Irish or British elections without recognising any need for cross-community deliberation within Northern Ireland. This rationale also supposes that a solution may be effected which can leave Nationalist and Unionist identities and traditions entirely untouched. It is difficult to see how this might serve as the basis for overcoming social division and building the practices of public reasoning required for stable democratic politics within Northern Ireland. While deeply implausible, this rationale for joint sovereignty is entirely consistent with the apolitical view of cultural identity central to the culturalist outlook. This is not at all to say, however, that joint-sovereignty is not a legitimate option – my criticism centres only on the culturalist rationale which may be offered for it. Indeed, not only is it legitimate, it may even turn out to be a solution acceptable to both Nationalists and Unionists in the long run, but the rationale for judging this solution to be legitimate is, on my account, a matter of the extent to which it facilitates democratic government, and not the symmetry such a solution possesses with respect to Irish and British identities.

In principle, the traditional alternatives, belonging to a unitary state, British or Irish, may also be legitimate options however difficult they may be to achieve in practice. In this case the task for Nationalists and Unionists is first to build robustly inclusive practices of public reasoning within Northern Ireland, but then to build Northern Irish concerns into the public imaginations of the larger polity – whether Irish or British. For Nationalists, this will be a matter of building Northern Ireland into the public imagination of the Republic, as a part of the project of persuading Unionists that their interests will be given equal consideration within any future united Ireland, a move that will obviously require some transformation both within the public imaginations of both Northern Nationalists and the Southern citizens. For Unionists, a similarly dual aspect approach will be needed in order to assure Nationalists that their interests may be given equal consideration within the existing institutions.

This may seem to hand Unionists a clear advantage in that they need only defend the status quo, but this overlooks a key problem for Unionists – not only must they overcome Nationalist distrust, but building Northern Ireland into the public imagination of the wider UK will be an uphill struggle in the face of the indifference and often ignorance of the wider British public concerning Northern Ireland. To the extent that Northern Ireland is on the margins of the larger British public imagination it will be difficult to claim that Northern Irish interests receive equal consideration within the UK. Equally, Nationalists should not underestimate the resistance of many in the Republic to getting more closely involved in the affairs of Northern Ireland. While Northern Ireland is much more central to the political imagination of the Republic than it is to that of the wider UK, it is also the case that many Northern Nationalists are more closely engaged in the public affairs of the UK, than in those of the Republic (O'Connor, 1993: 347).[15]

Of course, pursuing these projects in the manner suggested here, rather than through the traditional Nationalist politics of identity assertion and mutual misrecognition, will be risky for both Nationalists and Unionists. To the extent that inclusive deliberation takes hold, the distinctiveness of each community's identity will be lessened, or at least, the salience of these differences, raising the prospect that each may be more easily assimilated into the other's preferred destination. Whether this makes Nationalist or Unionist projects more easily realisable, or whether, as is perhaps more likely, this simply facilitates the development of some sort of institutionally complex deliberative arrangements short of inclusion in either a British or an Irish nation-state, is a matter for speculation, but what is clear is that in contrast to the traditional nationalist conception of popular sovereignty, the theory advanced here can recognise all of the above as legitimate possible outcomes, provided that each were to embody sufficiently robust practices of public reasoning.

What this argument will have shown, however, is that an egalitarian theory does have something useful to say about the unity of democratic peoples which is neither unhelpfully utopian, nor resigned to presupposing the status-quo. It can conceive of a democratic politics which can make the limits of the demos a subject for democratic deliberation, and offer guidance on how this politics might legitimately be pursued. That existing states did not begin as democracies is not ultimately an insuperable logical or practical obstacle to their democratisation, and democrats need not be embarrassed at the apparent 'incompleteness' of democratic theory provided this theory can offer guidance on how best to proceed in the world in which we find ourselves. Rather than make identity the goal, or equally, the presupposition, of democratic politics, it takes the unity of a people, and the limits of a democracy to be internal to democratic politics itself, and to that extent open and unfinishable, such as the democratic conversation itself.

Notes

Earlier versions of this paper were presented at the ALSP annual conference, 'Aliens & Nations' Keele, 19-21 April 2007, the Recognition, Equality, Democracy workshop, QUB, 8 June, 2007, and the Beyond the Nation? Conference, QUB, 11–13 September 2007. I would like to thank all the participants in those events and, in particular, Jurgen De Wispelaere, John Horton, Paul Gilbert, Catherine Frost and Keith Breen for their valuable comments.

1. Following Barry, I reject the term 'neutralism', preferring 'impartialist' for the reason that policies issuing from impartialist procedures do not have to be 'neutral' in their effects.
2. Irish citizens have always been entitled to vote in UK general elections, for example, although this is a product of legal anomalies in the process of the Republic becoming independent rather than an expression of an explicit commitment to a strong model of inclusive citizenship. The Republic, for its part, now permits UK citizens to vote in elections, by way of reciprocating. It is clearly not unthinkable that EU citizens more generally will in time come to enjoy full voting rights in all member states. While the current practice is mixed, the idea that the national component of citizenship might be further sidelined, is not utopian.
3. That said, it is important to note the lack of symmetry between the primarily political interpretation of the conflict adopted by Irish Nationalists, and the more religiously inflected interpretation adopted amongst the Protestant, Unionist community. This lack of symmetry in interpretations of the nature of the conflict itself is directly related to the problem of misrecognition explored here.
4. Tamir's attempt to reconcile Palestinian and Israeli rights to national self-determination within the state of Israel conspicuously fails to offer the Palestinians an *equal* right to national self-determination.
5. This is clearly reflected in the division within unionism on whether to pursue an integrationist strategy, or a devolutionist, 'Northern Ireland nationalist' line.
6. Whether the devolutionist politics of the DUP will increasingly take on a civic character and relinquish its traditionally more loyalist flavour as the longer participation in power-sharing is sustained, remains to be seen.
7. The leading exponents of civic unionism, the UUP have, until very recently, been institutionally linked to the Orange Order (a tie broken by the Order in the end, rather than by the UUP). A similar confusion of British and Protestant identity surrounds the issue of marching, and the almost certainly doomed attempts to rebrand the 12th of July celebrations as 'Orangefest'.
8. This contradictory tendency is clearest in Sinn Féin, which combines both a traditional Gaelic cultural Irishness, evident in its extensive use of (often halting) Irish in its public pronouncements, with an official commitment to a secular tradition of Enlightenment republicanism, with strong internationalist elements. On the unionist side of the house the picture is less clear-cut, with Orangeism providing the central cultural element of Northern Irish British identity. The development of an interest in an the Ulster–Scots identity and language is a curious attempt to mimic the apparent success of the Gaelic revival in nationalism, but may prove less resistant to assimilation than its proponents believe. To the extent that the cultural component of unionism becomes focused on language and folk-dancing, and less on a commitment to the state-centred Whig nationalism of Protestant Succession then it will be easier to assimilate within a culturally pluralist Irish nationalism.
9. Responding to the facts, of course, should not mean capitulation to sectarianism: institutional design is a complex affair and will necessitate hard choices about trade-offs between values. Provided these are frankly acknowledged, we may hope, however, to build features into our institutions which can at least mitigate possible costs.
10. 'Discounting' as I call it here, is an essential feature of any piece of deliberation in which we must weigh a complex array of considerations, and assessments of the credibility or representativeness of spokesmen is just one of the criteria we apply in this process.
11. O'Neill notes that Rawls takes a bounded, Rousseauian view of the public reason as the reason of a given body of citizens, and regards this as presupposition of public reason. The view adopted here, follows the Kantian view set out by O'Neill, which views any such restriction as incompatible with genuine public reasoning. Contra Rawls, it is the practice of public reasoning that constitutes a people, through the mutual recognition involved.
12. I argue in McBride (European Journal of Political Theory – forthcoming) that the logic of esteem recognition actually tends to have the opposite effect – a view borne out in the Northern Ireland context by MacGinty and duToit.

13. My thinking here has been clarified by a paper on collective intentionality by Blain Neufeld (RIA presentation, 2006).
14. As Hardin (2006) points out, it is trustworthiness that is valuable, and not trust per se. We may tend to trust people who share features of our identity or culture, but to the extent that the practice of public reasoning can be sustained in the conduct of everyday politics, it serves to make manifest the *trustworthiness* required to forge a common citizenship out of a divided society.
15. Sinn Féin's failure to make further electoral advances in the recent election in the Republic has been plausibly attributed to misjudgements on the part of party strategists about the concerns of the Republic's citizens, and in particular, an overestimation of the importance of Northern Irish affairs to the Republic's politics.

References

Aughey, A. (1990) Recent Interpretations of Unionism, *Political Quarterly*, 61, pp. 188–199.

Barry, B. M. (2001) *Culture and Equality* (Cambridge, MA, Harvard University Press).

Benhabib, S. (2002) *The Claims of Culture* (Princeton, NJ, Princeton University Press).

Benhabib, S. (2004) *The Rights of Others: Aliens, Residents, and Citizens* (Cambridge: Cambridge University Press).

Buchanan, A. (1995) The Morality of Secession, in: W. Kymlicka (Ed.) *The Rights of Minority Cultures* (Oxford: Oxford University Press).

Cohen, J. (1997) Deliberation and Democratic Legitimacy, in: J. Bohman & W. Rehg (Eds) *Deliberative Democracy*, pp. 67–92 (Cambridge, MA: MIT Press).

Colley, L. (1992) *Britons: Forging the Nation* (New Haven, CT: Yale University Press).

Coulter, C. (1994) The Character of Unionism, *Irish Political Studies*, 9, pp. 1–24.

Elster, J. (1997) The Market and the Forum: Three Varieties of Political Theory, in: J. Bohman & W. Rehg (Eds) *Deliberative Democracy*, pp. 3–34 (Cambridge, MA: MIT Press).

Fraser, N. & Honneth, A. (2003) *Redistribution or Recognition?* (London: Verso).

Gallie, W. B. (1955–1956) Essentially Contested Concepts, in: *Proceedings of the Aristotelian Society*, 56, pp. 167–198.

Gellner, E. (1983) *Nations and Nationalism* (Oxford: Blackwell).

Goodin, R. (2000) Democratic Deliberation Within, *Philosophy and Public Affairs*, 29, pp. 81–109.

Goodin, R. (2007) Enfranchising All Affected Interests, and its Alternatives, *Philosophy and Public Affairs*, 35(1), pp. 40–68.

Habermas, J. (1998) On the Relation Between the Nation, the Rule of Law, and Democracy, in: C. Cronin & P. D. Greiff (Eds) *The Inclusion of the Other*, pp. 129–153 (Cambridge, MA: MIT Press).

Habermas, J. (2001) Constitutional Democracy: A Paradoxical Union of Contradictory Principles?, *Political Theory*, 29(3), pp. 766–781.

Hardin, R. (2006) *Trust* (Cambridge: Polity).

Honneth, A. (1992) Integrity and Disrespect: Principles of a Conception of Morality Based on the Theory of Recognition, *Political Theory*, 20, pp. 187–201.

Honneth, A. (1995) The Struggle for Recognition (Cambridge: Polity).

Kant, I. (1970) 'Perpetual Peace', in: H. Reiss (trans.) *Kant's Political Writings*, pp. 93–130 (Cambridge: Cambridge University Press).

Kymlicka, W. (1989) *Liberalism, Community and Culture* (Oxford: Oxford University Press).

Kymlicka, W. (1995) *Multicultural Citizenship* (Oxford: Oxford University Press).

MacGinty, R. & duToi, P. (2007) A Disparity of Esteem: Relative Group Status in Norther Ireland After the Agreement, *Political Psychology*, 28, pp. 13–31.

McBride, C. (2003) Consensus, Legitimacy, and the Exercise of Judgement in Political Deliberation, *Critical Review of Social and Political Philosophy*, 6(3), pp. 104–128.

McBride, C. (2005) Deliberative Democracy and the Politics of Recognition, *Political Studies*, 53, pp. 497–515.

McBride, C. (forthcoming) The Politics of Recognition: Corrective and Competitive, *European Journal of Political Theory* (forthcoming).
McGarry, J. & O'Leary, B. (1995) *Explaining Northern Ireland* (Oxford: Blackwell).
Miller, D. (1995) *On Nationality* (Oxford: Oxford University Press).
Neufeld, B. (2006) Social Diversity and the Idea of a Civic People, presented at Conflict, Dialogue, and Philosophy, Royal Irish Academy, 2–3 November.
O'Connor, F. (1993) *In Search of a State: Catholics in Northern Ireland* (Belfast: Blackstaff).
O'Neill, O. (1997) Political Liberalism and Public Reason: A Critical Notice of John Rawls, *Political Liberalism, The Philosophical Review,* 106(3), pp. 411–428.
Pateman, C. (1970) *Participation and Democratic Theory* (Cambridge: Cambridge University Press).
Pettit, P. (1993) *The Common Mind* (Oxford: Oxford University Press).
Pettit, P. (1997) *Republicanism* (Oxford: Oxford University Press).
Pettit, P. (1999) Republican Freedom and Contestatory Democratization, in: I. Shapiro & C. Hacker-Cordon (Eds) *Democracy's Value,* pp. 163–190 (Cambridge: Cambridge University Press).
Phillips, A. (1995) *The Politics of Presence* (Oxford: Oxford University Press).
Pogge, T. W. (1992) Cosmopolitanism and Sovereignty, *Ethics,* 103(1), pp. 48–75.
Rawls, J. (1993) *Political Liberalism* (New York: Columbia University Press).
Robbins, K. (1990) Varieties of Britishness, in: M. Crozier (Ed.) *Cultural Traditions in Northern Ireland* (Belfast: Institute of Irish Studies).
Ruane, J. & Todd, J. (1996) *The Dynamics of Conflict in Northern Ireland* (Cambridge: Cambridge University Press).
Searle, J. (1995) *The Construction of Social Reality* (New York: Free Press).
Sen, A. (2006) *Identity and Violence* (New York: Norton).
Spinner-Halev, J. (2000) *Surviving Diversity* (Baltimore, MD: Johns Hopkins University Press).
Sunstein, C. R. (2003) *Why Societies Need Dissent* (Cambridge, MA: Harvard Unversity Press).
Tamir, Y. (1993) *Liberal Nationalism* (Princeton, NJ: Princeton University Press).
Taylor, C. (1994) The Politics of Recognition, in: A. Gutmann (Ed.) *Multiculturalism,* pp. 25–74 (Princeton, NJ: Princeton Unversity Press).
Thompson, S. (2003) The Politics of Culture in Northern Ireland, *Constellations,* 10, pp. 53–74.
Todd, J. (1995) Beyond the Community Conflict: Historic Compromise of Emancipatory Process, I *rish Political Studies,* 10, pp. 161–178.
Tully, J. (1995) *Strange Multiplicity* (Cambridge: Cambridge University Press).
Whelan, F. J. (1983) Democratic Theory and the Boundary Problem, in: J. R. Pennock & J. W. Chapman (Eds) *Liberal Democracy Nomos XXV,* pp. 13–47 (New York: New York University Press.
Whelan, K. (1996) *The Tree of Liberty* (Cork: Cork University Press).
Young, I. M. (2000) *Inclusion and Democracy* (New York: Oxford University Press).

INDEX

Abortion Act 72–3
adoption, Constitutional Amendment proposals 117–18
Afghan asylum seekers, hunger strike 39–40
Agamben, Giorgio 41, 46, 48–9, 49, 54–5
agencies, insulating role 174–5, 186
Ahern, Bertie 115, 126
Ahern, Dermot 40
alienation, in ethno-national conflict 28–29
APNI (Alliance Party of Northern Ireland) 70
Arneil, Barbara 105
Assembly, Northern Irish *see* Northern Ireland Assembly
asylum applications, RoI statistics 43
asylum seekers: Luibhéid's argument 49–50; racialisation 42, 43; RoI control strategies 43–4; treatment of female 50
Australia 22, 127
autonomy: commitments to parental 80; in democratic principle 66–7; dimensions of 68–9; in domestic relationships 152–3; as important Irish value 152; Mill on liberal 83; principle of personal 65–6, *see also* political autonomy; women's autonomy
AV (alternative vote), gendered perspective 70
Ayers, Iain & Braithwaite, John 172, 177–9, *see also* enforcement pyramid

bare life, Agamben's concept 49
Barnardos 114
Belfast Agreement: bi-national framework 31–2; egalitarian critics' arguments 19–21; ethnic awareness 62; *jus soli* citizenship 47–8; power sharing model 61, *see also* peace process
Bentham, Jeremy 83
Beyond Conjugality (LCC) 157–8
biopower, Foucaultian concept 45–6
birth-right citizenship 40, 47
Blair administration, agencification 174
Bosnia 22
Boston/Berlin debate 41, 53–5
Brunette c. *Québec* 157
Bryan, Dominic 182

Callan, Eamonn 83–4, 88
Canada 22, 127, 157
Catholic Church: cross-community intolerance 162; position on education 80
cave analogy 2
CC v *Ireland* 112
children's rights: adoption 117–18, 119; Amendment contents battle 114–15; Amendment proposals 115–19; and autonomy 111; Barnardos' Amendment proposals 114; constitutional enumeration 116–17; court cases 104, 108–9, 112–13; court identification of enumerated 109; CRA 114, 117; CRC 103–4, 110, 111, 114, 119; discrimination in 110; empowerment theory 103; enumeration 109, 116–17, 119; family protection

107–8, 117; ICCL 116, 117; implications for parental authority 102; interest theory 103; international pressure for 113; interpretation of 'family' 114–15; judicial opposition 109–10; key themes 107; Kilkenny Incest Investigation 112; legal vs moral 103–4; moral weight 105; paternalism 110–12, 115; public support 113–14; referendum proposals 116; representation 104–5; 'special protection' constitution 102, 107, 110, 115, 119; to education 108, 112; Tobin's approaches 102; very young's ability to claim 104; and will/choice theory 103
citizen, Rawls' conception 82–3
citizenship: forging a common 191–3; *jus soli/jus sanguinis* 40, 41, 48, 194; Marshall's account 9; and recognition 205; requirements of equal 29–30; taskforce on active 96; territorial model 193–7; and voting rights 194
Citizenship Referendum 40–1, 49, 51, 55
Citizenship Studies, Ward & O'Shea's proposals 91
civic education: American context 84; choices 84; the 'common school' 85; conflict exploration 88–9; consequences of Millian position 88; constitutional provision 80; Irish school ethos 92; liberal conception 82–3; Rawlsian perspective 82–3, 84, 85–6, 87; relation with religious 80–1, 80–2; role of 79; syllabus proposals 81; as test for liberalism 83–4; values 87; Ward & O'Shea's approach 91–2
Clarke, Desmond M. 91
Coghlan, Deirdre 43
cohabitation: gender neutral rights 154; legality 152–3; sexual vs non-sexual relationships 156; siblings 155; and tenancy rights 154–6, *see also* domestic relationships; family law; marriage law
Commission on the Status of People with Disabilities 125
communitarianism 2, 199–200
community, and marriage 161–2
conflict: desirability of confrontation 181, 182; Irish pedagogical treatment 88–92
Constitution, Irish *see* Irish Constitution
contestatory democracy 136, 139
cosmopolitan criticisms, of Northern Ireland peace process 19–21, 32–4
CRA (Children's Rights Alliance) 114
CRC (UN Convention on the Rights of the Child) 103–4, 110, 111, 114, 119
creationism teaching 95
crisis racism 41
critical theory: distinctive features 18; emphasis on engagement 24–26; Marxian approach 3
CSPE (Civic, Social and Political Education Syllabus) 79, 81, 89, 94
culturalism, institutional recognition 191
Cyprus 22

DCLG (Disability Legislation Consultation Group) 138
deliberative democracy: components 203; and disability rights 137; limitations 204; Millian perspective 8; and public reasoning 7–9; recognition component 205; and social equality 9–10
democracy: components of deliberative model 203; egalitarian 19–21; equality principle 66, 67; liberal-egalitarian model 192–3, 200–1; O'Flynn's definition 66; as ongoing learning process 65; personal autonomy principle 66–7

diaspora nation: Boston/Berlin debate 53–5; Feldman's theorisation 40, 50; Gray on 50–1; Griffith on 51
Disability Act (RoI, 2005) 123; accessibility benchmarks 139; appeals process 139–40; dignity/ empowerment/publicity scores 140; and EHCR 141; evaluation 138–42; as missed opportunity 142–3
disability rights: discrimination protection 127, 140–1; and empowerment 137; fair proceduralism 133–4, 135; and human dignity 136–7; impairment thresholds 138; individuals' 132; Irish government's commitment 127; Irish legal development 125–6; justiciability debate 124, 133; needs assessment 127–8, 138, 139; and publicity 137; resource availability model 129; resource commitment model 129; right to challenge model *see* right to challenge; service delivery 128–30; vs social welfare model 127, 136
discrimination: in children's rights 110; disability protection 127, 140–1; European Court treatment 154; in school system 93
Diswellstown, Co. Dublin 81, 93, 96–7
diversity: and educational demand 92; Mill's encouragement 86–7, 90, 91; pedagogical celebration of 81; and politics of recognition 5; state recognition 79
domestic relationships: autonomy in choice of 152–3; case studies 152–3, 155–7, 164; health care rights 158–60; ICGU status 163, 164; interdependence and care 163–5; Irish vs Canadian law 158; legal distinctions 159–60; principle of recognition 160–5; protection against violence 158; recognition of homosexual 151, *see also* cohabitation; family law; marriage law
domestic violence, Irish legislation 158
Drumcree 173
duck-rabbit drawing 24–5
DUP (Democratic Unionist Party) 69, 70–1
duty of civility 202–3

ECHR (European Convention on Human Rights) 141, 155
education: civic *see* civic education; demand for secular 92; Irish constitutional rights 108, 112; Millian perspective 4, 83, 86–7, 87–8, 89, 93, 94, 95–6; and political power 96; state-controlled 86
educational institutions, denominational nature of Irish 81
egalitarian democracy 19–21
Éire *see* Ireland
emigration, Lenihan's justification 51–2
enforcement pyramid: effectiveness of lower level 182–3; and localisation of communities 183–4; Parades Commission taxonomy 179–81; purpose 179, 180–1; and sense of law 184–5
Ennis v *Butterly* 152–3
Equal Citizens: Proposals for Core Elements of Disability Legislation (NDA) 126
equal citizenship, requirements of 29–30
equality: in marriage law 154–60; Northern Irish communities 30–1
ethnic groups: patriarchy in 62, 65; and rights of veto 73; social attitudes 68
ethnic politics: Northern Ireland as representative of 21; typology 21–23
ethnicity: and collective polity 191; and egalitarianism 193–4

ethno-national conflict: *about* a state 21, 22–3; *beyond* a state 23; conclusions about Northern Irish 34–35; constitutional requirements 29–30; critically engaged approach 24–26; dismantling causes of in Northern Ireland 26–30; distinctiveness retention 27–8; in immigrant societies 21–22; key dimensions 26; Northern Ireland peace process as model 30–34; ontological considerations 27–28; overview 17–18; political alienation experiences 28–29; post-colonial 22; third-party intervention 23; *within* a state 21–2; Wittgenstein's duck-rabbit drawing 24–5
European Union 127
evolutionary biology teaching 95

fair proceduralism, in disability rights 133–4, 135
faith schools, management concerns 94–5
family, constitutional interpretation 114–15, 164–5
family law: marginalisation of single persons 164–5; overhaul requirements of Irish 151–2, *see also* cohabitation; domestic relationships; marriage law
Famine 50
Federle, Katherine H. 103
Feinberg, Joel 104
Feldman, Alice 40, 50
Fishkin, James S. 8
Fitzpatrick v *Sterling* 156
Foucault, Michel 3, 45
Frankfurt School 3
Fraser, Nancy 3
freedom, and positive group recognition 27
Freeman, M.D.A. 105, 111

Garvaghy Road 173
Gilligan, Carol 63–4
Goldberg, David T. 41, 44–5
Good Friday Agreement (GFA) *see* Belfast Agreement
Goodin, Robert 67, 204
governance, agencification 174–5
Gray, Breda 50–1
Green Party 70
Griffith, Arthur 51
Gutmann, Amy 8, 89

Habermas, Jürgen 3
Hamilton, Michael 177, 186
Hanafin, Mary 81
Harney, Mary 53
Harvey, Colin 42
Helvétius 83
hermeneutics of suspicion 26
historical materialism 1
Holmes, Stephen & Sunstein, Cass 129
homo sacer 49
homosexual couples, state recognition 151
Honneth, Axel 6
Hotak, Osman 39
hunger strike, Afghan asylum seekers 39–40, 55
Hyde, Douglas 162

ICCL (Irish Council for Civil Liberties) 116, 117
ICGU (intimate care giving union) 163
'The Idea of Public Reason Revisited' (Rawls) 82
identity cards, Irish proposals 54
IHRC (Irish Human Rights Commission) 126, 127, 138
immigrant societies, ethno-political conflict 22
immigration: illegal Irish 40, 43, 51–3; Irish state's approach to 42; residency rights 48–9; RoI legislation proposals 54
immigration statistics, RoI 42

INIS (Irish Naturalisation and Immigration Service) 44
institutions, configuring 207
intervention, third-party 23
Iraq 22
Ireland: Boston/Berlin debate 41, 53–5; diversity in 79; immigration and race in 42–4; Northern *see* Northern Ireland; polarisation of wealth 54; racial state of exception 44–50; refugee policies 43
Irish Constitution: children's rights *see* children's rights; citizenship referendum 40–1, 49, 51, 55
Irish Leaving Certificate 79, 81, 90, 91, 92
Irishness: diaspora inclusion 40–1, 50–1; O'Toole on 51; racialisation of 41, 42–4
Israel/Palestine 22

Jarman, Neil 172
Joram Developments v *Sharratt* 156
jus sanguinis citizenship 40, 41, 48, 194
justice: in political theory 3–4; Rawls' theory 85–6

Keane, Ronan 48
Kennedy, Ted 53
Kilkenny Incest Investigation 112
Kymlicka, Will 6

Lebanon 22
Lenihan, Brian 114
liberal autonomy, Mill on 83
liberal egalitarianism: in multicultural model of citizenship 200–1; and state boundaries 192–3
liberalism: Rawls' charge on comprehensive 84; and the teaching of values 82–8; and values teaching 82–8
Lo, Anna 70
local government, Northern Ireland 187–8

McCain, John 53
MacCormick, Neil 103
McDowell, Michael 43
McGillivray, Ann 104
MacIntyre, Alasdair 162
McVeigh, Robbie & Lentin, Ronit 46–7, 49
McWilliams, Monica 70
majoritarianism, vs power sharing 62
Make a Difference! (Harrison/Wilson) 89
marriage: and the community 161–2; Hegel's view 160; instrumental benefit investigation 157–8; instrumental vs constitutive status 153, 160–3
marriage law: Canadian experience 157–8; equality in 154–60; function 153
Marxism 1, 5
Metz, Tamara 153, 160–1, 162, 163
Mill, James 83
Mill, John Stuart 67, 74, 83, 86–7, 87–8, 95–6
minority groups: democratic principles 66–7; and right of veto 73
Moriarty, Elaine 40, 51
Mozert v *Hawkins County Public Schools* 84
Mullally, Siobhán 48
multiculturalism: limits of 199–201; vs nationalism 197

national identity: limits of democratic politics 193–7; limits of multiculturalism 199–201; practicality of multiculturalist solutions 199
nationalism: demos/ethnos parity 193; divisiveness of motivational force 193; inclusivity 191–3; limits of

197–9; public culture account of liberal 206
nationalists, resistance to domination 27, 28
NDA (National Disability Authority) 126
Neill, John 39
New Zealand 22, 127
NIWC (Northern Ireland Women's Coalition) 70, 71
North, Peter 173
Northern Ireland: Agreement *see* Belfast Agreement; conflict analysis 195; deconstructive emphasis of critical perspectives 18–21; dismantling causes of ethno-national conflict 26–30; electoral system 69–71, 74; joint-sovereignty model 209; key obstacles to human freedom 27; nationalist perspective 197; parliamentary structure 71–4; peace process *see* peace process; power-sharing 32, 62, 69–74; public space regulation *see* Parades Commission; transformation requirements 26–30; unionist perspective 197–8
Northern Ireland Assembly: members' registration of ethnicity 71; representation and equality 32–3, 70–1; restoration 187
Northern Ireland Parades Commission *see* Parades Commission

Oakeshott, Michael 2
O'Dowd, Niall 52
Oliver, Mike 128
On Liberty (Mill) 90
O'Neill, Shane 186, 204
O'Neill, Tip 52
Orange Order: attitudes to mediation 181–2; political perspective 182
Orange parades, rerouting 171–2, 173
Ormeau Road 184
O'Toole, Fintan 50, 51

Parades Commission: 2005 Orange parade ruling 171–2; adjudicative role and criteria 174, 179; as agency 174–5; categorisation 175–6; Code of Conduct 182–3; conclusions 188–9; enforcement pyramid model *see* enforcement pyramid; impact on violence 176; insulating role 176–7, 185; and legitimacy 185–8; long term perspective 185; mediation emphasis 174; monitoring system 183; origins 173–4; political benefits 177; primary motivation for establishment 174–5; problems with mediated agreements 181–2; as public body 173–7; as regulator 177–85; responses to violence 186–7; responsive regulation model 172, 177
parallel consent rule 71
parents: educational responsibilities 86, 90; implications of children's rights 102
Parker, Christine 178–9, 181
paternalism, in children's rights context 110–12
patriarchy, of ethnic groups 62, 65
peace, requirements of 19
peace process: as conflict resolution model 30–34; cosmopolitan criticism 19–21, 32–4; critical perspectives 18–21; normative imperative 29, *see also* Belfast Agreement
Pettit, Philip 136, 139
Plato 2, 83
pluralism, Rawls' concerns 8, 82
political autonomy: and institutional legitimacy 201–2; nationalist/multiculturalist accounts of 201; term analysis 202
political equality, as central value of democracy 66, 67

Political Liberalism (Rawls) 82
political philosophy: communitarian view 2–3; Oakeshott on 2
political theory: Rawlsian approach 3, 4; theory-context relationship 1, 2
politics, Irish pedagogical treatment 89
Portadown 182, 184
positive group recognition, and social movements 27
power sharing: enabling features of Agreement 32; and normative individualism 202; vs majoritarianism 62
PR (proportional representation) 69
The Primary School Curriculum (RoI) 80
primary schools, introduction of state-run 81
public reasoning: and deliberative democracy 7–9; recognition through 203–8; term analysis 204–5
public space regulation *see* Parades Commission

Quinn, Gerard 108, 125

race/racialisation/racism, term analysis 44
racial states: and biopower concept 45–6; conceptualisation of migrants 50; Goldberg's theorisation 44–5
racialisation, of Irishness 41, 42–4
racism: denying 41; Foucault's theory 46
Rawls, John 4, 7, 82–3, 84, 85–6, 137, 202
recognition: concern of politics of 205–6; as guiding principle of relationships 160; and public reasoning 203–8; respect 205; and social movements 27
recognition politics: Honneth's model 6–7; multiculturalism in 6; Taylor's formulation 5
referenda: children's rights 116; citizenship 40–1, 49, 51, 55
reflective equilibrium 4
refugee policies, RoI 43
refugees, Agamben's argument 48–9
regulation, Cabinet Office definition 175
relationships, domestic *see* domestic relationships
religion: constitutional commitments to non-discrimination 80; and Irish educational provision 108
religious education: Catholic Church's perspective 80; Irish syllabus 81; relation with civic 80–2
religious freedom, in Irish education 90–1, 94
reproductive rights 125; Abortion Act 72–3
Republic of Ireland *see* Ireland
residency rights, RoI Supreme Court rulings 48–9
responsive regulation model 172, 177, *see also* enforcement pyramid
Ricoeur, P. 26
right to challenge: central properties 131–7; in Disability Act 140, 141–2; fair proceduralism 133–4, 135, 142; implications 130–1; independent redress requirements 135; individualised 132; justiciability requirements 132–3; justification 135–7; as precedent 134; vs social welfare model 136
Rights, Safeguards and Equality of Opportunity (Belfast Agreement) 31
rights-protection, questions of fairness 129
rites of passage, dangers of community control 162
Robinson, Mary 40–1, 50

Schmitt, Carl 46

Schumer, Chuck 53
SDLP (Social and Democratic Labour Party) 69
secession, liberal-egalitarian model 207–8
self-determination, under Belfast Agreement 31
September 2005 riots 171–2
single persons, marginalisation 164–5
Sinn Féin 69, 199
social issues, ethnic attitudes 68
social movements, and positive group recognition 27
social welfare model, of disability services 127, 136
society, Mill's doctrine 83, 86
Society Must Be Defended (Foucault) 45
sovereignty: Agreement dispute resolutions 31; bi-polar disputes 22–23; in ethno-national conflict 17
Sri Lanka 22
state education, Mill's view 86–7
states of exception: Agamben's theory 41, 46, 54–5; Ireland as 44–50
STV (single transferable vote): criticisms 69–70; gendered perspective 69, 70–1

Taskforce on Active Citizenship 96
Taylor, Charles 5
tenancy rights, and cohabitation 154–6
textbooks, conflict in Irish 88–9
A Theory of Justice (Rawls) 82
Tobin, John W. 102, 106, 107, 110, 118–19, 119
tolerance, in CSPE syllabus 81
Tormey, Roland 81
tribalism 200
tribunals: disability rights 140–1; for grievance resolution 131–2

Ulster *see* Northern Ireland
UN Convention on the Rights of Persons with Disabilities 123, 127
unionism, and national identity 198
unionists, resistance to incorporation 27
US (United States of America): benign intervention 23; disability legislation 127; education court cases 84; ethno-political conflict 22; illegal Irish immigrants 40, 43, 51–3
UUP (Ulster Unionist Party) 69

values, inculcation of 91, 92, 97
violence: in ethno-national conflict 23; impact of Parades Commission on 176; in marches and parades 171–2; Parades Commission responses to 186–7
Volk, MacIntyre's perspective 162

Walzer, Michael 2, 4
Ward, Eilís & O'Shea, Karen 91–2
Waters, John 50
welfare state 165
will/choice theory of rights 103
Williams, Kevin 80, 81
Wisconsin v *Yoder* 84
Wittgenstein, Ludwig 24
women: dimensions of democratic engagement 68–9; immigration control perspective 49, 50; interpretations of ethnicity 65; and right of veto 73
women's autonomy: and NI Assembly rules 71–4; and the NI electoral system 69–71, 74; power sharing context 69–74
women's interests: conceptualising 63–6; democratic autonomy and 66–9; essentialist approaches 63; relational approach 64, 65, 74; reproductive rights 72–3

Young, Iris 3, 64, 73

For Product Safety Concerns and Information please contact our EU representative GPSR@taylorandfrancis.com Taylor & Francis Verlag GmbH, Kaufingerstraße 24, 80331 München, Germany

Batch number: 10725971

Printed by Printforce, the Netherlands